Translating Tolkien:
Text and Film

Translating Tolkien: Text and Film

edited by
Thomas Honegger

2011

Cormarë Series No. 6

Series Editors: Peter Buchs • Thomas Honegger • Andrew Moglestue • Johanna Schön

Library of Congress Cataloging-in-Publication Data

Honegger, Thomas
Translating Tolkien: Text and Film
ISBN 978-3-905703-16-0

Subject headings:
Tolkien, J.R.R. (John Ronald Reuel), 1892-1973 - Criticism and interpretation
Tolkien, J.R.R. (John Ronald Reuel), 1892-1973 - Language
Translation
Literature, Comparative

First published 2004
Second edition 2011

Cormarë Series No. 6

© Walking Tree Publishers, Zurich and Jena, 2004, 2011

All rights reserved. No portion of this book may be reproduced, by any process or technique, without the express written consent of the publisher

Cover illustration: "Ithilien", Anke Eißmann 1999

Set in Adobe Garamond Pro and Shannon by Walking Tree Publishers
Printed by Lightning Source in the United Kingdom and United States

Editor's Preface

It's over – December '03 saw the release of the third and final part of Peter Jackson's adaptation of *The Lord of the Rings*. There will be, of course, the release of the extended version in August '04, and we can expect more material in the director's cut which will appear sometime in the future. For the time being, however, it is possible to take stock and make a first assessment of Jackson's achievement (or failure). Five out of twelve contributions united in this volume thus deal with the movie under the aspect of 'translation'.

As in the preceding volume (*Tolkien in Translation*), the studies presented here deal with a wide range of problems and challenges connected with the task of translating Tolkien's work. The brief abstracts that precede each article will help the reader to find the paper of his or her choice.

Finally, I would like to direct the reader interested in scholarly studies on further aspects of Tolkien's work to the other volumes of the Cormarë Series. Volume 5, Mark T. Hooker's *Tolkien Through Russian Eyes*, was published last year, and volume 7, Christopher Garbowski's *Recovery and Transcendence for the Contemporary Mythmaker* will appear in 2004. Also, due to WTP's new policy of publishing with a 'print-on-demand' company, we are or will soon be able to provide reprints of the earliest volumes of the Cormarë Series.

Thomas Honegger

Jena, Spring 2004

Acknowledgments

I would like to express my thanks to all the contributors for their cooperation and patience during all stages of the preparation of the manuscript.

I would also like to thank Johanna Schön who proofread the articles with great care and with an eye for editorial mishaps.

Finally, I wish to express my gratitude to Walking Tree Publishers for making this venture possible.

Contents

Editor's Preface ... i

Acknowledgments ... ii

The Westron Turned into Modern English: ... 1
The Translator and Tolkien's Web of Languages
   Thomas Honegger

"The New One Wants to Assimilate the Alien" – ... 19
Different Interpretations of a Source Text
as a Reason for Controversy: The 'Old' and the 'New'
German Translation of *The Lord of the Rings*
   Rainer Nagel

The Israeli Translation Controversy – What About and ... 49
Where To?
   Danny Orbach

Estne Tolkien Latine Reddendus? ... 65
A Light-Hearted Look at Some of the Challenges
   Richard Sturch

Dutch *Samizdat*: The Mensink–van Warmelo ... 79
Translation of *The Lord of he Rings*
   Mark T. Hooker

The Treatment of Proper Names in the German Edition(s) ... 89
of *The Lord of the Rings* as an Example of Norms in
Translation Practice
   Rainer Nagel

Tolkien in Swedish Translation: 109
From *Hompen* to *Ringarnas herre*
   Beregond, Anders Stenström

Tolkien, our Judge of Peter Jackson 119
   Vincent Ferré

Humiliated Heroes: Peter Jackson's Interpretation 129
of *The Lord of the Rings*
   Anthony S. Burdge & Jessica Burke

The Adaptation of *The Lord of the Rings* – A Critical Comment 159
   Øystein Høgset

The Professor and the Director 177
and Good vs. Evil in Middle-earth
   James Dunning

The Soundtrack Lyrics of Peter Jackson's *The Lord of the Rings* – 209
A Legitimate 'Translation' of Tolkien
   Alexandra Velten

Thomas Honegger

The Westron Turned into Modern English: The Translator and Tolkien's Web of Languages

Abstract

Tolkien's presentation of *The Lord of the Rings* as a translation out of the original Westron into modern English inspired him to go one step further and reproduce the relationship between the various languages of Middle-earth by means of linguistic transposition (e.g. Rohirric = Old English, Language of Dale = Old Norse). The resulting 'web of languages' presents itself as a highly complex and not always fully coherent structure and poses an additional challenge to every translator.

> In presenting the matter of the Red Book, as a history for people of today to read, the whole of the linguistic setting has been translated as far as possible into terms of our own times.
> ('On Translation', Tolkien 1992a:1167)

I

Tolkien presents his account of the War of the Rings as a translation going back to a copy of the Red Book, for which he provides an elaborate textual history in the Prologue. By doing so, he inscribes himself in a venerable medieval tradition of authors hiding their own poetic, literary or scholarly achievements behind references to (often fictitious) originals and models. Geoffrey of Monmouth, for example, claims to have used an ancient Breton/Briton book as the main source for his *Historia Regnum Britanniae* (c. 1136). Wolfram von Eschenbach, in his *Parzival* (c. 1210), makes reference to an elusive Kyot as his informant on the Grail, and even Geoffrey Chaucer, in his *Troilus and Criseyde* (c. 1380), names an equally enigmatic Lollius as one of the authors on whom he relies for his account of the Trojan War. All three authors intend to imbue their works with greater credibility by referring to these supposedly older and, therefore, more authoritative sources. Furthermore, the fabrication of a source has the welcome side effect of providing protection against criticism of all sorts:

the blame can be passed on to the alleged model. Tolkien, then, knew about the uses and misuses of such a device. But he was not after playing games with his readers, in contrast to some of the medieval authors mentioned, nor did he feel any need to hide behind his 'sources'. Nevertheless, he must have felt grateful for being able to point out occasionally that he must not be expected to know all the answers to questions concerning Middle-earth[1] and that the opinions of his characters must not be equated with his own.[2] He considered himself merely a humble sub-creator who re-constructs the lost tales and chronicles of an older age.[3] The claim that *The Lord of the Rings*, as well as *The Hobbit* and *The Silmarillion*, as we know them, are but translations from the Red Book and other sources, is the expression of this self-same attitude though in a different form.

II

Tolkien, as part of his sub-creative project, provided a complex pedigree for the major languages of Middle-earth.[4] The linguistic history of Elvish has been relatively well researched, not least since the Eldarin tongues were at the centre of Tolkien's preoccupation with invented languages and the extant corpus of Elvish offers sufficient material for linguistic-philological inquiries.[5] Other languages remain peripheral and, until recently, no comprehensive study of even the major Mannish language, i.e. the Westron, was available.[6] These matters may seem, at first sight, of little import for the task of a translator who, as the

---

1 See, for example, Tolkien's admittance of ignorance concerning the fate of the Entwives in his letter to Naomi Mitchison from 25 April 1954 (Carpenter 1981:179) or his "I have yet to discover anything about the cats of Queen Berúthiel" (Letter to W.H. Auden, 7 June 1955, Carpenter 1981:217).
2 See his discussion of 'creation by evil' in his letter (draft) to Peter Hastings (September 1954; Carpenter 1981:190): "Treebeard is a *character* in my story, not me; and though he has a great memory and some earthy wisdom, he is not one of the Wise, and there is quite a lot he does not know or understand."
3 See, for example, the letter to Peter Hastings (draft September 1954; Carpenter 1981:189) where Tolkien comments: "[...] it [i.e. his work of sub-creation] seems to have grown out of hand, so that parts seem (to me) rather revealed through me than by me [...]."
4 Scholars differ as to the exact number of languages. Ruth S. Noel lists fourteen languages. Helge K. Fauskanger (http://www.ardalambion.com, accessed 27 July 2002) discusses this problem in depth and comes to the conclusion that there are two 'usable' languages (i.e. languages sufficiently developed to be used in communication) and eight to ten other languages, often with a very limited corpus. Tolkien, in Appendix F, mentions, for the Third Age, the Westron (the 'Common Speech', and Adûnaic as its ancestor), Drúadanic, Dunlendish, Rohirric, Quenya and Sindarin (as the two representatives of the Eldarin tongues), Entish, Orkish, Black Speech, and Dwarvish.
5 See Allan (1978), Kloczko (1995), Krege (2003), Noel (1980), and Pesch (2003).
6 See now Kloczko (2002). See http://www.ardalambion.com for an overview of what is known.

contributions to this volume show, faces difficulties enough on his or her way towards a 'readable' rendering of Tolkien's works. Yet since the foundation of Tolkien's world is basically linguistic,[7] a translator is well advised to take into consideration the linguistic setting as outlined and illustrated by Tolkien himself. In the following, I will concentrate on delineating the relationship between the different languages, real and invented, as they occur in *The Lord of the Rings*, and the possible implications for translations into other real languages in general. I will limit myself to the linguistic side of the problem and do not intend to explore the questions that arise in connection with attempts at translations into cultural settings other than those of Western Europe.[8]

Tolkien's first major act as 'translator' – which is of importance for all subsequent translators – is the division of the tongues of Middle-earth into two groups. The first comprises "languages alien to the Common Speech" (LotR p. 1167), which have been left unchanged, whereas the second group is made up of the Westron and related languages, which have been translated into English. A translator is therefore expected to retain the words and quotations from the Eldarin tongues, Black Speech, Dwarvish, etc. in their original form, yet render all other passages in his or her target language. This seems to tally with Tolkien's own point of view as made explicit in his 'Guide to the Names in *The Lord of the Rings*'. The retention of the 'alien languages' in their original form is unproblematic in the great majority of instances because the distance between 'alien languages' and the target language is very likely sufficient to reproduce the effect achieved in the original setting with English as the backdrop. The aesthetic quality, though, may be judged differently. Tolkien, in a letter to Naomi Mitchison (25 April 1954), points out that his Elvish tongues are "intended [...] to be specially pleasant" (Carpenter 1981:175). Quenya and Sindarin reflect Tolkien's personal 'phonaesthetic' predilections,[9] whereas Black Speech, with its harsh and guttural sounds, represents the very opposite. At worst it may happen that a new target-language

---

7 See his comment made in a letter to his son Christopher (21 February 1958): "my long book [i.e. LotR] is an attempt to create a world in which a form of language agreeable to my personal aesthetic might seem real" (Carpenter 1981:264).
8 See Bigger (1999) for a discussion of the problems likely to occur when attempting a translation of *The Lord of the Rings* into Hindi.
9 Quenya, as Tolkien writes in a letter to Naomi Mitchison (25 April 1954) is "composed on a Latin basis with two other (main) ingredients that happen to give me 'phonaesthetic' pleasure: Finnish and Greek. It is however less consonantal than any of the three. [...] [And Sindarin possesses] a character very like (though not identical with) British-Welsh" (Carpenter 1981:176).

audience perceives, on the one hand, Tolkien's Eldarin tongues as 'phonaesthetically' unpleasant and, on the other, Black Speech as agreeable.

Furthermore, translators into Finnish and Welsh may feel that the Finnish and Welsh elements in Quenya and Sindarin respectively cause these 'alien languages' to lose part of their 'otherness'. A speaker of Finnish is able to recognise some Quenya words or word-stems and would feel at home with the overall sound shape of Quenya. However, it seems that the similarities between 'late Quenya', as found in *The Lord of the Rings*, and Finnish are not sufficient to place them into the same language family (Finno-Ugric).[10]

The problems and complications connected with the wholesale transfer of 'alien languages' belonging to the first group are marginal when compared with the challenges that arise in the process of translating the Westron and languages related to it. Luckily, Tolkien has not only set the example in his own 'translation', but also provided helpful comments, as in 'On Translation' (Appendix F, Tolkien 1992a:1167-72), or even explicit guidelines, as in his 'Guide to the Names in *The Lord of the Rings*'.

The Common Speech, as used by the Hobbits for their narratives, has been turned into modern English. Tolkien points out that the variety spoken by the Hobbits is "for the most part a rustic dialect, whereas in Gondor and Rohan a more antique language was used, more formal and more terse" (Tolkien 1992a:1167). This difference in tone has been retained in the English 'translation' and is clearly noticeable in a comparison between Tolkien's depiction of the 'Hobbit talk' in the first chapter, and the loftier diction of the people of Gondor and Rohan later on. A careful translation into another language must take this difference in tone and register into account and dialectal markers as typical elements of Hobbit speech may be used to achieve this purpose.[11] Tolkien himself applied this device so coherently and skilfully that it has been possible to identify Shire talk with a dialect in the Oxfordshire and Warwickshire area.[12]

---

[10] I would like to thank Manu Paavola of the Finnish Tolkien Society for patiently answering my questions and pointing me to Harri Perälä's elucidating article on this subject.
[11] The use of dialectal varieties is not without dangers and requires a detailed knowledge of the affective connotations. Anecdotal (?) oral tradition has it that a dubber, in order to adapt an American movie for the German market, substituted the Bronx dialect of some Afro-American actors with the Bavarian dialect.
[12] See Johannesson (1997).

An enterprising translator may reproduce not only these differences in tone and register as given in the English version, but may even attempt a reconstruction of the original divergence, which "was greater than has been shown in this book" (Tolkien 1992a:1167). Pursuing this line of thought, a translator may also try and depict the one diverging point that Tolkien considered impossible to represent in modern English, namely the distinction in the pronouns of the second (and sometimes third) person between 'familiar' and 'deferential' forms. Neither Tolkien's brief sketch of the situation of the pronouns of address in Appendix F of *The Lord of the Rings* (Tolkien 1992a:1167) nor his notes in *The Peoples of Middle-earth* (Tolkien 1996:42-43) provide sufficient information for the reconstruction of the complete system of address. Yet we may be able to appreciate its complexity by means of a comparison with the forms of pronominal address in Middle English times. It actually seems a likely supposition that Tolkien took his inspiration for the Westron system of pronominal address from the one current in England in the 14th and 15th centuries. I will therefore, in a first step, briefly outline the situation in high to late Middle English times[13] and, in a second step, discuss the parallels and differences to the Westron.

In Old English the pronoun *þu* and its associated forms *þy* and *þyne* were used of the second-person singular while *ye, you, your* and *yours* were used of the second-person plural. Thus a speaker of Old English would invariably address one person with *þu*, several persons with *ye*. After the Norman Conquest in 1066, French became the dominant language of the high nobility, administration and literature for almost three centuries. It was probably under the influence of the French model (*tu* vs. *vous*) that the plural pronoun in Middle English[14] extended its use to singular contexts. Middle English thus offered a choice of a singular (*thou*) and a plural pronoun (*ye*) for addressing a *single* individual. Speakers of German or French may recognise parallels to their own systems of pronominal address.[15] Yet the use of Middle English *thou* and *ye* differs greatly from those languages in at least one point: it is possible to switch back and forth

---

13 The standard study on forms of address in the history of English is still Finkenstaedt (1963). See also Burnley (2003) and Honegger (2003).
14 I will use *ye* and *thou* when talking about Middle English pronouns of address used for individual persons, but I will use V (< vos) and T (< tu) as generic designators for the polite and the familiar pronouns respectively in any language (cf. Brown and Gilman 1960:254).
15 See German *du* vs. *Sie* and French *tu* vs. *vous*.

between the two forms. A speaker of Middle English may start out by addressing a foreigner with the 'deferential' *ye*, switch occasionally to the 'familiar' *thou* in moments of emotional closeness or anger, and then return to *ye* again.

In time, the pronoun became an important means to express social and interactional-emotional categories such as 'superordination vs. subordination', 'distance vs. intimacy', 'respect vs. disrespect', 'emotional involvement (positive or negative) vs. emotional distance', 'upper class usage vs. lower class usage', etc. A lord would typically use *thou* to a servant, who would give back the respectful *ye*. Children, too, would use *ye* towards their parents, but receive *thou*. Members of the nobility would habitually address each other with *ye*, occasionally switching to *thou* in emotionally charged situations or in private. Lower-class and rustic people, by contrast, generally employed *thou* among themselves and may not even have been familiar with the 'new' polite form *ye*.[16] The 'deferential' *ye* spread slowly from the upper classes and the courtly centres to the lower classes and the periphery. For decades, if not centuries, there existed varieties of English that knew only *thou* for addressing a single individual next to varieties that used both *thou* and *ye*. So it might have happened that a merchant from London would address a rustic from Yorkshire with *ye*, wishing to be polite, but receive *thou*. Not that the Yorkshireman wanted to insult the polite merchant, but he simply would know no better and was probably wondering why the Londoner was addressing him, an individual man, in the plural. The choice of the pronouns in such cases tells us not so much about the speakers' relative interactional position (e.g. superior vs. inferior), but is rather an indicator to their geographic origin (centre vs. periphery) and social standing (upwardly mobile middle class vs. rustic peasant).

Comparing the situation in Middle English with the one in the Westron, we can observe parallels as well as points of divergence.

The Westron spoken by the men of Gondor and Rohan features a 'deferential' and a 'familiar' form of the second person pronoun. In this it is similar to the more progressive varieties of Middle English. Unfortunately, Tolkien neither comments explicitly on the possibility of 'switching' between the forms of

---

16 Braun (1988:20) points out that in Jordanic Arabic, for example, rural speakers do not have a V form and thus, when speaking to an urban higher status addressee, cannot but use the T form.

pronominal address nor does he provide clear examples in any of the dialogues in *The Lord of the Rings*. He mentions that "the sudden use of *thou, thee* in the dialogue of Faramir and Éowyn [a private affair] is meant to represent (there being no other means of doing this in English) a significant change from the courteous to the familiar" (Tolkien 1996:43). Yet the published version of the dialogue (Tolkien 1992a:1000) shows no longer any use of *thou* and we are also not told whether Faramir was intended to change back to *ye* when speaking to Éowyn in public settings. It is my (educated) guess that Tolkien would have been in favour of such a flexible use of the pronouns of address.

The surviving instances of *thou* in *The Lord of the Rings* can be divided into five categories.[17]

Firstly, *thou* occurs in poetry and songs, such as the 'Hymn to Elbereth' ('Three is Company', Tolkien 1992a:92-93), Sam's 'Troll Song', ('The Flight to the Ford', Tolkien 1992a:223-24), Galadriel's 'Namárië' ('Farewell to Lórien', Tolkien 1992a:398), and the 'Song of the Ents' ('Treebeard', Tolkien 1992a:498-499).

Secondly, we encounter *thou* in archaic, formal or formulaic speech. Examples of this category are Galadriel's messages to Aragorn, Legolas and Gimli ('The White Rider', Tolkien 1992a:524-25) and those by Elrond and Arwen to Aragorn ('The Passing of the Grey Company', Tolkien 1992a:806). Tolkien's use of *thou* in these passages may have been inspired by the widespread use of the 'clerical *thou*' in medieval wisdom and 'advice' literature ('gnomic sayings'). Éowyn's "Health be with thee at thy going and coming!" ('The King of the Golden Hall', Tolkien 1992a:545) as well as Aragorn's "That office is not ended, and it shall be thine and thy heirs' as long as my line shall last. Do now thy office!" ('The Steward and the King', Tolkien 1992a:1003) are instances of formulaic use.

Thirdly, *thou* is used to express contempt ('negative emotional involvement'). Isildur, laying the curse on the King of the Mountains ('The Passing of the Grey Company', Tolkien 1992a:813), uses *thou*.[18] So do the Witchking of Angmar ('The Battle of the Pelennor Fields', Tolkien 1992a:874) when addressing Éowyn, and Sauron's messenger, who talks to Gandalf and Aragorn before the Black

---

17 I would like to thank Dieter Bachmann for providing me with all the passages in *The Lord of the Rings* containing *thou*.
18 The *thou* carries, of course, overtones of hatred and anger, too.

Gate ('The Black Gate Opens', Tolkien 1992a:923). Denethor, in his madness and grief, also addresses Gandalf contemptuously and provocatively with *thou*,[19] while Gandalf keeps his calm and gives *you* ('The Pyre of Denethor', Tolkien 1992a:886-88).

Fourthly, we find *thou* as an indicator of high emotion. Faramir, calling out to the dead Boromir ('The Window in the West', Tolkien 1992a:692), addresses him with *thou* in his first grief.[20] The dialogue between Éowyn and Aragorn ('The Passing of the Grey Company', Tolkien 1992a:816-17), then, contains a switch from *you* to *thou*. Éowyn, addressing Aragorn with *you*, begs him to be allowed to ride with him to battle, yet he steadfastly refuses. In her final turn, Éowyn changes to *thou* and comes close to openly confessing her love to Aragorn:

> 'Neither have those others who go with thee. They go only because they would not be parted from thee – because they love thee.' Then she turned and vanished into the night. (Tolkien 1992a:816)

Although Éowyn's switch from *you* to *thou* carries overtones of 'increased familiarity', it is predominantly a sign of her emotional turmoil and agitated state of mind. Aragorn continues to address her with *you*.

Fifthly, *thou* is employed to express 'familiarity' or emotional closeness. As we have seen, some of the preceding examples could have been included in this category, too. The one typical example of *thou* expressing familiarity is Aragorn's. Throughout the book, he addresses Éowyn consistently with *you* and it is only at the official betrothal of Faramir and Éowyn that he uses *thou* ('Many Partings', Tolkien 1992a:1014). By that time it is safe for him to give expression to his emotional closeness because Éowyn no longer desires his love.[21]

---

19 See Tolkien's note on a loose page: "[...] its use [i.e. of *thou*] by Denethor in his last madness to Gandalf, and by the Messenger of Sauron, was in both cases intended to be contemptuous" (Tolkien 1996:68). However, as Christopher Tolkien observes (Tolkien 1996:68), there remain some uncorrected occurrences of *you* in Denethor's speech (cf. Tolkien 1992a:887: "Do I not know that you commanded this halfling here to keep silence? That you brought him hither to be a spy within my very chamber?").

20 Otherwise, Faramir does not automatically address his brother with *thou*. See "'*Boromir, O Boromir!*' he cried. '*What did she say to you, the Lady that dies not? [...]*'." ('The Window on the West', Tolkien 1992a:693).

21 See Honegger (1999) for a detailed analysis of the relationship between Éowyn and Aragorn.

Our discussion of *thou* and *ye* in Middle English has enabled us to see things more clearly in these instances and we have been able to guess Tolkien's intention(s) behind his choice of *thou*. However, I have my doubts about the general reader's ability to appreciate these fine distinctions. Most speakers of English are familiar with the 'biblical *thou*' only and associate this form with archaic and ceremonious speech. Tolkien obviously found these connotations not conducive to his purpose and replaced *thou* in most cases by *you*.[22]

It is, therefore, no wonder that Tolkien did not plan to try and recreate the complications that arise when speakers of the Hobbit variety of the Westron address Gondorians, though he comments on the problem in 'On Translation'. He points out that the idiom of the Shire no longer features a differentiation into a deferential and a familiar form. All individual persons[23] are addressed with the 'familiar' pronoun.[24] This is reminiscent of the situation in Old English and in the older and less 'progressive' varieties of Middle English and provides the background for Tolkien's 'philological anecdote' about Pippin's linguistic *faux-pas*:

> Peregrin Took, for instance, in his first few days in Minas Tirith used the familiar forms to people of all ranks, including the Lord Denethor himself. This may have amused the aged Steward, but it must have astonished his servants. No doubt this free use of the familiar forms helped to spread the popular rumour that Peregrin was a person of very high rank in his own country. ('On Translation', Appendix F, Tolkien 1992a:1167)

If British English had retained the Old and early Middle English usage of addressing all individual people with *thou*, and if, let's say, American English, had developed and retained the late Middle English system of *thou* vs. *ye*, then we could attain a fairly close reconstruction of the situation as found in the Westron. Yet since English on either side of the Atlantic has kept only one pronoun of address, we lack contemporary linguistic means to represent the distinction and, as a consequence, the contrast between Pippin and Denethor

---

22 It would have been more consistent if Tolkien had restricted his use of *thou* entirely to ceremonious occasions. See also Christopher Tolkien's comment on Tolkien's use of *thou* and *you* (Tolkien 1996:67-68).
23 Tolkien (Tolkien 1992a:1167) mentions some few dialectal exceptions.
24 It is, of course, not quite appropriate to call this form 'familiar' since it was, at that time, the one in universal use and could no longer be contrasted with a 'deferential' form. The situation in the Hobbit Westron corresponds, in this aspect, to the one in modern English. There we have only one form of pronominal address (*you*) and cannot make a distinction between 'familiar' and 'deferential'.

cannot be shown. Tolkien could have presented the Gondorians as speaking a kind of Shakespearean early modern English, which still possessed a *thou* vs. *ye* dichotomy, but being no great admirer of Shakespeare, he decided against this option and preferred to leave the problem unresolved – and unresolved it is likely to remain. Even translations into modern languages that make the distinction in pronominal address cannot reproduce the coexistence of the Hobbit Westron and the Gondorian variety adequately. The 'deferential' form, for obvious reasons, is out of the question; but neither would it do to have the hobbit simply use the 'familiar' form because it does not possess the 'neutral' value of the Hobbit Common Speech form.

III

Tolkien, as we have seen, decided against taking recourse to an older stage of English to bring out some of the differences between the varieties of the Westron. Yet he saw no problem in using Old English (his 'ancient English') in order to represent Rohirric, the language of the Riders of the Mark:

> Having gone so far in my attempt to modernize and make familiar the language and names of Hobbits, I found myself involved in a further process. The Mannish languages that were related to the Westron should, it seemed to me, be turned into forms related to English. The language of Rohan I have accordingly made to resemble ancient English, since it was related both (more distantly) to the Common Speech, and (very closely) to the former tongue of the northern Hobbits, and was in comparison with the Westron archaic. In the Red Book it is noted in several places that when Hobbits heard the speech of Rohan they recognized many words and felt the language to be akin to their own, so that it seemed absurd to leave the recorded names and words of the Rohirrim in a wholly alien style.
> ('On Translation', Appendix F, Tolkien 1992a:1170)

However, the equation of the Hobbit Westron with modern English is not meant to imply that their respective developments have been identical (see the diagrams on the following pages).

Simplified Depiction of the Development of Some Mannish Languages

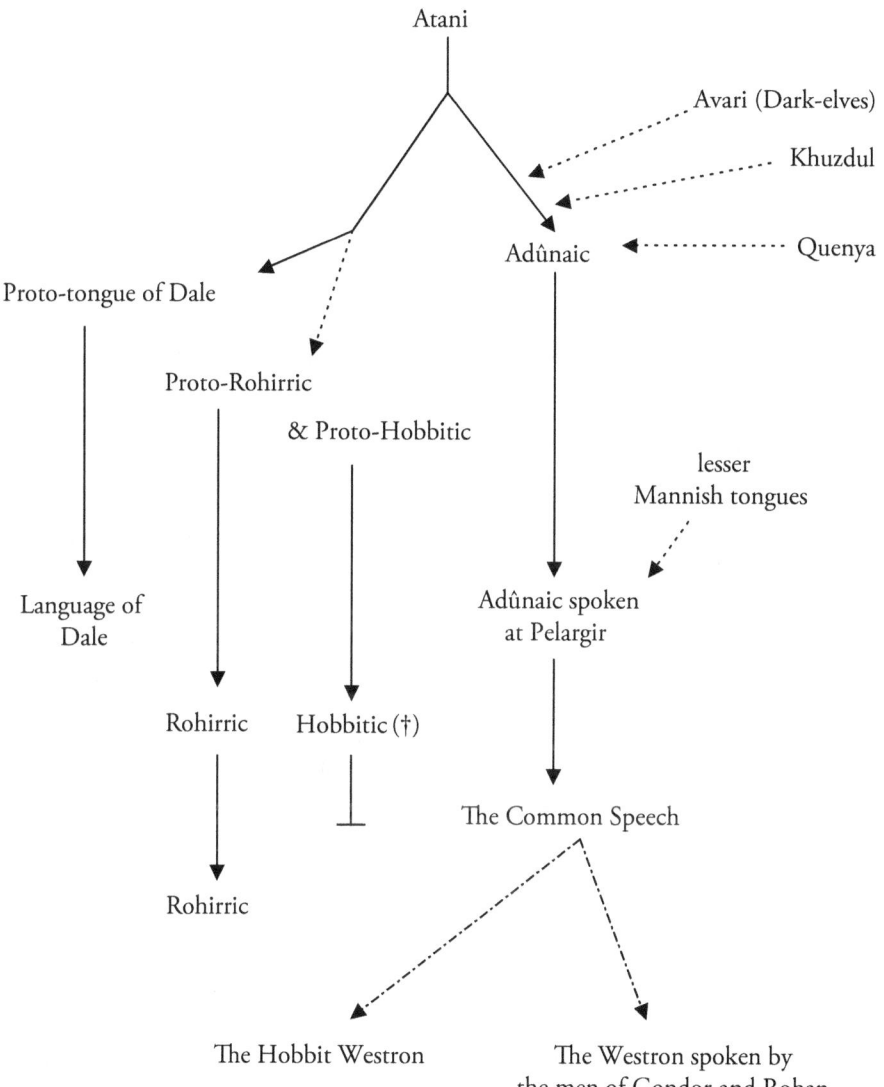

Simplified Depiction of the Development of the Germanic Languages

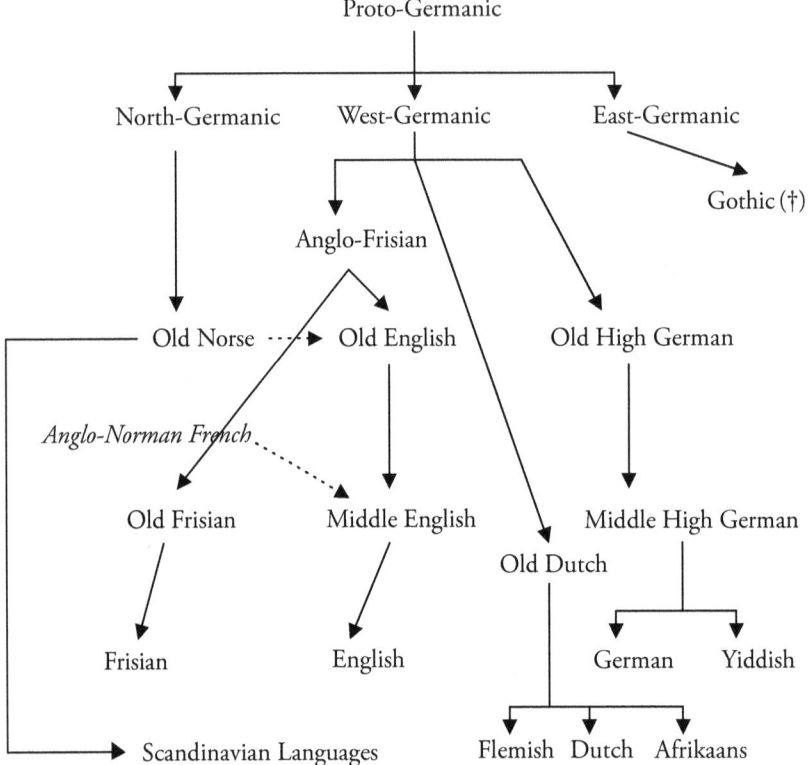

The northern Hobbits, before emigrating into the land around Bree and then further into the area of the Shire, had dwelt in close proximity to the ancestors of the Rohirrim in the upper vales of Anduin. Both peoples spoke closely associated Mannish tongues that were related to Adûnaic, the ancestral Mannish tongue of the Númenoreans.[25] When the Hobbits entered the area of the Shire, they soon abandoned their original tongue and adopted the Common Speech. This process was made easier by the fact that their original language showed a likeness to the Common Speech, which had developed out of Adûnaic as spoken at Pelargir "and mingled with many words of the languages of lesser men" ('Of Men', Appendix F, Tolkien 1992a:1163).[26] This account differs in important

---

25 'Lowdham's Report on the Adunaic Language' (Tolkien 1992b:413-440), though never completed, represents the most comprehensive description of Adûnaic.
26 See Christopher Tolkien's commentary (Tolkien 1996:64-65) on the origin of the Common Speech.

points from the development of Old English into Modern English. Firstly, the Germanic tribes that invaded Britain in the 5th century did not abandon their native tongue (proto-Old English). Secondly, the Anglo-Saxons themselves had in turn to deal with two invasions that made a lasting impact on Old English and shaped the future development of the English tongue: the Viking invasion and settlement in the 9th and 10th centuries, and the Norman conquest in 1066. These differences make clear that Tolkien obviously did not wish to model the development of the tongues of Middle-earth too closely on the development of real languages, although he incorporated many recognisably historical elements and kept within the limits of philological credibility.

What he wanted to achieve is the representation of the 'relative linguistic distance' between the languages in question. The idea of equating the Common Speech with modern English and, as a logical conclusion, to represent Rohirric by Old English, also suggested the solution to his problem of how to accommodate the "rabble of Eddaic-named dwarves out of Völuspá" that he had inherited from *The Hobbit* (Tolkien in a letter to G.E. Selby on 14 December 1937, quoted in Tolkien 1988:7). Christopher Tolkien comments:

> But now this inescapable Norse element had to be accounted for; and from that 'rabble of Eddaic-named dwarves out of Völuspá' the conception emerged that the Dwarves had 'outer names' derived from the tongues of Men with whom they had dealings, concealing their true names which they kept altogether secret. And this was very evidently an important component in the theory of the 'transposition of languages': for the Dwarves had *Norse* names because they lived among Men who *were represented* in *The Lord of the Rings* as speaking Norse. (Tolkien 1996:71)

By February 1942, i.e. the time he was working on the chapters introducing the Riders of Rohan, he had worked out the following list of correspondences:

Language of Shire = modern English
Language of Dale = Norse (used by Dwarves of that region)
Language of Rohan = Old English
'Modern English' is *lingua franca* spoken by all people (except a few secluded folk like Lórien) – but little and ill by orcs.
(Tolkien 1996:70)

We have now, instead of isolated languages, a complex series of correspondences.[27] A translator, then, cannot simply replace one element without upsetting the entire logical structure. So if the Common Speech is equated, for example, with modern French, then a conscientious translator should redress the balance by providing the French equivalents to Norse and Old English. Such a 'transposition' could look as follows:

> Language of Shire = modern French
> Language of Dale = Picard (used by Dwarves of that region)
> Language of Rohan = medieval (Vulgar) Latin
> 'Modern French' is *lingua franca* spoken by all people (except a few secluded folk like Lórien) – but little and ill by orcs.

As a consequence, the names and quotations from those languages would also have to be translated accordingly.[28] The problem of translating names is dealt with in detail in Rainer Nagel's contribution in this volume, so I will concentrate on the question of 'quotations'.

The great majority of 'foreign language quotations' in *The Lord of the Rings* is from tongues alien to the Westron, and they have therefore to be left in their original form. The only specimens from a related language are snatches of Rohirric. We have Éomer's joyous greeting of his lord "Westu Théoden hál!" (Tolkien 1992a:540), which echoes Beowulf's greeting to Hrothgar "Wæs þu, Hroðgar, hal!" in the Old English epic poem *Beowulf* (l.407), and Éowyn's wish for health to Théoden, "Ferthu Théoden hál!" (Tolkien 1992a:545), which is easily recognisable as Old English (Mercian?)[29] for 'Fare thou well, Théoden!'. These should be translated into the target language's equivalent to Old English,

---

27 See Kloczko (2002:169-170) on the role of Gothic. Although we have some Gothic elements, e.g. in the names of some hobbits and of the early king and princes of the Northmen and Éothéod, Gothic does not seem to play a systematic role in Tolkien's concept of language-transposition.

28 Tolkien's early view on how to treat the nomenclature is reflected in a letter to Rayner Unwin (3 July 1956; Carpenter 1981:249-250): "*In principle* I object as strongly as is possible to the 'translation' of the *nomenclature* at all (even by a competent person)." Yet this did not keep him from compiling his 'Guide to the Names in *The Lord of the Rings*' for the use of translators.

29 The 'corpus' of spoken Rohirric sentences, namely the two greetings quoted above, is too small to allow a definitive classification (see Toon 1992 for an in-depth discussion of the characteristics of Old English dialects). Yet since the names of the Rohirrim, at least, are clearly Mercian, as Tom Shippey (1992:112 and 2000:92) has pointed out, it is likely that Tolkien intended to represent Rohirric by means of the Mercian dialect of Old English. This would be very right and proper for people who inhabit a land called 'the Mark'.

for example Old High German in a German translation.³⁰ Needless to say that no translator known to me has as yet bothered to do so and though this 'translatorial negligence' is deplorable from a strictly systematic point of view, it makes good common sense from a cultural viewpoint. Tolkien's description of the Riders of Rohan contains too many historical and cultural parallels to the Anglo-Saxons as to make it likely that his choice of Old English was motivated merely by linguistic convenience. He must have been aware of this and tried to play down the impact:

> This linguistic procedure [i.e. translating Rohirric into Old English] does not imply that the Rohirrim closely resembled the ancient English otherwise, in culture or art, in weapons or modes of warfare, except in a general way due to their circumstances: a simpler and more primitive people living in contact with a higher and more venerable culture, and occupying lands that had once been part of its domain. ('On Translation', Appendix F, Tolkien 1992a:1170, fn 1)

As Tom Shippey (1992:111-119 and 2000:90-102) has convincingly shown, "this claim is totally untrue" (Shippey 1992:106), and Christopher Tolkien, too, concurs that a limitation to the linguistic level "is difficult to accept" (Tolkien 1996:71). There is no denying that the Rohirrim are Anglo-Saxons. Yet at the same time it must be pointed out that Tolkien did not model the Riders of Rohan so much on the historical ancestors of the English as on the Anglo-Saxons of poetry, which allows for the presence of horses and some other non-historical traits.³¹

(Mercian) Old English is, therefore, no mere linguistic *accidentia* that can be replaced by any other ancient language, but it is closely linked to the culture and character of the Rohirrim and, as a consequence, the Rohirric names and quotations are better left unchanged.³² This seems to be also Tolkien's point of view, as becomes evident from his comments in 'Guide to the Names in *The Lord of the Rings*'. Most of the names of the Rohirrim are not listed, which means that they "should be left *entirely* unchanged in any language used in translation" (Tolkien 1975:168). Furthermore, Tolkien often instructs potential

---

30 What would a translator into a Scandinavian language do? Rohirric would correspond to Old Norse in such a set-up, which leaves us in the lurch for finding an equivalent for the Language of Dale.
31 See Shippey (1992:111-119 and 181-182) for an in-depth discussion of this point. The historical Anglo-Saxons kept horses but did not use them in battle.
32 This applies even more to names that are meaningful in Old English (Rohirric) as well as in Elvish, such as *Orthanc* and *Eärendil*.

translators to leave Old English names unchanged because they are from the language of Rohan,[33] or even to use the original Rohirric names instead of the 'modernised' forms found in *The Lord of the Rings*.[34] This, of course, stands in contradiction to the system of correspondences based on the 'relative linguistic distance'. Tolkien may have sensed this contradiction, yet he seemed unwilling to give up either of the two positions and unable to find a satisfactory explanation that would harmonise these mutually incompatible viewpoints.

IV

Tolkien's 'fiction of authenticity', as has become clear in the course of my discussion, is not equally consistent in all points. The main contradiction is between Tolkien's theoretical conception of the 'relative linguistic distance' between the Mannish languages and his concrete implementation of these languages as Old English (for Rohirric) and modern English (for the Westron) in his narrative works. This unresolved tension is hardly ever noticed by the average reader, yet comes to the fore if a transposition into another language is attempted. It would be unfair, therefore, to expect consistency from a translator in a question that Tolkien himself had not been able to answer satisfactorily.[35] The indecisiveness remains, and a translator has, in the end, to make his or her own decisions how to deal with this problem. I don't mind Éomer greeting his lord unanimously with 'Westu, Théoden, hal!' in translations of *The Lord of the Rings* all over the world, but sometimes a bit of linguistic adaptation to the target language might not have been a bad idea. It would certainly do no harm to the German translation if Éomer were to utter his greetings in Old High German:

'Sî dû, Thioden, heil!'

---

[33] See, for example, the entries under *Scatha, Windfola, Eastemnet, Firien, Folde,* and *Halifirien*.
[34] See, for example, the entry under *Fenmarch* and Tolkien's deliberations under *Shadowfax*.
[35] The contradiction remains even if we differentiate between an 'editor/translator' persona for the Prologue and the Appendices, and an 'authorial' persona for the 'Guide to the Names in *The Lord of the Rings*'. See also Turner (2003).

About the author

Thomas Honegger holds a Ph.D. from the University of Zurich where he had been working as assistant and where he taught Old and Middle English. He is the author of *From Phoenix to Chauntecleer: Medieval English Animal Poetry* (1996) and has edited *News from the Shire and Beyond – Studies on Tolkien* (1997, together with Peter Buchs), *Root and Branch – Approaches towards Understanding Tolkien* (1999), *Authors, Heroes and Lovers* (2001), *Tolkien in Translation* (2003), and *Riddles, Knights, and Cross-Dressing Saints* (2004). Apart from his publications on animals and Tolkien, he has written about Chaucer, Shakespeare, and medieval romance. His 'Habilitationsschrift' focused on the interaction between lovers in medieval narrative fiction. He is, since April 2002, Professor for Medieval Studies at the Friedrich-Schiller-University (Jena) and currently head of the department.

Homepage: http://www2.uni-jena.de/fsu/anglistik/Struktur%20&%20Personal/Bereiche/Mediaevistik.html

References

ALLAN, Jim, *An Introduction to Elvish*, Bran's Head Books, 1978, reprinted 1995.

BIGGER, Andreas, 'Love Song of the Dark Lord: Some Musings on the Reception of Tolkien in an Indian Context', In: Thomas Honegger (ed.), *Root and Branch – Approaches towards Understanding Tolkien*, Zurich and Berne: Walking Tree Publishers, 1999, 165-79.

BRAUN, Fredericke, *Terms of Address: Problems of Patterns and Usage in Various Languages and Cultures*, Berlin: Mouton de Gruyter, 1988.

BROWN, Roger and Albert Gilman, 'The Pronouns of Power and Solidarity', In: Thomas A. Sebeok (ed.), *Style in Language*, New York and London: The Technology Press of Massachusetts Institute of Technology and John Wiley & Sons, 1960, 253-76.

BURNLEY, David, 'The T/V pronouns in Later Middle English Literature', In: Irma Taavitsainen and Andreas H. Jucker (eds.), *Diachronic Perspectives on Address Term Systems*, (Pragmatics & Beyond), Amsterdam: Benjamins, 2003, 27-45.

CARPENTER, Humphrey (ed., with the assistance of Christopher Tolkien), *The Letters of J.R.R. Tolkien*, Boston and New York: Houghton Mifflin, 1981, (paperback edition 2000).

FINKENSTAEDT, Thomas, You *und* thou: *Studien zur Anrede im Englischen*, Berlin: Walter de Gruyter, 1963.

HONEGGER, Thomas, 'Éowyn, Aragorn and the Hidden Dangers of Drink', In: *Inklings* 17, (Jahrbuch für Literatur und Ästhetik), (1999), 217-25.

  '"And if ye wol nat so, my lady sweete, Thanne preye I thee, [...]." Forms of address in Chaucer's *The Knight's Tale*', In: Irma Taavitsainen and Andreas H.

Jucker (eds.), *Diachronic Perspectives on Address Term Systems*, (Pragmatics & Beyond), Amsterdam: Benjamins, 2003, 61-84.

JOHANNESSON, Nils-Lennart, 'The Speech of the Individual and of the Community in *The Lord of the Rings*', In: Peter Buchs and Thomas Honegger (eds.), *News from the Shire and Beyond – Studies on Tolkien*, Zurich and Berne: Walking Tree Publishers, 1997, 11-47.

KLOCZKO, Edouard, *Dictionnaire des langues elfiques*, Toulon: Tamise Productions, 1995.

Dictionnaire des langues des Hobbits, des Nains, des Orques et autres créatures de la Terre du Milieu, de Númenor et d'Aman, Argenteuil: A.R.D.A., 2002.

KREGE, Wolfgang, *Elbisches Wörterbuch nach J.R.R. Tolkien*, Stuttgart: Klett-Cotta, 2003.

NOEL, Ruth S., *The Languages of Tolkien's Middle-earth: A complete guide to all fourteen of the languages Tolkien invented*, Boston: Houghton Mifflin, 1980.

PERÄLÄ, Harri, 'Are High Elves Finno-Ugric?', 2000, accessed 24 July 2002. http://www.sci.fi/~alboin/finn_que.htm

PESCH, Helmut W., *Elbisch*, Bergisch Gladbach: Bastei Lübbe, 2003.

SHIPPEY, Tom A., *The Road to Middle-earth*, (second edition), London: HarperCollins, 1992.

J.R.R. Tolkien: Author of the Century, London: HarperCollins, 2000.

TOLKIEN, J.R.R., 'Guide to the Names in *The Lord of the Rings*', In: Jared Lobdell (ed.), *A Tolkien Compass*, New York: Ballantine Books, 1975, reprinted 1980, 168-216.

The Return of the Shadow, (Volume 6 of *The History of Middle-earth*, edited by Christopher Tolkien), London: HarperCollins, 1988.

The Lord of the Rings, (text of the second edition of 1966; one-volume centenary edition), London: HarperCollins., 1992a.

Sauron Defeated, (Volume 9 of *The History of Middle-earth*, edited by Christopher Tolkien), London: HarperCollins, 1992b.

The Peoples of Middle-earth, (Volume 12 of *The History of Middle-earth*, edited by Christopher Tolkien), London: HarperCollins, 1996.

TOON, Thomas E., 'Old English Dialects', In: Richard M. Hogg (ed.), *The Cambridge History of the English Language, Volume 1: The Beginnings to 1066*, Cambridge: Cambridge University Press, 1992, 409-51.

TURNER, Allan, 'A Theoretical Model for Tolkien Translation Criticism', In: Thomas Honegger (ed.), *Tolkien in Translation*, Zurich and Berne: Walking Tree Publishers, 2003, 1-30.

Rainer Nagel

"The New One Wants to Assimilate the Alien"[1] — Different Interpretations of a Source Text as a Reason for Controversy: The 'Old' and the 'New' German Translation of *The Lord of the Rings*

Abstract

In 2000, Klett-Cotta, the German publisher of *The Lord of the Rings*, ventured forth with a new translation of the novel. This translation caused a big controversy among fans and casual readers alike. The 'new' translator, Wolfgang Krege, defended his version on grounds of his translation "assimilating the alien", whereas the first one (by Margaret Carroux) had just "rendered the text" from one language into another. From this point of view, it would appear that the major differences between the two texts are those of interpreting the source text, the author's intention, and the expectations of the potential audience. The article traces these factors against the backdrop of modern translation theory, contrasting especially J.R.R. Tolkien's intentions with the intentions and interpretation of Wolfgang Krege. Comparisons will be made on the levels of morphology, syntax, semantics, and stylistics, if necessary back-translated from one of the German versions into English should major differences arise.

1. Interpretation as the Cornerstone of Translation

From the point of view of text linguistics, any text starts out as a dichotomy between text producer and text recipient. In this model, the translator occupies what might best be described as an intermediary position between the two. As such, he shares a niche with others who modify an existing text (editors, censors, rewriters, etc.).[2] The specific mediation a translator performs is that of

---

1 This is the translation of a statement made by Wolfgang Krege in an email sent by Klett-Cotta to customers complaining about the new translation. The quote can be found at:
http://www.tolkiengesellschaft.de/alleszutolkien/uebersetzung/uebersetzungverlagoff.shtml
The original text was published in *Tolkien Times*, 11 August 2000; and there is also a full rendition of Wolfgang Krege's text in Buelles (2001), along with a selection of fan reaction and a few remarks by Tolkien about the use of 'modern English'). The German text (contrasting the old and new translations) is: "Die neue will das Fremde assimilieren."
My translation of "das Fremde" with "the alien" (and not "the foreign") is influenced by the notion of "Fremdartigkeit" (*alienness*) in the sense of intercultural transfer of information (Lönker [1992 passim]).
2 On the basis of this broader classification, it might be a good idea to adopt the larger system of classification as presented by Sager (1991). Sager opts for a general theory of text modification by creating four large subgroups: monolingual modification of the text without change of text type (e.g., editing); monolingual modification of the text with change of text type (e.g., summary); translation without change of text type; and translation with change of text type (e.g., translation of a letter by content rather than wording).

mediating between the speakers of two languages, implying that speakers of the target language (TL), the one he is translating for, are not (or at least not sufficiently) familiar with the source language (SL). This means that first he has to process and understand (and interpret) the SL text before he can go on to produce a derived version of that text in the target language. This makes the translator's task a lot more difficult, for not only does he have to satisfy his own "threshold of termination" in the words of Beaugrande/Dressler (1981:43), but also has to anticipate the readers'. Part of this anticipation is not only a thorough knowledge of both the source language and the target language (with knowledge of the target language being the more important one[3]), but also substantial inferential knowledge about both the source language and the target language's cultures, in order to be able to properly translate the text without confusing the target reader with concepts strange or even alien to his culture. As a basic model of the process, the one proposed as early as Stein (1980:62) will do for purposes of this article.[4]

The producer of the SL text writes from within a particular situation (read: extra-linguistic reality) with a certain intention, having a particular audience in mind; this text is composed of linguistic signs from the source language. The SL reader then decodes the text and tries to understand the text producer's intentions. This SL text recipient, in case of the translator, then becomes the new text producer, creating a derived text on the basis of the SL text. Whatever the text producer's original intention was, the translator's is now different: it is to render the text understandable (and acceptable) to the text recipient the translator is writing for. Thus, the translator has to understand not only intention and situation of the text producer, but also has to take into account the situation of the TL text recipient, allowing for the fact that the cultural situation may not be the same between the two. At the end of the process, ideally the TL text recipient understands the text exactly in the way the SL text producer intended it to be, while at the same time the TL text remains as close as possible to the SL text.[5]

---

3 Cf. especially Hönig/Kußmaul (1996⁴:passim) and Lang (1992).
4 A much broader and better-developed model, taking into account the various stages of reading, understanding, and translating, is offered in Hellwig (1995: 405).
5 Nord (1993) uses the term 'loyalty' for such adherence to the SL text; Hermanns 1991 opts for "translational correctness". In a somewhat innovative approach, Gramlich (2003) views the translator as the "co-author" of the translated text.

This is, of course, the ideal case of translation, with the translator trying to be as "loyal" to the SL text as possible and without any motivations (internal or external ones) that might lead him into modifying the SL text[6] (i.e., Sager's translation without change of text type).

2. Tolkien's Intentions When Writing *The Lord of the Rings*

Even without taking a closer look at Tolkien's guidelines for translators as expressed in Tolkien (1980)[7], we need to approach his intentions in writing the book *per se*, in order to be able to deal with how the translators interpreted these.

As summarised neatly in the first two chapters of Shippey (1992), Tolkien's main impetus for writing *The Lord of the Rings* was his desire to showcase his languages, to put them into a world where they could 'naturally' exist (and not *vice versa*). In Tolkien's own words, taken from his correspondence, as published posthumously in 1981, hereafter referred to as *Letters* (*Letters* 219f.):

> The invention of languages is the foundation. The 'stories' were made rather to provide a world for the languages than the reverse. To me a name comes first and the story follows. [...] It is to me, anyway, an essay in 'linguistic aesthetic', as I sometimes say to people who ask me 'what is it all about?'

The same thought, governing the relation of the various elements in *The Lord of the Rings*, is expressed even more clearly in a letter from Tolkien to his son Christopher from 21 February 1958[8] (*Letters* 264; Tolkien's italics):

> All the same, I suddenly realized that I am a *pure* philologist. I like history, and am moved by it, but its finest moments for me are those in which it throws light on words and names! Several people (and I agree) spoke to me of the art with which you made the beady-eyed Attila on his couch almost vividly present. Yet oddly, I find the thing that really thrills my nerves is the one you mentioned casually: *atta, attila*. Without these syllables the whole great drama both of history and legend loses savour for me – or would.

---

6 See footnote 31 on page 110 (*Raise the Titanic*) for an example of text modification (without change of text class) by internal motivation (i.e., the translator's decision). An example of external modification (change of text class at the behest of an editor) can be found in early American translations of Jules Verne's *20,000 Leagues Beneath the Sea*, from which all references to Ned Land being a socialist were cut because the publisher wanted to treat this as a children's book.
7 These have been covered in much greater detail elsewhere in this book (cf. pp. 93-113 of this volume). I will only bring them into the course of this treatment where they are needed.
8 Referring to a presentation given by Christopher Tolkien on 'Barbarians and Citizens', his subject being the heroes of northern legend as seen in different ways by Germanic poets and Roman writers.

Shippey, in his *Afterword* (1992:292), puts it like this: "The real horror for Tolkien would probably have come when he realised that there were people writing about him who could not tell Old English from Old Norse, and genuinely thought the difference didn't matter."

This line of thinking is further evidenced in Tolkien's dealing with translations. After being dissatisfied with the Dutch (1956) and Swedish (1959) translations (*Letters* 304-307; cf. also Carpenter [1977:300]), Tolkien devised a glossary of what he regarded as the most important proper names (the above-mentioned Tolkien [1980]), which had to be used by all subsequent translators. As Tolkien himself summed up his view in a letter of 24 January 1961 (regarding the problems of the Swedish translation): "The original is my only protection against the translators" (*Letters* 304). Thus, Tolkien (1980:154) starts out with (Tolkien's italics):

> It is desirable that the translator should read Appendix F in Volume III of *The Lord of the Rings* and follow the theory there set out. In the original text English represents the Common Speech of the supposed period. Names that are given in modern English therefore represent names in the Common Speech, often but not always being translations of older names in other languages, especially Sindarin (Grey-Elven). The language of translation now replaces English as the equivalent of the Common Speech; the names in English form should therefore be translated into the other language *according to their meaning* (as closely as possible).

All of this makes it abundantly clear that any translation of *The Lord of the Rings* is to be judged by the way it treats Tolkien's use of language.

3. The Positions of the German Translators

Not much is known about the positions held by Margaret Carroux when working on her translation of *The Lord of the Rings* in 1968, except for her occasional remark in footnotes in the German appendices. As I have pointed out elsewhere in this publication[9], she remained, on the whole, true to the stipulations given

---

9 On page 106, I quote Carroux's probably best-known of these notes. Another one deals with the translation process in general, but does not get beyond a con-committal "[d]ieser Prozeß fand dann natürlich nochmals in der Übersetzung vom Englischen ins Deutsche statt." (My translation: "This process, of course, took place once again when translating from English into German.") – *Anh.* 123. In a similar vein, there is a brief note in *Anh.* 103 mentioning that the chapter on pronunciation had to be deleted, and that the *Silmarillion* has advice on the pronunciation of Elvish names.

by Tolkien in his notes for translators, thus, with very few exceptions, remaining as 'loyal' to the text as was possible without sacrificing the need to create a readable German text.

It is interesting that Wolfgang Krege starts out his rationalisation of his own translation by setting it against that of Margaret Carroux. In the publishing company's email referenced in footnote 1, he has the following to say:[10]

> Die Übersetzerin Margaret Carroux hat also an etlichen Stellen die auch aus meiner Sicht richtigen Worte schon gefunden. Dies waren die schwierigsten Momente in meiner Arbeit. Abschreiben tut weh.
>
> Dennoch wird der Leser auch ohne peniblen Textvergleich Unterschiede bemerken. Die alte Fassung ist nachvollziehend; sie bildet den fremden Text in der eigenen Sprache getreu ab, wobei als unvermeidlich in Kauf genommen wird, dass der Ausdruck ein wenig blasser, das Tempo langsamer, der Stil gleichförmiger wird. Die neue will das Fremde assimilieren. Der Text soll, obwohl Übersetzung, ein gewisses Eigentempo in den Spielräumen der deutschen Sprache gewinnen: Farben, Tempo, Kontraste. Die Blässe der durchschnittlichen guten Übersetzung im Vergleich zum Original ist hier nicht mehr entschuldbar.

This is a tall order, especially taking into account that part of the statement renouncing the concept of 'loyalty' developed so far. On the other hand, this is basically a statement of adapting a text more closely to the cultural situation of the target language it is being translated into – all in all, not a bad proposition. The problem here is to find the right balance.[11] It is also a question of choosing the appropriate linguistic means in the target language. In this regard, another statement given by Wolfgang Krege during a radio interview (WDR 5) on

---

10 My translation: "Thus, translator Margaret Carroux has already found the right words, even from my point of view, in quite a few places. These were the hardest moments in my task. Having to copy hurts. And yet, even without minute comparisons, the reader will notice some differences. The old version is reconstructing; it transfers the text faithfully into the target language, taking it for granted that expressions fade a bit, speed slows down, style gets levelled. The new one wants to assimilate the alien. The text, despite being a translation, is to gain a certain life of its own within the limits of the German language: colour, speed, contrasts. The blandness of the average, good translation in comparison to the original text can no longer be excused here."

11 This is, of course, not a new problem. There were, for instance, heated discussions in the sixties and seventies on whether a crime novel set in London should, after translation, still be set in London, or whether it should rather be transferred (or, as Krege would say, "assimilated") into a Berlin setting. The same thing happened to the German translation of *Pygmalion*, when Eliza Doolittle's Cockney accent was turned into a Berlin accent (see Hönig/Kussmaul [1996:126]).

10 December 2001 is very instructive with regard to his views on both English and German as relevant for *The Lord of the Rings*:[12]

> Vor allem das *Silmarillion* ist in einem Englisch [verfaßt], das heute nirgends mehr gesprochen und geschrieben [wird], einem sehr stark archaischen Englisch, das auch von der englischen Kritik, die ganz auf ihre moderne Spra[che], auf die Modernität ihrer Sprache stolz ist, fürchterlich beschimpft wurde. *Der Hobbit* dagegen ist in ganz normalem modernen Englisch geschrieben. Und im *Herrn der Ringe* stoßen diese beiden Dinge aufeinander. Man kann daraus als Übersetzer die Konsequenz ziehen, eine mittlere Linie zwischen beiden zu befolgen. Dann bekommt man so eine gleichmäßige, etwas patinierte Sprache – nicht geradezu altertümlich, aber auch nicht so ganz modern –, die sich dann mit wenig Variationen durch das ganze Buch hindurchzieht. Oder man kann im Gegenteil den Kontrast zwischen beiden besonders stark herausarbeiten.

Besides the fact that it once again points out the difference between Carroux's (implied) "uniform" and "patinated" translation and Krege's "contrasting" one (which then, by default is neither "uniform" nor "patinated"), this statement does contain a few interesting insights into the source language (English) that Krege was to assimilate. *The Hobbit* may have been written in "plain and simple English" from the point of view of a speaker of 1937's English, but even then only to a certain degree. Even *The Hobbit* contains linguistic features that were out of date at the time of its composition, for instance the use of be + past participle to express a state of things (e.g., "We are met to discuss our plans, our ways, means, policy and devices." – *Hobbit* 26).[13] Also, it introduces Tolkien's retro-actively coined plural form, *dwarves*, which did not exist anymore at the time of his writing *The Hobbit*, the standard form being *dwarfs*.[14] As regards the "widely lambasted" English of the *Silmarillion*, at least the

---

12 Quoted from: http://www.tolkiengesellschaft.de/alleszutolkien/uebersetzung/uebersetzungradio.shtml. My translation: "*The Silmarillion* especially is written in a variety of English that is neither spoken nor written anywhere, anymore, a strongly archaic variety of English that was terribly lambasted by English criticism, which is proud of its modern language, of the modernity of its language. *The Hobbit*, on the other hand, is written in plain and simple modern English. And with *The Lord of the Rings*, the two varieties clash. It is perfectly within your rights as a translator to follow a middle line between the two. This leads you to a uniform, slightly patinated use of language – not exactly archaic, but not really modern, either – within the course of the entire book, with only a small amount of variation. Or, on the other hand, you can work out the contrast between the two in a clearly defined fashion."
13 Faiß (1989:298) classifies such constructions as "stark eingeschränkt" ("highly restricted") in Present-Day English, setting them off from constructions using "have", describing the end of an action; see also Lamprecht (1986:§514, note). The phenomenon is not even treated anymore in the 1999 edition of the *CGEL*, probably *the* standard grammar of English.
14 Tolkien's spelling was even corrected by the typesetters back into the standard form. The *OED* still lists only *dwarfs* as the correct plural form; cf. also Nagel (1993:265).

Daily Mail ("Passages of sublime poetic expression") and the *Sunday Telegraph* ("The mythology gives his writings their indisputable grandeur and power.") seemed to think otherwise, and *The Guardian* asked the (rhetorical) question: "How, given little over half a century of work, did one man become the creative equivalent of a people."[15]

In the end, it would appear that Wolfgang Krege approached his translation not merely as a translation, but as a modernisation of Tolkien's text to make it acceptable (I presume) for what he believed to be a 'new' generation of readers. What needs to be seen now is how Wolfgang Krege set about modifying the Carroux translation.

4. An Introductory Example: *The Prancing Pony*

In the *Tolkien Times* from 11 August 2000, along with the general remarks about his mode of translating, Wolfgang Krege juxtaposes part of the scene at the *Prancing Pony* in Bree (p. 4). I rely in the following on examples from Gloge (2003:52), adding full back-translations on the basis of Gloge's footnotes, with "OV" = "Original Version" (as quoted from *LotR* 150), "OT" = "Old Translation" (as quoted from the *Tolkien Times*, p. 4), "NT" = "New Translation" (as quoted from the *Tolkien Times*, p. 4), and "BT" = "Back-Translation (of NT)".

Excerpt 1:

OV 'Where are you, you woolly-footed slow-coach?'
OT "Wo steckst du denn, du wollfüßiges Faultier?"
NT "Wo steckst du denn, du flaumfüßiger Penner?"
BT 'Where are you, you fluffy-footed dosser?'

This is one of these instances where OT fails to get the direct equivalent across, instead resorting *sloth*, where German "Faulpelz" would have been more acceptable. "Penner" / *dosser*, on the other hand, shifts the focus onto a lower stylistic level, acceptable in young persons' speech, but not expected in the language of an elderly innkeeper.

---

15 Quotes are from the back of *The Silmarillion* (*Sil*). There are six other statements on the back of this edition, with the *Financial Times* and the *Glasgow Herald* praising the mythology presented in the *Silmarillion*. The statements from the *Washington Post*, the *Toronto Globe & Mail*, the *New York Times Book Review*, and the *Sydney Morning Herald* cannot really count here, since these are not English papers.

Excerpt 2:

OV 'A cheery-looking hobbit bobbed out of a door [...]'
OT "Ein vergnügt aussehender Hobbit schoß aus der Tür heraus [...]"
NT "Ein aufgeweckt aussehender Hobbit kam aus einer Tür geschossen [...]"
BT 'A bright-looking hobbit came bobbing out of a door [...]'

Here, "kam aus einer Tür geschossen" (as the back-translation shows) is stylistically inferior to "schoß aus der Tür heraus". While NT successfully corrects OT's impression that there was only one door in the *Prancing Pony* for the servants to use, "aufgeweckt" / *bright* is not exactly within the span of meaning of "cheery" (and besides, Nob, who we are talking about here, is not exactly bright, anyway).

Excerpt 3:

OV 'But we've got a room or two in the north wing that were made special for hobbits, when this place was built.'
OT "Aber wir haben ein paar Zimmer im Nordflügel, die eigens für Hobbits vorgesehen wurden, als dieses Haus gebaut wurde."
NT "Aber im Nordflügel haben wir ein paar Zimmer, die wurden speziell für Hobbits angelegt, als dieser Laden hier gebaut wurde."
BT 'But in the north wing, we've got a room or two that were made special for hobbits, when this here pile was built.'

None of the two translations takes particular care of the zero-marked adverb "special" in Butterbur's speech (a clear indication of him being somewhat elderly and using rather old-fashioned language), so in fact they have both lost one feature of the archaic quality inherent in Tolkien's language. OT's translation of *place* with "Haus" is acceptable, as are both "vorgesehen" and "angelegt" for multi-functional *made*. And while NT's shift of emphasis (in OT, as in the original text, the emphasis is on the rooms being made for hobbits, while in NT, the emphasis is on the rooms being in the north wing), it is once again the style of Butterbur's language that has been reduced to that of a young speaker of German, evidenced both in "Laden" / *pile* for *place* and in the linking of the subordinate clause (positioning the verb at the beginning of the subordinate clause to render communication easier).

Excerpt 4:

OV 'Here is a nice little parlour.'
OT "Hier ist eine kleine nette Gaststube."

NT "Hier haben wir ein nettes kleines Klubzimmer."
BT 'Here we have a nice little parlour.'

Here, NT actually is an improvement on OT. First, the different sentence structure of NT conveys the somewhat condescending tone Butterbur uses on the hobbits ("nice little") by using "hier haben wir". Second, the meaning of *parlour* is more specified than simply "Gaststube" (according to the *OED*: "A room in an inn, more private than the taproom, where people may converse apart"); while "Klubzimmer" may sound too modern[16], the alternative "Gesellschaftszimmer" does seem a bit clumsy, while "Sitzungszimmer" would once again come off too 'modern'.

Excerpt 5:

OV 'If he don't come, ring and shout.'
OT "Wenn er nicht kommt, läutet und ruft."
NT "Wenn er nicht kommt, noch mal lauter bimmeln und brüllen."
BT 'If he doesn't come, jangle the bell again, louder, and yell.'

Granted, Butterbur's use of "he don't" instead of "he doesn't" is substandard, but then again displays a typical feature of rural English dialects, which is in no way tied to age or social group (and hard to render adequately into German, since German does not have a grammatical structure comparable to the *do* paraphrase for question and negation). And thus, OT does a good job of rendering Butterbur's meaning; if the German translation is 'bland', then, unfortunately, so is the original. NT's emendation of "ruft" to "brüllen" is unnecessary, since the semantic range of *shout* covers either. Once again, though, we see the recourse to the speech patterns of younger Germans: simplified sentence structure (infinite verb-forms replacing finite ones) and a shift of stylistic level from standard (but somewhat old-fashioned) "läuten" to colloquial "bimmeln".

With only a slight bias (and a bit of melodrama), Gloge (2003:52) sums up his observations:

---

16 Then again, we are talking about hobbits here, and there are quite a lot of things about hobbits that would be considered 'too modern' for a fantasy setting. Just think of the Shire post, auctioneering firms, potatoes, or fish and chips; cf. also Shippey (1992: chapter 3). Thus, Gloge's (2003:52) attempt at ridiculing this translation by back-translating it as "club room" is missing its target, especially with the first usage of *parlour* as a private room in public houses coming as late as 1870 (according to the *OED*, the word originally meant "An apartment in a monastery for conversation with persons from outside, or among the inmates" [*a*1225]), and thus being still rather topical in Tolkien's day.

> A clear tendency to update Tolkien's language can be seen. The text is adapted to modern German thus altogether disregarding Tolkien's intentional old-world quality of the language and its special effect. […]
>
> Of course, these are only small changes but even in these few passages a more or less subliminal imitation of modern German usage is revealed. Even though the hobbits can be said to communicate in the most modern form compared to all other peoples in Middle-earth, too modern a translation of Tolkien's carefully selected prose runs the risk of destroying the magic of this remote world by making the language sound too vulgar.

On the other hand, this is no more than what Krege had intended to set out to do in the first place, and as far as a 'modernisation' of the text is concerned, he has achieved his goal – a goal, quite obviously, being to address the new translation towards a younger circle of readers by trying to imitate their speech patterns, or at least those speech patterns that the translator feels to be used or seen as attractive or desirable by those readers.

This, in itself, is part of the translator's job: trying to figure out the needs and desires of his audience and adjust his translation accordingly. If Krege regards the language of *The Hobbit* as "plain and simple" English, and wants his translation of the *Lord of the Rings* to sound similar, then such 'modernisation' (in fact a reduction of vocabulary and stylistic level) might well be the path to take. This would, then, indicate that by 'assimilating' the novel Krege actually means "assimilating it into a particular variety of German", i.e., the German used by the younger generations.

From the point of view of translation theory, Krege has thus limited the range of potential addressees down to one particular subset of readers. There are probably sound reasons for that (like publisher's demographics requiring concentration on this particular age group specifically by choosing appropriate language). If that were the case, the peculiarities of the translation we have seen so far would not be the result of translatorial failure, but of a conscious decision to modify the text to make it more accessible to certain readers, and less accessible to others (i.e., those belonging to less prominent demographic groups).

5. An In-Depth Comparison

Given the results we have obtained so far, we would expect the new German translation to be a conscious modernisation of the original, adapting it to a younger audience by deliberately changing Tolkien's sometimes old-fashioned choice of words and phrases to a text easier to read for younger people and, at the same time, more 'in tune' with current German. Given his views about language as used in his novel (and, as has been pointed out, its ultimate focus and reason of existence), Tolkien himself would probably have disapproved on these grounds already.[17] And yet, if done consequently and correctly, there may at least a point to be made about a valid 'modern' interpretation of a 'literary classic'.

To investigate this claim further, I will now take a look at the beginning of one of those chapters already intensively discussed: Chapter VII of Book Two of *The Fellowship of the Ring*, 'The Mirror of Galadriel'.[18] The excerpt treated here is largely descriptive, allowing me to focus on yet another facet of the translation process. Discussion will be paragraph by paragraph; sources are: OV – *LotR* 344-5; OT – *HdR 1 (C)* 426; NT – *HdR 1 (K)* 457-8. Back-translations to NT will be added as necessary.

> OV
> The sun was sinking behind the mountains, and the shadows were deepening in the woods, when they went on again. Their paths went now into thickets where the dusk had already gathered. Night came beneath the trees as they walked, and the Elves uncovered their silver lamps.
>
> OT
> Die Sonne ging hinter dem Gebirge unter und die Schatten wurden dunkler in den Wäldern, als sie wieder weitergingen. Ihre Pfade führten sie nun in Dickichte, wo sich die Dämmerung schon sammelte. Nacht wurde es unter

---

17 Tolkien's views on 'modernising' (his) language are clearly expressed in a letter to Hugh Brogan from December 1955 (*Letters* 225f.). The following passage (p. 226) is revealing (Tolkien's italics): "But there would be an insincerity of thought, a disunion of word and meaning. For a King who spoke in a modern style would not really think in such terms at all [...]. I can see no more reason for not using the much *terser* and more vivid ancient *style*, than for changing the obsolete weapons, helms, shields, hauberks into modern uniforms." It should be noted that Wolfgang Krege, who translated the *Letters* into German, must have been aware of this statement.

18 The German Tolkien Society organised two workshops on the new translation, resulting not only in an encompassing list of criticism, but also of a direct comparison between the two version of this chapter. I am deeply indebted to Marcel Buelles and Dr. Christian Weichmann for valuable analytical work on this chapter, on which I draw rather heavily here.

den Bäumen während sie wanderten, und die Elben zündeten ihre silbernen Lampen an.

NT
Die Sonne versank schon hinter den Bergen und die Schatten im Wald wurden dunkler, als sie weitergingen. Ihre Wege führten nun durch dichte Gehölze, in denen die Dämmerung schon fortgeschritten war. Unter den Bäumen wurde es Nacht, und die Elben holten ihre Lämpchen hervor.

Commentary

It is obvious at first glance that OT tries to convey Tolkien's old-fashioned syntax, while NT modernises syntactic structures almost wherever possible. While this usually takes away from the intended atmosphere of the text, it sometimes helps to convey syntactic functions, for instance by adding "schon" to get across the progressive aspect not available in German. The last sentence is curious: While NT emends an inaccuracy of OT (*uncovered* implies the lamps are already lit), it also adds diminutive "-chen" (while deleting *silver*), thus possibly creating a more endearing, also diminutive, depiction of the elves. The change from "Dickichte" to "dichte Gehölze" probably results from the fact that "Dickicht" actually does not have a plural in German.

> OV
> Suddenly they came out into the open again and found themselves under a pale evening sky pricked by a few early stars. There was a wide treeless space before them, running in a great circle and bending away on either hand. Beyond it was a deep fosse lost in soft shadow, but the grass upon its brink was green, as if it glowed still in memory of the sun that had gone. Upon the further side there rose to a great height a green wall encircling a green hill thronged with mallorn-trees taller than any they had yet seen in the land. Their height could not be guessed, but they stood up in the twilight like living towers. In their many-tiered branches and amid their ever-moving leaves countless lights were gleaming, green and gold and silver. Haldir turned towards the Company.

> OT
> Plötzlich kamen sie wieder ins Freie und standen unter einem blassen Abendhimmel, an dem einige frühe Sterne blinkten. Vor ihnen erstreckte sich eine weite baumlose Fläche, die einen großen Kreis beschrieb und zu beiden Seiten abfiel. Dahinter lag in sanftem Schatten ein tiefer Graben, aber das Gras an seinem Rand war grün, als glühe es noch in der Erinnerung an die untergegangene Sonne. Auf der anderen Seite erhob sich zu großer Höhe eine grüne Mauer; sie umgab einen Berg, der dicht mit Mallorn, größer als alle, die sie bisher in diesem Land gesehen hatten, bestanden war. Ihre Höhe ließ sich nicht erraten, aber sie ragten in der Dämmerung empor wie lebende

Türme. In ihren reichverzweigten Ästen und zwischen den sich unablässig bewegenden Blättern schimmerten unzählige Lichter, grün, golden und silbern. Haldir wandte sich zu der Gemeinschaft um.

NT
Plötzlich kamen sie wieder ins Freie und sahen über sich einen blassen Abendhimmel, an dem erst wenige frühe Sterne standen. Sie gingen über eine große baumlose Fläche, die einen weiten Bogen beschrieb und sich zu beiden Seiten in den Hintergrund fortsetzte. In der Mitte stießen sie auf einen tiefen Graben, der schon in milde Dunkelheit versunken war, aber das Gras an seinem Rand war grün, als glühte es noch in Erinnerung an die untergegangene Sonne. Auf der anderen Seite erhob sich eine hohe grüne Mauer. Sie umfasste einen grünen Hügel, auf dem dicht an dicht die größten Mallornbäume standen, die sie in diesem Land bisher gesehen hatten. Ihre Höhe war schwer zu schätzen, aber in der Dämmerung ragten sie auf wie lebende Türme. Auf ihrem vielstufigen Geäst und dem unermüdlich wedelnden Laubwerk schimmerten unzählige Lichter hervor, grüne, goldene und silberne. Haldir wandte sich zu den Gefährten um.

Commentary

In the first sentence, NT emends a slight mistake of OT, by changing "blinkten" (BT: "a pale evening sky in which a few early stars were twinkling") to "standen" ("stood"). The rest of the translation, however, despite being lexically adequate, subtly shifts the meaning of the scene. In OV, the Company stop to examine what lies in front of them. It is actually not until two paragraphs later that they continue moving.[19] In NT, however, the Company continue at once (BT: "They walked across a wide treeless space."), taking the view of the scenery in as they go. This implies that, given the length of the description, their way to Caras Galadhon is a rather lengthy one, leading them once around the entire plain. (BT: "In the middle, they arrived at a deep fosse [...].") Judging from NT, Haldir only starts speaking once the Company have reached that fosse, welcoming them into Calas Galadhon not until after they have entered it, while OV conveys the impression that Haldir's welcome is pronounced at the edge of the "treeless space", before moving on.

Both versions have a problem with "mallorn-trees taller than any they had yet seen in all the land", both of them rather using "in this land" (implying they might have seen taller mallorn-trees in other lands; "im ganzen Land" would

---

[19] The corresponding scene in the movie depicts this scene rather adequately; the rendition in Wynn Fonstad (1991:131) leaves a similar impression.

have been closer to OV, since there is no place in Middle-earth that holds higher mallorn-trees than Lórien). However, NT compounds the problem a bit more by putting "bisher" in a post-position, stressing "in this land" even more.

Lexically speaking, NT's "vielstufig" is closer to *many-tiered* as OT's "reichverzweigt" (BT: "widely branching"), but as regards trees is too technical (the range of meaning of *tier* is larger than that of German "Stufe"). In this sentence, both translations are hard-pressed to find adequately brief renditions of "ever-moving". OT, despite having to take recourse to a full subordinate clause, manages to do slightly better; NT's "unermüdlich wedelnden" (BT: "tirelessly waving") is shorter, but the choice of words is inappropriate for leaves (both "unermüdlich" and "wedeln" imply animate agents, or at least free volition).

Finally, the choice of "Gefährten" for *Company* is problematic. OV has a clear distinction between "Company of the Ring" ("Ringgemeinschaft") and "Fellowship of the Ring" ("Die Gefährten", as per the title of the book). This is, of course, a direct offshoot of NT's elimination of the "Nine Walkers" Elrond mentions in his speech to Frodo in Rivendell, where NT replaces "Nine Walkers" with "Bund der Neun Gefährten", with "Bund" (*alliance*) naturally being inappropriate for Haldir to address a body of people.[20]

> OV
> 'Welcome to Caras Galadhon!' he said. 'Here is the city of the Galadhrim where dwell the Lord Celeborn and Galadriel, the Lady of Lórien. But we cannot enter here, for the gates do not look northward. We must go round to the southern side, and the way is not short, for the city is great.'
>
> OT
> "Willkommen in Caras Galadhon!" sagte er. "Hier ist die Stadt der Galadhrim, wo der Herr Celeborn und Galadriel, die Herrin von Lórien, wohnen. Doch können wir hier nicht hinein, weil die Tore nicht nach Norden schauen. Wir müssen herumgehen, zur Südseite, und der Weg ist nicht kurz, denn die Stadt ist groß."

---

20 OV 268: 'The Company of the Ring shall be Nine; and the Nine Walkers shall be set against the Nine Riders that are evil.'
OT 335: "Die Gemeinschaft des Ringes soll aus Neun bestehen; und die Neun Wanderer sollen es mit den Neun Reitern aufnehmen, die böse sind."
NT 359: "Neun sollen es sein, die mit dem Ring auf die Fahrt gehen: der Bund der Neun Gefährten gegen die Neun Reiter, die des Bösen sind."
BT 'Nine it shall be who will go on the quest of the Ring: the Alliance of the Nine Companions against the Nine Riders, who are of evil.'

NT

"Willkommen in Caras Galadhon!" sagte er. "Dies ist die Stadt der Galadhrim, wo der Herr Celeborn und die Frau Galadriel wohnen, der Herr und die Herrin von Lórien. Doch können wir hier nicht eintreten, denn nicht an der Nordseite steht das Tor, sondern nach Süden. So müssen wir die halbe Mauer umrunden, was, da die Stadt groß ist, kein kurzer Weg ist."

Commentary

It is obvious from OV that Galadriel is ruler of Lórien, while Celeborn is not. He is called "Lord" as a title of honour, but the qualification "of Lórien" is applied to Galadriel alone; thus, NT overgeneralises. This may be due to the fact that NT does have a certain tendency of explaining things to the reader in places where further explanations are not really necessary. Also, the capitalisation in "Lady" points to this being a much stronger title than simply "Frau".

The rendition of the second part of Haldir's speech is a strange amalgam of old-fashioned speech elements ("denn nicht an der Nordseite steht das Tor" – "for not to the northern side stands the gate"[21]), misleading preposition use ("sondern nach Süden" – "but to the south"), and modernisation of Haldir's speech rhythm (the subordinative relations in Haldir's last sentence in NT result in a BT of: "Thus, we must go halfway round the wall, which, since the city is great, is not a short way.")

OV

There was a road paved with white stone running on the outer brink of the fosse. Along this they went westward, with the city ever climbing up like a green cloud upon their left; and as the night deepened more lights sprang forth, until all the hill seemed afire with stars. They came at last to a white bridge, and crossing found the great gates of the city: they faced south-west, set between the ends of the encircling wall that here overlapped, and they were tall and strong, and hung with many lamps.

OT

Eine mit weißen Steinen gepflasterte Straße führte am äußeren Rand des Grabens entlang. Auf dieser gingen sie nach Westen, während sich die Stadt wie eine grüne Wolke zu ihrer Linken erhob; und als die Nacht dunkler wurde, leuchteten immer mehr Lichter auf, bis der ganze Berg mit Sternen übersät zu sein

---

21 And yet, this is probably what Wolfgang Krege meant when he spoke of "man kann den Kontrast besonders stark herausarbeiten": colloquial German to represent the language of the simple folk (hobbits, Breelanders), but old-fashioned language for elves, wizards, and dwarves. It is also quite often the case that, as seen here with Haldir, this intention is disturbed by modern grammar, or by colloquialisms.

schien. Schließlich kamen sie zu einer weißen Brücke, und als sie sie überquert hatten, zu den großen Toren der Stadt: diese schauten nach Südwesten und lagen zwischen den Enden der umgebenden Mauer, die sich hier überschnitten und sie waren hoch und stark und mit vielen Lampen behängt.

NT
Eine mit weißen Steinen gepflasterte Straße führte am äußeren Rand des Burggrabens entlang. Darauf gingen sie nach Westen, die Stadt immer wie eine grüne Wolke zur Linken; und als die Nacht dunkler wurde, flammten immer mehr Lichter auf, bis der ganze Hügel von Sternen durchglüht zu sein schien. Endlich kamen sie an eine weiße Brücke, überschritten sie und standen vor dem großen Stadttor. Es lag nach Südwesten, und zwar zwischen die beiden Enden der Umfassungsmauer eingelassen, die ein Stück gegeneinander überstanden: ein hohes, festes Tor, und mit vielen Lampen behangen.

Commentary

Suddenly, *fosse* is turned into "Burggraben" in NT. While this is lexically correct, it also looks slightly out of place with a tree city; and it is somewhat puzzling why NT uses "Graben" earlier and now emends to "Burggraben". While both translations retain the cloud image, NT deletes the "climbing up" aspect of OV's description (both OT and NT ignore the intensifying "ever") – probably because in modern German clouds do not climb up. Nor do they in modern English. However, the image of the cloud is intended to stress the height of the city, climbing *ever* (my italics) up until it finally reaches cloud level. The imagery of NT is far weaker than that of OT (or OV, for that matter).

Both OT and NT do not seem too happy having to deal with "until all the hill seemed afire with stars." OT's "bis der ganze Berg mit Sternen übersät zu sein schien" neglects the "afire" aspect (juxtaposing the stars dotting the hill with those described at the beginning of the chapter, especially as these are already described as "twinkling" in OT). NT's morphologically creative "durchglüht" (BT: "glowing all over"), while not really a German word, is a bit more appropriate for the situation, but is still too weak as compared to OV's "afire".

NT's rendition of "crossing" is, in fact, more elegant than that of OT, doing away with the somewhat awkward syntactic construction of OT. Towards the end of the passage, the interpolated "und zwar" in NT conveys the impression of the translator needing to insert himself into the text by means of a meta-language reference to make certain that the reader does not fail to understand what looks like a rather complicated description. This is the second instance of the 'explanation' tendency of NT within just one page of OV.[22]

As a brief analysis of a longer passage in context, this will have to do for purposes of this article. The analysis of a descriptive passage points to the fact that there is more to NT's changes in the text than simply modernising the language. The treatment of "Company" and "Fellowship" reveals inconsistencies of decisions made in earlier parts of the text, while the description of the view of the elven city (characters stationary in OT, while moving in NT) and the rearrangement of the rulership conditions in Lórien hint at substantial re-interpretations on the part of the translator, not all of which seem to be justifiable in the context of the novel.

Another aspect that needs to be mentioned here is text length. A standard formula used by typesetters for comparing the length of English and German texts is to calculate the average English word at five characters, but the average German word at six.[23] In the four paragraphs given above[24], OV has a total length of 1,845 characters (including spaces). Applying this formula yields an expected 2,227 characters for a standard German translation; any translation longer than these additional 20 per cent would run the risk of being accused of over-specification[25], a mistake rather often made by translators who want to make absolutely certain that the readers understand what they want to tell them. In fact, both are shorter: OT has 2,058 characters, NT 2,119. Divided per paragraph, the following listing emerges:

Paragraph	OV	OT	NT
1	272	299	274
2	779	857	912
3	289	310	355
4	505	592	578

---

22 Tolkien himself would have disapproved of too much explaining to his readers, as evidenced in Anderson (2002:76, note 18).
23 This is due to the fact that the most frequent words of English are shorter than their equivalents in German; just compare the three letters of *I am* to the six letters of "ich bin" or *we go* to "wir gehen".
24 Which, of course, do not even begin to constitute a representative sample of either text; in fact, the length relations seem to be levelled out throughout the entirety of the text(s): this entire chapter, for instance, has 35,272 characters in OV, 40,201 characters in OT, and 39,585 characters in NT.
25 See Hönig/Kussmaul (1996 passim) and, for a (non-Tolkien related) clear case of over-specification, Nagel (2003).

In two out of four paragraphs, OT is actually longer than NT; this is especially striking in the (rather short) first paragraph. However, NT achieves its conciseness mostly either due to syntactic modernisation or, almost as often, by leaving out words. Sometimes, as in the first paragraphs, these are words that are not strictly necessary for the text but still present in OV to convey atmosphere (such as "again", in OT represented as "wieder", in NT omitted), but usually the omissions simply narrow down the tone of passage as given in OV ("silver" in paragraph 1, "climbing up" in paragraph 4, etc.), creating stylistic levelling not too far removed from what Wolfgang Krege might have meant by OT's 'uniform' language.

That the two translations are more or less equal in length (despite NT's shortenings) may be because NT's 'modern' German is in places more long-winding than OT's 'patinated' language; however, it may also be a result of NT's aforementioned tendency to give explanations to the reader, thus possibly falling prey to a form (albeit disguised) of over-specification after all.[26]

6. An Etymological Excursion: Differences in Naming

When talking about style and giving explanations, a short word about NT's treatment of proper names is in order. In general, Wolfgang Krege has stated[27]:

> Einen wichtigen Teil der Arbeit hatte mir die alte Übersetzung schon abgenommen: die Verdeutschung der Namen. Darin verbergen sich einige Vorentscheidungen über den Stil. Und an den Namen gab es nicht viel zu ändern. Die meisten sind

---

26 Another case in point, from the end of the chapter analysed here, is the following sentence spoken by Galadriel:
OV (*LotR* 357): 'Did not Gandalf tell you that the rings give power according to the measure of each possessor?'
OT (*HdR 1 (C)* 442): "Hat Gandalf dir nicht gesagt, daß der Ring Macht verleiht entsprechend der Natur jedes Besitzers?"
NT (*HdR 1 (K)* 474: "Hat dir Gandalf nicht gesagt, dass der Ring nur nach den Maßen seines Besitzers Macht verleiht?"
NT adds "nur" ("only"), giving an explanation (or rather, qualification) that OV does not deem necessary.
27 Klett-Cotta email, op. cit. My translation: "One important aspect of my work had already been taken care of by the old translation: the rendering of the names into German. This already conceals some decisions about the style of the translation. And as regards the names, not much needed to be changed. Most of them have been well chosen and cling to people's memories (although quite a few characters have two or more names); and I had even grown accustomed to some of those that might seem questionable. Only with a few minor characters, and a few lesser known places, were small changes possible without overdue force."

gut gewählt und haften im Gedächtnis (obwohl nicht wenige Figuren zwei oder mehr Namen haben); und auch an manche vielleicht anfechtbare hatte ich mich gewöhnt. Nur bei Nebenfiguren und selten erwähnten Orten waren kleine Umbenennungen ohne Gewaltsamkeit möglich.

One of these changes comes in the case of the hobbit family name, "Proudfeet". Tolkien (1980:171) simply states: "A Hobbit surname (it is an English surname). Translate." which is not too helpful either way. The respective context (*LotR* 29) has Bilbo use the (deliberately obscured) wording "Proudfoots", causing Odo to yell, "Proudfeet!" in order to remind Bilbo of the 'correct' plural form. Thus, OT uses "Stolzfüße". NT emends this to "Stolzfüsser" (BT: "Proudfooter"), which may be more acceptable as regards the processes of proper name development out of descriptive words, but does take away from the humour of the scene.[28]

Another name change that has come under quite some criticism is NT's re-translation of "Cotton" (OT: "Hüttinger"; NT: "Kattun"). Some critics (especially on the internet) have pointed out (quite rightly) that "Cotton" is to be derived from *cottage*, thus correctly leading to OT's "Hüttinger" (BT: "somebody coming from / living in a cottage"). Tolkien (1980:162f.) states:

> This is a place-name in origin (as are many modern surnames), from *cot*, a cottage or humble dwelling, and *-ton*, the usual shortening of 'town' in place names (Old English *tún* 'village'). It should be translated in these terms.
>
> It is a common English surname and has, of course, in origin no connection with *cotton* the textile material, though it is naturally associated with it at the present day.

---

28 Wolfgang Krege was a bit less successful in what might be considered an overdose of humour when re-translating the names of the trolls in *The Hobbit*:
OV: Bert, Tom, William
OT: Bert, Bill, Tom
NT: Berti, Hucki, Toni
The OV troll names are everyday names (exactly the type of language Krege was looking for in *The Hobbit*), with no indication of children's language. Probably, Krege was induced by the trolls' 'funny' dialect (and the fact that *The Hobbit* was aimed at children) to give them somewhat more endearing names. However, this takes away from Tolkien's original intentions, as stated by Anderson (2002:70, note 15): "Tolkien presents the Trolls' speech in a comic, lower-class dialect. This linguistic joke shows a perception for language similar to that which Tolkien ascribed to Geoffrey Chaucer in a long paper presented to the Philological Society in Oxford on May 16, 1931. This paper, entitled 'Chaucer as a Philologist: *The Reeve's Tale*,' shows how Chaucer used the northern dialect of Middle English as a source of humor for his (southern) London audience."
This idea is lost in the German translation of *The Hobbit* (understandably in a children's book), leading to yet another shift of focus (or change of scope – "Skoposfestlegung", as Reiss/Vermeer (1984) would have it).

> [...] Since it is highly improbable that in any other language a normal and frequent village name should in any way resemble the equivalent of *cotton* (the material), this resemblance in the original text may be passed over. It has no importance for the narrative.

OT, consequently, opted for deleting the 'textile' aspect of the name, centring on the *cot* part. NT, on the other hand, found a way to incorporate both by using "Kattun", a lesser-known German term to indicate a garment made from a particular type of cotton (see Kluge [1975:358]), both words going back to the same (Arabic) origin. The relation to *cot* is preserved by referring back to "Kate", a term for a small hut rather similar to English *cot* (and also sharing the same origin; v. Kluge [1975:397]). Thus, NT's translation is in fact even closer to OV's name, albeit a bit less transparent than OT's "Hüttinger".[29]

However, despite the (as in Krege's own words, few) improvements observed so far, there is another tendency found in NT's name translation that needs mentioning: the obscuring of etymology in favour of phonological similarity between OV and NT.[30] This feature is best illustrated with "Brockhouse" (OT: "Dachsbau"; NT: "Brockhaus"), related to the place-name, "Brockenborings" ("Dachsbauten" in both translations). The element "brock" in both names goes ultimately back to Old English *brocca*, a Celtic loanword meaning (and later replaced by) "badger". German "Brock", on the other hand, has no relation to this Celtic word, the lexical niche for the badger being long since blocked by Old High German *dahs* (from Middle Latin *taxus, taxo*). German "Brock", on the other hand, is derived from either Old High German *bruoch* or Middle High german *brók* "swamp, moor", thus rather denominating a "house in (or near) a swamp" (i.e., as a personal name, "someone living in a house in or near a swamp"). Since the Brockhouses live in and around Brockenborings, which is nowhere even near a swamp, NT's re-translation does not make any sense etymologically, thus violating Tolkien's dictum about 'telling names' as quoted at the end of chapter 2.[31]

---

29 I am indebted to Alexandra Velten of Johannes Gutenberg University Mainz for bringing this to my attention in the first place. – The same applies to the Hobbit name "Cotman", commented upon in Tolkien (1980:163) as: "It is an old word meaning 'cottager', 'cot-dweller', and is to be found in larger dictionaries. It is also a well-known English surname." OT has "Hüttner" (following the "Hüttinger" reasoning), while NT has "Katuner" (following the "Kattun" reasoning); cf. also Foster (2002:402): "abgeleitet von einem Wort für Kate."
30 A process called "phonologische Kalkierung" in Gläser (1989) and treated in more detail on page 107.
31 Tolkien (1980:161f.) gives a lengthy etymological discursion on the name "Brockhaus" and offers "Dachsbau" as the German equivalent.

Then again, NT's tendency of 'de-etymologisation' sometimes works in favour of Tolkien's wishes, as in the treatment of OV's "Sharkey", the name of Saruman after his flight to the Shire. Tolkien (1980:173) remarks:

> This is supposed to be a nickname modified to fit the Common Speech (in the English text anglicized), based on orkish *sharkû* 'old man'. The word should therefore be kept with modification of spelling to fit the language of translation; alteration of the diminutive and quasi-affectionate ending *–ey* to fit that language would also be in place.

Neither OT ("Scharrer") nor NT ("Scharker") retain the "diminutive and quasi-endearing ending" (which would have been something like '-i' or '-ie'); however, OT adds a new set of meaning by referring to an older meaning of German "scharren" ("kratzen" – *to scrape*), while NT here sticks closer to Tolkien's intentions.

A final remark on the translation of names is to deal with OV's "Neekerbreekers", according to Tolkien (1980:170): "Invented insect name; represent it by some invention of similar sound (supposed to be like that of a cricket)." OT has "Kirperzirper", while NT opts for "Niiikerzriiiker". OT's translation centres not so much on the actual sound but instead on a description of it, while NT tries to mimic the sound as such, in a way that NT deems fitting for a name created by hobbits (as per the picture of hobbits given in NT, which will concern us in the next chapter). The onomatopoetic use of three vowels characters in a row treads a fine line between acceptable name and silly nonce-word.

7. A Closer Look at Style and Tone

Having by now established NT's broad intentions as well as general treatment of those, all that remains is to see whether these intentions are realised consequently. We have already found that there is a tendency of simplifying speech patters, mainly those of hobbits and rural folk (see chapter 4). A general indication of such overall stylistic matters is forms of address, especially those between persons of unequal social standing. While there is not much of a social difference between the inhabitants of Bree and the hobbits from the Shire, consider the following question put by Frodo to Galadriel when enquiring whether to look into the Mirror:

>   OV (*LotR* 354): 'Do you advise me to look?'
>   OT (*HdR 1 (C)* 438): "Ratet Ihr mir, hineinzuschauen?"
>   NT (*HdR 1 (K)* 470): "Rätst du mir zu?"

Frodo and Galadriel are not of the same social standing: one is a (socially rather insignificant) hobbit, the other is a 9,000-year-old elven queen, one of the few Noldor still remaining in Middle-earth who have seen the light of the Trees. It may be for Galadriel to level this social difference by allowing Frodo a more intimate form of address, but it is certainly not for Frodo to impinge on her like that.

English does not really have the means to distinguish between these two forms of address, but German still has. Granted, old-fashioned English still uses "thou, thee, thine" to indicate 'archaic' forms of address (the missing of which probably prompted Krege to disregard OT's "Ihr"), but historically speaking, "thou" (the former singular form) and it accompanying forms were used to address people of the same or lower social standing, while "you" (originally a plural form) and its accompanying forms were used to address people of higher standing, and for polite forms of addressing others.[32]

Another feature of the 'modernisation' of the text causing problems with forms of address is Sam's habit in NT of addressing Frodo, or speaking about him to others:

>   OV (*LotR* 62): 'Mr. Frodo, sir!'
>   OT (*HdR 1 (C)* 87): "Herr, Herr Frodo!"
>   NT (*HdR I (K)* 92): "Herr Frodo, Chef!"

>   OV (*LotR* 357): 'But if you pardon my speaking out, I think my master was right.'
>   OT (*HdR 1 (C)* 442): "Aber wenn Ihr mir verzeihen wollt, daß ich es anspreche: ich glaube, mein Herr hat recht gehabt."
>   NT (*HdR 1 (K)* 474): "Aber wenn du mir ein offenes Wort gestattest, dann würd' ich sagen, dass mein Chef schon Recht hatte."

Tolkien takes great pain in describing Sam not only as Frodo's friend, but also as somebody who regards himself as a loyal servant.[33] Given all this, the relation

---

32 This distinction figures prominently in the *Canterbury Tales* and the relations are still basically intact in the works of William Shakespeare; it is not until well after Shakespeare that *thou* is being phased out of the language, with *you* taking over address in general; cf. Freeborn (1998:310-12 & 334-6) and Honegger (in this volume, esp. pages 5-9).
33 Much has been written on this, especially with regard to the "officer-batsman relation" Tolkien must have known from his experiences in World War One; for rather current surveys, see Chance (2001) and Garth (2003). All of this background and the corresponding allusions are lost in NT.

between the two, by using the more 'youthful' "Chef" (BT: "boss"), is shifted to one of playful equality (the idea that Sam may somehow be 'employed' by Frodo and thus refer to him jovially as "boss" is neither supported by the novel nor true in the purely technical sense, despite Sam acting as Frodo's gardener). The use of "Chef" instead of "Herr" (*master*) signals the most significant breach of the stylistic level of OV so far, totally levelling the social relations between the two main protagonists.[34]

Unfortunately, there are other such stylistic inaccuracies, of which only three shall be mentioned here:

>   OV (*LotR* 353): 'Like as not,' said the Lady with a gentle laugh.
>   OT (*HdR 1 (C)* 437): "Höchstwahrscheinlich", sagte die Herrin und lachte leise.
>   NT (*HdR 1 (K)* 468): "Na klar!" sagte die hohe Frau leise kichernd.
>   BT 'But of course!' said the Lady, giggling softly.

>   OV (*LotR* 29): Most of them bore the mark *dale* on them [...]
>   OT (*HdR 1 (C)* 45): Die meisten trugen die Herkunftsbezeichnung *thal* [...]
>   NT (*HdR 1 (K)* 47f.): [...] die meisten mit dem Herkunftsstempel *made in thal* [...]
>   BT [...] most of them with the mark *made in dale* [...]

>   OV (*LotR* 435): 'I hope Strider or someone will come and claim us!'
>   OT (*HdR 2 (C)* 51): "Ich hoffe, Streicher oder sonst wer wird kommen und uns abholen!"

---

34 Generally, Sam's way of speaking exemplifies NT's treatment of the 'rustic' language of the hobbits and other rural folk (like the Breelanders). Tolkien draws heavily on the Warwickshire/Oxforshire dialect (see Johannesson [1997]) to set their speech apart from that of elves, wizards, dwarves, noble men, etc. (cf. also Einhaus [1986] as regards Tolkien's uses of style and dialect). This dialect, while distinguishable for what it is, shares quite a few features with other rural dialects of England. German dialects, on the other hand, have less of a common ground between them, and thus choosing one would have been restricted to non-localizable features such as contractions and elisions (as done in OT). NT's solution is instead almost invariably to use younger-generation language. This is despite the fact that not only is Frodo socially superior, but also older than Sam (50 years, to be precise; Sam, on the other hand, at 38 has barely come of age), something that is often overlooked especially after the choice of actors for the movie trilogy became known; this difference in age is lost by the verbal depiction of their social relations in NT. However, even the movies (the German versions of which use OT after all, despite the fact that Klett-Cotta produced a special edition for the movie – "Sonderausgabe zum Film" – of NT in paperback) preserve the social relations between Frodo and Sam. And yet, there are some strange quirks in NT's treatment of Sam's way of speaking. Just one example:
OV (*LotR* 70): 'There is a dry fir-wood ahead, if I remember rightly.'
OT (*HdR 1 (C)* 97): "Da vorn ist ein trockener Tannenwald, wenn ich mich recht erinnere."
NT (*HdR 1 (K)* 103): "Da vorn kommt ein Tann mit trockenem Boden, wenn ich mich recht erinnere."
"Tann" for "fir-wood" is rather archaic and not really fitting for somebody whose speech is probably the most 'modern' of all in the book. In a way, this is a reversal of the 'elvish colloquialism' as mentioned in footnote 20, both phenomena equally breaking the established stylistic mould.

NT (*HdR 2 (K)* 54): "Hoffentlich kommt Streicher und holt uns vom Fundbüro ab."
BT 'I hope Strider will come and claim us from the lost-and-found.'

"Kichern" (*giggle*) is nowhere near within the span of meaning of "to laugh gently", and in this context (the "Lady" is Galadriel) provides the elven ruler with some kind of 'girlish' image. Also, the translation of OV's somewhat archaic "like as not" with a more youthful "Na klar!" (one of the 'elvish colloquialisms' mentioned in footnote 20), while trying to expand on Galadriel not meaning what she says, is stylistically out of place.

"Made in Thal" is an example of present-day German 'trend' speech, out of place in a fantasy world; also, it does not make much sense to import English phrases into a German translation of an English text, despite this being done rather frequently in modern German.

And finally, the "lost-and-found" is not only an anachronism in Middle-earth; it is also a stark misinterpretation of OV: how would Pippin, dragged away by the Uruk-hai, hope to get into a lost-and found (even if he knew of the concept)? Or is this meant to be a joking reference to the Uruk-hai casting the hobbit away, or delivering him into a place for lost goods? It might be a not-so-subtle pun on Pippin regarding Merry and himself as "pieces of luggage", which both translations render as "Gepäckstücke". It seems that NT's orcs have a tendency of depositing unwanted baggage (like hobbits) in the lost-and-found. If so, the joke is well beyond the textual scope of OV.

It would appear that in some way or another, NT is clearly overstepping the boundaries of a translation befitting the SL text in all three cases, aiming too much at reflecting the speech patterns of the younger generation(s) obviously intended to be the main target group. Examples such as these not only distort the original linguistic intention of the text (as expanded on in chapter 2), but also makes the translation dated, since the speech patterns reflected here are sure to go out of style in the foreseeable future. It would appear that, in the end, a conflict seems to be emerging between the translator's 'loyalty' to the text and his need to modernise it.

8. Conclusion

The following sentence (taken from the temptation of Galadriel) nicely sums up next to everything that is to say about the two translations: OT is closer to OV, if need be up to the point of producing awkward German, while NT's German is more fluent, but takes unnecessary liberties with OV:

> OV (*LotR* 356): 'Would not that have been a noble deed to set to the credit of his Ring, if I had taken it by force or fear from my guest?'
> OT (*HdR 1 (C)* 441): "Würde das nicht eine edle Tat gewesen sein, die dem Einfluß seines Ringes zuzuschreiben wäre, wenn ich ihn meinem Gast mit Gewalt oder unter Drohungen abgenommen hätte?"
> NT (*HdR 1 (K)* 473): "Wäre es nicht ein schöner Beweis für des Ringes Kraft, wenn ich ihn mit Gewalt oder List meinem Gast abnähme?"

While OT closely mirrors the syntactic relations of OV, its (for purposes of strict 'loyalty' necessary) choice of the present perfect subjunctive, even less frequent in German as it is in English, makes for somewhat hard reading, while NT's syntactic simplification (BT: "Would that not be good proof of the Ring's power, if I took it from my guest by force or cunning?") still gets Galadriel's meaning across. And yet, this example also shows the weaknesses of NT's over-simplification of OV's lexical structures and stylistic devices ("noble deed" becomes "good proof", and OT's "threat" – for "fear" – becomes NT's "cunning", watering down what Galadriel expresses in OV: her appearance is intimidating at that moment, not sly or cunning.

As a summary, I think it is fair to conclude that NT very often succeeds in purging mistakes from OT, but very often overshoots its target of modernising the text, of 'assimilating' it into a language the translator of NT feels to be appropriate, but that OV's text does not really lend itself to. Gramlich (2003:178) raises an interesting point when trying to balance the role of Krege not only as translator, but as co-author, claiming that the latter role takes precedence over the former too strongly (his italics)[35]:

> Denn entweder war er nicht fähig, textnah zu übersetzen und hat so Fehler an Fehler gehäuft, oder er hat etwas völlig unverzeihliches getan: Er versucht

---

35 My translation: "For either he was not able to stick closely to the text in his translation and thus heaped error upon error, or he has done something that is completely unforgivable: He has tried to set *his* work, *his* re-telling, so far apart from the original that it can be clearly recognised as *his* work."

sein Werk, *seine* Nacherzählung, bewusst so stark vom Original abzusetzen, dass es als *sein* Werk identifizierbar wird.

Thus, it might be possible to classify NT's 'assimilating' tendency as a translation with modification of text type (or rather, stylistic level and thus, genre), while OT is a translation without modification of text type or genre. Both may have their place in the world of the German reader (and thus, both are currently available on the German market), but judging from Tolkien's remarks as reflected in Tolkien (1980) and Carpenter (1977) and quoted in chapter 2, he would clearly have preferred the less translator-centred approach of OT.

Gramlich's statement, while once again being provocatively overstated, may actually have some truth to it, as so far as Wolfgang Krege seems to imply in his statements quoted in chapter 3 that he not only has a better view than Margaret Carroux of what modern German should be like, but also a better view than Tolkien what modern English should be like. If this were the truth (and statements such as "Abschreiben müssen tut weh". Or "ein gewisses Eigentempo in den Spielräumen der deutschen Sprache gewinnen" point in this direction), then NT is a translation as much as it is a re-interpretation of the original. Or, to use the concept of the translator as co-author again: the translator is much less visible in such capacity in OT that he is in NT.

This, probably, is the major difference between the two versions. To sum up the last chapter of the introduction to this article: It does appear that NT is as free of 'external motivation' as it should be for purposes of 'loyalty' to the SL text.

About the author

Rainer Nagel holds a PhD in English Linguistics from Johannes-Gutenberg University, Mainz. His PhD thesis was on word-formation in special languages. His research subjects are morphology/word-formation, historical linguistics, translation studies, and ESL studies. He currently teaches at Johannes Gutenberg-University, Mainz.

Primary sources

Anh. = *Der Herr der Ringe. Anhänge*, (second edition, first edition 1969), Stuttgart: Klett-Cotta, 1979.

HdR 1 (C) = *Der Herr der Ringe. Die Gefährten*, (second edition, first edition 1969), translated by Margaret Carroux, Stuttgart: Klett-Cotta.

HdR 2 (C) = *Der Herr der Ringe. Die zwei Türme*, (second edition, first edition 1969), translated by Margaret Carroux, Stuttgart: Klett-Cotta.

HdR 3 (C) = *Der Herr der Ringe. Die Rückkehr des Königs*, (second edition, first edition 1969), translated by Margaret Carroux, Stuttgart: Klett-Cotta.

HdR 1 (K) = *Der Herr der Ringe. Die Gefährten*, translated by Wolfgang Krege, Sonderausgabe zum Film, Stuttgart: Klett-Cotta, 2001.

HdR 2 (K) = *Der Herr der Ringe. Die zwei Türme*, translated by Wolfgang Krege, Sonderausgabe zum Film, Stuttgart: Klett-Cotta, 2001.

HdR 3 (K) = *Der Herr der Ringe. Die Wiederkehr des Königs*, translated by Wolfgang Krege, Stuttgart: Klett-Cotta, 2001.

Hobbit = *The Hobbit, or There and Back Again*, (fourth edition, first edition 1937), London, etc.: Unwin, 1981.

Letters = *The Letters of J.R.R. Tolkien*, Humphrey Carpenter and Christopher Tolkien (eds.), London, Boston & Sydney: Allen & Unwin, 1981.

LotR = *The Lord of the Rings*, (text of the second edition 1966, one-volume paperback edition; first edition 1954-55), London: HarperCollins, 1995.

Sil = *The Silmarillion*, (paperback edition, first published 1977), London, etc: Unwin, 1979.

Secondary sources

ANDERSON, Douglas A. (ed.), *The Annotated Hobbit*, (revised and expanded edition; first edition 1988), Boston & New York: Houghton Mifflin, 2002.

BEAUGRANDE, Robert de & Wolfgang Dressler, *Introduction to Text Linguistics*, London & New York: Longman, 1981.

BUELLES, Marcel, *'Der Herr der Ringe* oder *Der Chef mit den fetten Klunkern'* In: Hubert Strassl et al. (eds.), *Magira. Jahrbuch zur Fantasy 2001*, Norderstedt: Books on Demand, 187-201.

CARPENTER, Humphrey, *J.R.R. Tolkien: A Biography*, London: Allen & Unwin, 1977.

CGEL = QUIRK, Randolph et al. (eds), *A Comprehensive Grammar of the English Language*, (fifteenth impression, first edition 1985), Harlow: Longman, 1999.

CHANCE, Jane, *Lord of the Rings: The Mythology of Power*, Lexington: University Press of Kentucky, 2001.

EINHAUS, Barbara, *The Lord of the Rings: Logik der kreativen Imagination*, München: tuduv, 1986.

FAISS, Klaus, *Englische Sprachgeschichte*, Tübingen: Francke, 1989.

FOSTER, Robert, *Das große Mittelerde-Lexikon. Ein alphabetischer Führer zur Fantasy-Welt von J.R.R. Tolkien*, Bearbeitet und ergänzt von Helmut W. Pesch, Bergisch Gladbach: Bastei Lübbe, 2002.

FREEBORN, Dennis, *From Old English to Standard English. A Course Book in Language Variation across Time*, (second edition, first edition 1992), Basingstoke & New York: Palgrave, 1998.

GARTH, John, *Tolkien and the Great War. The Threshold of Middle-earth*, London: HarperCollins, 2003.

GLÄSER, Rosemarie, 'Zur Übersetzung von Eigennamen', In: Friedhelm Debus and Wilfried Seibicke (eds.), *Reader zur Namenkunde. Band I: Namentheorie*, Hildesheim, Zürich, New York: Olms, 1989, 67-78.

GLOGE, Andreas, 'Re-writing the Past – The Pillars of Middle-earth,' In: *Mallorn. The Journal of the Tolkien Society* 41, (July 2003), 44-52.

GRAMLICH, Thomas, 'Die verlorene Kunst der Übersetzung?', In: Hubert Strassl et al. (eds.), *Magira. Jahrbuch zur Fantasy 2003*, Marburg: Fantasy Club e.V., 171-80.

HELLWIG, Karlheinz, 'Freies Übersetzen englischsprachiger Gedichte – eine prozessorientierte Arbeitstechnik empirisch geprüft,' In: *Die Neueren Sprachen* 94, (1995), 402-27.

HERMANNS, Theo, 'Translational Norms and Correct Translation', In: Kitty Van Leuven-Zwart & Ton Naaijkens (eds.), *Translation Studies: The State of the Art. Proceedings of the First James S. Holmes Symposium on Translation Studies*, Amsterdam & Atlanta: Rodopi, 1991, 155-69.

HÖNIG, Hans G. & Paul Kussmaul, *Strategie der Übersetzung. Ein Arbeits- und Lehrbuch*, (fourth edition, first edition 1982), Tübingen: Narr, 1996.

JOHANNESSON, Nils-Lennart, 'The Speech of the Individual and of the Community in *The Lord of the Rings*', In: Peter Buchs and Thomas Honegger (eds.), *News from the Shire and Beyond – Studies on Tolkien*, (Cormarë Series 1), Zurich and Berne: Walking Tree Publishers, 1997, 11-47.

KLUGE, Friedrich, *Etymologisches Wörterbuch der deutschen Sprache*, (twenty-first edition, first edition 1883), Berlin & New York: de Gruyter, 1975.

LAMPRECHT, Adolf, *Grammatik der englischen Sprache*, (Neufassung, eighth edition, first edition 1971), Berlin: Cornelsen-Verhagen & Klasing, 1986.

LANG, Margaret, 'The problem of mother tongue competence in the training of translators', In: Mary Snell-Hornby et al. (eds.), *Translation Studies. An Interdiscipline*, Amsterdam & Philadelphia: Benjamins, 1992, 395-99.

LÖNKER, Fred (ed.), *Die literarische Übersetzung als Medium der Fremderfahrung*, Berlin: Schmidt, 1992.

NAGEL, Rainer, *Fachsprache der Fantasy-Rollenspiele. Wortbildungselemente und -prozesse*, Frankfurt: Lang, 1993.

'Perry Rhodan in der Übersetzung', In: Klaus Bollhöfener et al. (eds.), *Spurensuche im All. Perry Rhodan Studies*, Berlin: Archiv der Jugendkulturen, 2003, 48-67.

NORD, Christiane, *Einführung in das funktionale Übersetzen. Am Beispiel von Titeln und Überschriften*, Tübingen: Francke, 1993.

OED = *The Oxford English Dictionary*, (second edition, first edition 1929ff.), Oxford: Oxford University Press, 1989.

REISS, Katharina & Hans J. Vermeer, *Grundlegung einer allgemeinen Translationstheorie*, Tübingen: Niemeyer, 1984.

SAGER, Juan C., 'A Theory of Text Production, Modification, Reception', In: Hartmut Schröder (ed.), *Subject-oriented Texts. Languages for Special Purposes and Text Theory*, Berlin & New York: deGruyter, 1991, 244-53.

SHIPPEY, Tom, *The Road to Middle-earth. How J.R.R. Tolkien created a new mythology*, (second edition, first edition 1982), London: HarperCollins, 1992.

STEIN, Dieter, *Theoretische Grundlagen der Übersetzungswissenschaft*, Tübingen: Narr, 1980.

TOLKIEN, J.R.R., 'Guide to the Names in *The Lord of the Rings*', In: Jared Lobdell (ed.), *A Tolkien Compass*, New York: Ballantine, 1980, 153-201.

WYNN FONSTAD, Karen, *The Atlas of Middle-earth. Revised Edition*, (second edition; first edition 1981), New York: Houghton Mifflin, 1991.

Danny Orbach

The Israeli Translation Controversy – What About and Where To?

With contributions by Yuval Kfir and Yuval Welis

Abstract

This article looks into the controversy around the two Israeli translations of *The Lord of the Rings* into Hebrew. The older (and more archaic-literary) translation by Ruth Livnit is compared with the more recent (and more modern-technical) one by Emanuel Lottem. Supporters of each translation are given the opportunity to voice their opinions.

Our story begins in 1977, when the well-known Israeli translator Mrs. Ruth Livnit made a tempting suggestion to "Zmora-Bitan" publishers: To translate J.R.R. Tolkien's classic, *The Lord of the Rings*, into Hebrew. Israel has its own fair share of Tolkien fans, and Livnit's translation thrilled them and was received with enthusiasm. It is estimated that some 90,000 Israelis read this admirable book since Livnit translated it, and the numbers have been growing ever since.

What made this 'old translation' so special?

Most of the Israeli Tolkien fans and experts consider Livnit the best Hebrew Tolkien translator ever. Livnit believed that in order to translate a text on such an epic scale into Hebrew, one must use Jewish mythological terms – mostly Biblical ones. Only they can parallel the richness and splendour of Tolkien's language. Livnit used old, traditional and literary Hebrew. Like the greatest Hebrew authors and poets (Bialik, Tschernichovsky and others) she played with the language like a magician, and created beautiful literary forms. She did not always stick to the original text, but changed it a little in order to create the correct Hebrew impression and atmosphere. The Hebrew word chosen for the translation of "horn", for example, is "shofar" (literally 'a Ram's horn', used in Jewish religious ceremonies), which carries Jewish and religious connotations, unlike the word "keren" (literally 'horn'), which is a neutral term and carries no religious connotations. The black Numenorean kings were called "Malchei Ha'arelim" (Arelim – meaning, literally, 'uncircumsized'). These terms evoke strong cultural and religious associations among traditional Jews and educated Israelis. This fact, among others, helped to create the 'magic' of the Livnit translation, which filled thousands of Israelis in the 70s and the 80s with enthusiasm, and caused them to fall in love with Tolkien and his magnificent Legendarium. However, despite the traditional terms and the high register used, the accuracy of the translation was often compromised. This led, twenty years later, to the idea that a new translation was needed. Most of the members of the Israeli Tolkien Society have grown up on Livnit's translation, and for them Livnit *is* Tolkien in Hebrew. The poems were translated by Uriel Ofek, an admired poet, scholar and poetry translator. Like Livnit, he was a linguistic magician, with an incredible skill – which was needed to recreate the atmosphere and the beauty of the original. Ofek, too, used archaic and rich Hebrew, with many Jewish and Biblical terms.

But the Livnit – Ofek translation was not without its problems. Livnit, who had never read the *Silmarillion*, made many mistakes. Words were misplaced, a paragraph about Beren and Lúthien was completely misunderstood, and many mistranslations in the text itself occured. Worst of all, the Appendices were not translated at all. It is estimated that all in all Livnit made more than a hundred different mistakes in her translation. These were (usually) minor ones, but Ofek's mistakes were more severe. Although he was a great poetry translator, he was ignorant about the true character of the Legendarium. In the poems, Elves were sometimes translated as "nanasim" or "gamadim" (literally 'dwarves, gnomes' – there is no 'accurate' translation for Elves in Hebrew, not in the sense that Tolkien intended at least, but that is a debate in itself), Tom Bombadil brought water lilies "to the town" (what town?), and Elbereth was referred to as a male (in the text) or in the plural (in the verse).

Many fans admired Livnit's translation, but others were bothered by these inaccuracies and by the missing Appendices. Dr. Emanuel Lottem, a famous Israeli translator who is known for his excellent translations of popular science, fantasy and science-fiction books, offered the publishers to make a brand new translation of *LotR*. This being too expensive for the publishers, Lottem was appointed *editor* of Livnit's translation. Most Israeli fans were very excited to hear about the new edition. As Ms. Shirli Liron, a member of the Israeli Tolkien

Society wrote, "We were standing in book shops for hours, looking for our favorite passages". But for many the disappointment was enormous.

Lottem, as *editor* of Livnit's text, tried to combine his modern style with the archaic and rich diction of Livnit's translation, and the result was odd. The new edition combines two different styles, namely a modern-technical one and an archaic-literary one.

Lottem made changes in almost every paragraph. While he did correct many of the mistakes in the old edition, many fans believe that he did not pay attention to the spirit of the story and to the mythical atmosphere. No one claims that he worked carelessly. The opposite is true. Everyone knows that Lottem researched for an entire year and that he gave careful thought to his new translation. The main problem is that his translation tends to be technical. Many of the Biblical and traditional terms were removed, and slang expressions were introduced (words like "Tinofot" – meaning 'scum' in English). Most of the adult members of the Israeli Tolkien Society consider Lottem's changes a deterioration. It is important to say, however, that most of the new readers prefer Lottem's translation. These are usually young readers, aged 12-16 years, who cannot appreciate the beauty of Livnit's Hebrew, or readers that prefer accuracy to beauty in translation. There are also some who believe that Lottem's translation is better and more beautiful in style, but these are few in number.

Many Israeli fans, however, were angry and disappointed. Many of them liked Lottem's translations of *The Silmarillion* and *The Unfinished Tales*, and everybody admired his translations of classic science-fiction books such as *Dune*. Their anger arose not just because of Lottem's translation, but also due to the fact that the old edition, their favourite, had disappeared completely from the book shops. Currently, only one Hebrew edition of *LotR* is being published – Lottem's translation.

Livnit's fans went to war. Numerous articles were written against Lottem's translation, some of them too polemic and using language not suited to scholarly or literary discourse. As a reaction, the main supporter of Lottem came forth with a fierce counter attack. Yuval Kfir, Lottem's assistant for the *LotR* translation, wrote an article called "Hooray! The aged good translation!" (punning on

Livnit's odd translation for "alas!" and for "good old Merry"). Kfir demonstrated that Livnit and Ofek had made grave mistakes, and that Lottem had corrected them all. He emphasized in his article that Lottem's edition is the 'correct' and the 'accurate' one, in contrast to the 'faulty' edition of Livnit.

Kfir has a point. Livnit has, indeed, made many mistakes, more than Lottem. So the question is asked: Why? Why is Livnit's translation so loved in contrast to Lottem's translation?

This article will present the controversial opinions of Welis, one of the main supporters of Livnit, and of Kfir, by means of written contributions. We will begin with the contribution of Yuval Kfir, Lottem's assistant and defender of the new Hebrew *LotR* edition.

Of the Ruin of Tolkien, or the Two Translations

Yuval Kfir

Several years ago I posted a semi-flame to the rec.arts.books.tolkien newsgroup, concerning Ms. Ruth Livnit's Hebrew translation to *The Lord of the Rings*. I said I would be surprised if there is anyone who has read Tolkien in English and Livnit's translation and would be willing to speak in favour of the translation.

Four years later, a new Hebrew edition of *LotR* was published, in which I proudly took part (as voluntary assistant to the editor, Dr. Emanuel Lottem). Only then did I realise, with great surprise indeed, that this new translation upset a lot of people – most of the adult online community of the Israeli Tolkien readers, it seems.

I will not enter here into the debate of whether or not the old edition should be brought back into print. My goal in this contribution is to show that the only merits of the old translation are its rarity and the nostalgia it evokes in readers who grew up on it.

I believe the personal experience of the Israeli Tolkienians has had an important part in establishing their 'loyalty' to Livnit's translation – just as my experience definitely had a part in establishing *my* loyalty. In a nutshell, it is this: the majority of the adult Israeli Tolkienians became acquainted with Tolkien and *LotR*, came to love them, and grew up with them, through the old translation. For them, as has been said, Livnit *is* Tolkien, or even more than Tolkien, for she speaks their mother tongue.

I, too, read Livnit's translation in my early teens – but then I read the original, in English, a couple of years later, and I have resented Livnit ever since for robbing me of the real Tolkien experience. The old translation, I found out soon enough, is extremely flawed. Further investigation over the years revealed that another good adjective for it would be 'sloppy'. I will, of course, explain these accusations.

Even as a young boy, reading Livnit's translation without knowing the original text, I noticed some problems in the book: names were transcribed inconsistently ("Anathorn" and "Minas Thirith" are two examples); the maps were of very poor quality (roughly photocopied, white-out generously applied, Hebrew names written approximately in the correct places, some names obliterated entirely); "Alas!" was often translated as "Hooray!" (just imagine Aragorn saying "Hooray! Thus passes the heir of Denethor …"); and there were not always diacritical marks (Hebrew vowels) to help pronounce the strange names.

But the real shock came a few years later, when my father gave me *The Silmarillion* and *The Lord of the Rings* in English. Suddenly I found out what the maps *really* looked like, how "Celeborn" should be pronounced (Livnit transcribed it as "Tseleborn"), and, most importantly, I was shocked to discover that *The Lord of the Rings* has a set of appendices with a wealth of information about Tolkien's world.

You see, for some unknown reason, Livnit did not translate or even acknowledge the existence of the Appendices to *LotR*. It would seem, from information gained by Israeli Tolkienians years later, that her copy of *LotR* contained only "The Tale of Aragorn and Arwen" as an appendix. Nonetheless, she herself admitted in a letter that she did not think the Appendices (of whose existence she was dimly aware) were worth reading or translating. She treated the book as a literary work of art *and no more*. While we can certainly agree with the first half, the dismissal of the links to Tolkien's greater mythological work seems unforgivable. Livnit's translation had almost robbed me of the discovery of Tolkien's world in all its richness – in fact, it probably pulled a blind over the eyes of many other Israeli readers, who did not read English books, or did not think to seek out the original because they were confident of the quality of the Hebrew translation. They *didn't even know* what they were missing.

Livnit's ignorance of the Appendices and of *The Silmarillion* has been offered as an excuse for the many mistakes in her translation. But the sad fact is that she made many blunders that have nothing to do with being familiar with Tolkien, and everything to do with a disregard of the original text. Forget "Tseleborn" and "Izildur" – which are explained by not reading Appendix E – and consider "Bookland", "Brei" (or "Vrei"), "Arglav" and "Arvidui" kings of the "Dunadain", etc. And the Silvan Elves were left with the adjective *Silvan* transcribed, not translated, since Livnit failed to recognize this as a word meaning 'of the woods'.

Although Elbereth is referred to in two places as female, she is male in one place (the same place where Frodo says, "Those are mountain-Elves!" – Livnit's mistranslation of "High Elves"). The Valar undergo a transformation: when Damrod cries "May the Valar turn him [the Oliphaunt] aside!" Livnit translated this unfamiliar word as "rider". Then, when Théoden is described as "Oromë in the battle of the Valar", she decided it must be a place-name and translated "the battle of Valar". But when faced finally with "while the thrones of the Valar endure" (when Elessar is crowned), she translated it as "throne [*sic*] of the Valar". A good translator would have recognized by now that "Valar" is a plural proper name, and would have gone back and corrected the earlier occurrences, but Livnit did not bother to do so.

Nor is there consistency between verse and prose: when Saruman mocks Galadriel with "what ship will bear you back across so wide a sea?" readers of Livnit cannot recognize the quote, because it was translated quite differently in Galadriel's lament. And when Théoden is buried with the same words that Éomer sang, "Out of dark, out of doubt, to the day's rising", the Hebrew opening lines for both songs only remotely resemble each other. And Frodo's cry in Cirith Ungol "What have I said? What have I done?" which echoes Boromir's cry on Amon Hen, is translated differently.

More confusing still, Arwen, according to Livnit, was called Undómiel because she was "the Morning-Star of her people". It is true that the morning and evening star are the same planet, but the meaning is exactly opposite. And, like Bilbo in Rivendell, Livnit had no idea why Aragorn insisted on putting in a green stone in his song of Eärendil – so she turned it into a red stone in the translation. The connection to the Elessar, the Elfstone that Aragorn later bore and which gave him his name, was completely lost on her. In one place she translated Galadriel's words "the Elfstone of the house of Elendil" as "Prince of Elves, heir of the house of Elendil". Since when is Aragorn a prince of Elves?

Another example of 'twisted interpretation' can be found in Pippin's words about Shadowfax's lack of harness: "'None is rich and fair enough for him,' said Pippin. 'He will have none.'" In Livnit's translation, Pippin says '… therefore he will have none.' This small addition twists the original meaning of the sentence, and instead of being a 'wisecrack' about Shadowfax never wearing a harness, it becomes a comment on Shadowfax's vanity. Again, a small slip, but it demonstrates Livnit's lack of understanding of the text she was translating.

Indeed, many fans of the old translations acknowledge these mistakes. But, they say, Livnit's language is so much richer than Lottem's, using Biblical and Talmudic idioms and giving the book a high air.

This is partly true: Lottem removed some – definitely not all! – of the Biblical, Talmudic and Jewish references in Livnit's translation. And, in places, this reduces the 'grandeur' of the text. But *The Lord of the Rings* is not all 'grandeur' and pomposity! When Gollum or the orcs speak, they do not speak the Queen's English, nor do they quote Shakespeare and the Bible. And when Sam speaks, as he himself said, he is no poet. Secondly, there are many places where Livnit's style suddenly takes a dive, in mid-sentence, and changes from high, literary phrases to common, everyday speech. Thirdly, sometimes the Jewish connotations are simply out of place. And finally, some of the 'high language' which Livnit introduced may sound well, but it is inaccurate. I will attempt to 'reverse-translate' some of Livnit's Hebrew to demonstrate this.

For starters, Livnit corrected all of Gollum's English mistakes. Originally, Gollum's speech is full of "we wants it" and "we hates him" – but in Livnit's Hebrew, he just says, "we want it". Similarly, Sam's mimicking of Gollum's speech "I asks … I begs" was 'corrected' to "I ask … I beg". The reader of Livnit misses this little 'poke' Sam takes at Gollum.

But worse than that, Livnit's Gollum speaks Hebrew that even an Israeli lawyer would not dream of using – in speech, at least. "He lied on me, yes he did. I did escape, all by my poor self" says Tolkien's Gollum, where Livnit's Gollum has *"He hath slandered me, yes yes."* and continues with the formal, 'grand' form of 'I' in the second sentence (a form almost never used in speech). Gollum's speech is thus made at least as literary as Gandalf's, in form at least.

Uglúk, the Uruk leader, also speaks rather fancy Hebrew. "If you're afraid of the Whiteskins, run! Run! There's the forest," shouts Tolkien's Uglúk. "Get to it! It's your best hope. Off you go!" In Livnit's translation, Uglúk sounds less like a vicious, enraged platoon sergeant and more like a civilized officer calmly explaining matters. *"If you fear the Whiteskins, run! Make you haste and run! The forest lies yonder. That be your best chance. Get thee gone!"* – again, I am attempting to reach the same level of English as Livnit's level of Hebrew in this case. Formal sentence forms, use of literary expressions in speech – these devices are common in Hebrew literature, but the life they breathe into Gollum and Uglúk gives these characters – and other "low-life" in *LotR* – a style and class which they never had originally.

On the other hand, there are instances of lapses in style: from the high, antiquated and formal Hebrew to modern, informal language even within the same sentence. This is even harder to convey in English, and I will show just one small example to demonstrate what I mean: it is as if Théoden, instead of saying to Merry "And your friend is gone, who should also be here", said "And that friend of yours is gone …". Both say the same thing, but they have quite a different ring.

Some of Livnit's Jewish connotations are simply out of place. One of the most hotly debated examples is her translation of Elves into *"Bnei-Lilith"*, i.e. "sons of Lilith". Men are called in Hebrew *"Bnei-Adam"*, literally 'Sons of Adam'.

But Lilith, in Jewish mythology, was not only Adam's first, 'undocumented' wife – she is also the Devil's own spouse in many tales. There are many who feel that linking Elves with Satan is out of place.

Some Jewish associations are even more ridiculous, such as translating "renegade [Númenoreans]" as *"Meshumadim"* – this Jewish term is used solely to describe Jews who converted to Christianity, either under pressure from the Inquisition or of their own volition. The "heathen kings" that Gandalf speaks of to Denethor are *"Arelim"* – literally, 'uncircumcised', a word meaning 'non-Jews'. And the horn-calls appearing so frequently in the book are often translated as *"Shofarot"*, i.e. the ancient Jewish ram's horn used in religious ceremonies. It is true that using phrases and terms from the Bible and the Talmud gives a book, any book, an air of antiquity and grandeur. But in some places this simply goes too far: the Númenoreans and their descendants are not the Bnai-Brith, just as the followers of Sauron are not Goyim. There is no place for this distinction in a book so closely tied to Northern European myths and folklore.

In other places the Jewish phrases are not out of place, they are just incorrect or inaccurate. One such example is Aragorn saying of Gollum "I do not doubt that he was allowed to leave Mordor on some evil errand." Livnit turned "evil errand" into "errand of sabotage", which connects nicely to a Jewish term about "messengers [angels] of sabotage" – but Gollum's errand was not, in fact, one of sabotage but rather one of espionage and treachery.

There are many more examples, of all kinds. I have only skimmed them here. My main point remains that Livnit was not just ignorant of Tolkien's world: her whole approach to the translation was one of an 'intuitively flowing' translation. In some places her intuition was good. In many other places, it caused mistakes and inconsistencies, both in content and in style. Tolkien was a master of style and storytelling, but also a master of detail. Livnit paid no attention to detail.

I would like to make one final point regarding the new edition's unpopularity in the Israeli online Tolkien community. The "young readers" that Danny Orbach disparages, saying that they cannot "appreciate the beauty" of Livnit nor "see the mistakes" in Lottem – those young readers are of the same age, and, I daresay, generally of the same intellectual level, as many Livnit-supporters were when they first read Livnit's translation. They have their own tastes, and some of them like Lottem's edition better in its own right – until they are 'corrected' by the online community elders, most of them Livnitians. Group pressure, especially in a close-knit community like our Israeli Tolkien community, is not to be underestimated. I find myself agreeing with Danny Orbach, in fact: the young age of these readers does matter. It makes them much more susceptible to such persuasions, especially when coming from older, more authoritative figures (who really do know much more about Tolkien and his world than the new readers).

This, then, is the situation as I view it. The Livnitians' argument is not, in fact, with Emanuel Lottem: it is with the publisher, whom they want to persuade to reprint the old translation. But in its current form, unrevised and uncorrected, the old translation is better off the bookstores' shelves than on them.

As we have seen, Yuval Kfir has proved that Livnit was often wrong in her translation or failed in her understanding of the original text. Kfir has also claimed that the "grandeur" of Livnit's translation does not take into account the diversity of stylistic levels in the original text. And Livnit's supporters? Do they have an answer to these accusations? Yuwal Welis tries to answer on Livnit's behalf.

Livnit's *Lord of the Rings* Translation – A Unique Masterpiece

Yuval Welis

I think the main difference between the translations of *The Lord of the Rings* in Germany and Israel is that the new Hebrew edition of *LotR* is actually a *disguise* for a new translation. Lottem's work was so thorough that almost every third sentence was rewritten or modified; the terminology changed (among them was the Hebrew word for 'Elves'); a different pronunciation-system was used and many mistakes crept in (for example, 'Isildur' is now pronounced 'Ysildur' and so every name that begins with an I; 'Isengard' and 'Isen' are now pronounced with an 's' sound instead of a 'z' sound as found in the old version, which was made by a translator who knew German).

In other respects, I find many similarities between the situations in Israel and Germany. The original Hebrew translation was made, as mentioned, by a German-speaking translator, who grew up as a young girl in Germany (in the 30s). She had an extraordinary command of the Hebrew language and, as was the custom then, of the Jewish religious terms and texts. She did not know much about Tolkien (apart from having read *The Hobbit* and *LotR*) and it seems that the edition she worked from (the one-volume edition containing the text of the 2nd edition, printed in 1973) was missing the Appendices (only the story of Aragorn and Arwen was given). Nonetheless, she produced a most admirable translation that deserves to be recognized as a work of art in its own right. She used largely Jewish religious expressions (found in the Bible and other Rabbinical sources) to convey Tolkien's deep sense of the grandeur of the past. In this matter, I think, she went much along the same lines as Mrs. Carroux, her German counterpart. It is perhaps a quality unique to Tolkien's work that his style invokes in creative translators (mostly of the old generation) the desire to resort to expressions that are rooted in the past and have religious connotations. In Mrs. Livnit's translation, for example, 'Heathens' became "Arelim" (literally, 'uncircumsized') and many expressions were taken from the Bible and other ancient Hebrew sources. The Jewish tradition does not have a mythology like the European nations. There are mainly two sources at disposal, namely the Bible and the Babylonian legends and 'fairy stories' that were preserved in the Talmud and the Midrashim (dating from 200 to 700 AD). The latter contains stories about demons of many sorts. Some, for instance, tell of King Solomon and his dealings with these demons (he was considered a most wise and holy man, and therefore capable of controlling and using them for purposes of his own). Mrs. Livnit used a term taken from these legends to translate 'Elves': 'Bney-Lilith', which means 'of the kind of Lilith'. Lilith is a Babylonian demon, usually portrayed as a beautiful red-haired woman who tempts men and steals babies from their cribs. The "Lilin", another word used for demons, are thought to have wings. Mrs. Livnit did not coin this term. She found it in a German-Hebrew dictionary from 1929, compiled by a Bible scholar who later became a well-known professor of Ancient Eastern studies in Israel.

Thus, by creating an atmosphere of antiquity and evoking the feeling of a glorious, heroic and mythical past, Mrs. Livnit created a unique work of art, a masterpiece of Hebrew that, to my mind, is one of the finest that were ever written in Modern Hebrew.

The new edition, in contrast, did its utmost to eradicate all these terms and expressions and went sometimes as far as to adopt English sentence structures just to be as faithful as possible to Tolkien's original. It seems that nowadays translators feel uneasy with anything that carries even a faint smell of the past. Maybe they are afraid that younger readers would not understand such language or that they would be repelled from reading the book by any such remainders of the past. But in doing so they are obliterating the very impression Tolkien was striving to make with his unique language and expressions; they are discarding the *spirit* of the book.

The argument between Welis and Kfir, and the other supporters of the two translations, was long and hard and lasted many years. I have tried to present evenly the main issues in this controversy. For my part, I think that both sides have somewhat missed the point. Both Welis and Kfir are too busy pointing out minor mistakes, such as whether how one should pronounce correctly the name "Isildur", or what the correct Hebrew term for Elves is. These issues were very important, indeed, for Tolkien himself, and are very important and of interest to experts and fans. But the spirit of the translation, only mentioned in passing in both arguments, is, for my part, the most important issue at stake. One good answer was given by Shirli Liron, a member of the Israeli Tolkien Society, who wrote yet another article, called 'The Secret of Livnit's Magic'. In this article she addresses the question of what constitutes the spirit and the atmosphere of Tolkien's work – a question that both Kfir and Welis ignored. According to Liron, the crucial point is whether a translation succeeds in recreating the special atmosphere (Livnit's translation does) and not whether it is accurate (Lottem's translation). She claims that Lottem's main flaws are not his textual mistakes (of which he made a few), but concern matters of style and atmosphere. Lottem, for example, writes extremely long and complicated sentences. This is a technique that may sound good in English, but it makes for very awkward and uncomfortable Hebrew. She further argues that Lottem cared for the accuracy so much that he forgot the essence of the book. In most cases, she writes, Lottem translated word for word, without giving any thought to matters of atmosphere and lyric beauty.

I agree with her arguments, and believe Lottem's translation to be too technical. He has sacrificed the special Tolkinian spirit for a 'perfect accuracy', which is impossible to achieve anyway. Yet it is, according to Liron, this very Tolkienian spirit that causes so many people to love his books. I agree with Kfir in his main point – that Lottem is more accurate than Livnit. But I disagree with him on the importance given to accuracy. If the spirit of the book is betrayed, then accuracy, as I see it, is pointless and futile.

I believe in the choices Livnit and Ofek made, despite their many flaws. In my view, when translating a text on such an epic scale, one must make use of the correct mythological terms of the target language. Accordingly, an Arabic translation of *LotR* must use old Islamic terminology, a Japanese translation must use Shinto and Samurai terminology (as the Japanese translator, Mr. Teji Seta, actually did), and a Hebrew one should make use of Jewish and Biblical terminology. In Carroux's German translation, for example, 'Harry', the door-warden of Bree, was translated as 'Heinrich'. 'Baggins' was rendered as 'Beutlin', and 'Andy', Sam's uncle, was translated as 'Adolf', not to mention 'Elben' for 'Elves', 'Bruchtal' for 'Rivendell' and others. The reason for doing so is to be found in Carroux's intention to create a rural German atmosphere for the Shire, an atmosphere rooted in her language and culture. She aimed at tying the translated text to the rich mythological Germanic tradition, which Tolkien was greatly influenced by. Livnit did the same in Hebrew, and in that point her true success lies. Kfir has pointed out that Livnit used high language also for orcs and for Gollum. However, he ignores an important problem that any Hebrew translator has to face. The Hebrew language, except as the idiom of religious literature and prayer, had been dead for 2000 years and it had not been used as a living colloquial language until the rise of Zionism at the turn of the century. Modern Hebrew, which is just seventy or eighty years old, lacks the richness of its ancestor, and therefore would not do for a book like *LotR*. English, in contrast, has a long history of popular speech, so even 'low' English has a richness and beauty, as *LotR* illustrates. Since Hebrew lacks such a 'traditional' low style, a translator must use the high and ancient levels of the language, because there lies the richness of Hebrew. As a consequence, Livnit was correct in using a high level in the book as a whole. When Lottem tried to use popular Hebrew terms for the orcs and for Gollum, the results were problematic, to say the least. The whole atmosphere of *LotR* has been 'modernised', and that is the main problem of the new translation.

Conclusion

In this article, I have tried to summarize the different views concerning the existent translations of *LotR* into Hebrew. I have not mentioned translations of *The Hobbit* or the ones of *The Silmarillion* and *The Unfinished Tales* respectively, because they are not really controversially discussed. The positions of Welis, Kfir and Liron, along with my own arguments, summarize the Israeli translation controversy in brief.

The controversy, however, is not just limited to the translation of *LotR* but has a more general impact and raises far-reaching questions concerning the art of translation as a whole. Is beauty more important than accuracy? Does linguistic correctness matter more than atmosphere? I believe that these questions are at the core of the disagreement between the supporters of Lottem and Livnit respectively. I have encountered similar problems when translating "The Lay of Leithan" into Hebrew (a translation which has, as yet, not been published), and so will every translator who accepts the onerous and dangerous task of transfering high works of art from one language to another. Wilhelm von Humboldt's dictum still hold true: "Mehrere Sprachen sind nicht ebenso viele Bezeichnungen einer Sache. Es sind verschiedene Ansichten derselben". The art of translation is not a science, but an art, and that approach should inspire us to evaluate literary translations in general as 'works of art'. We should, therefore, not be too pedantic about 'mistakes' and 'misunderstandings' on the level of vocabulary, but try and appreciate the work in its entirety as a work of art and discover its beauty. That is what literature is all about, isn't it?

About the author

Danny Orbach is currently studying History and East-Asian studies at Tel-Aviv university. He is a translator and freelance author and, at the time, writing a book about the German resistance against Hitler. Furthermore, he is a board member of the Israeli Tolkien Society and author of several articles about philosophy, fate and religion in Tolkien's works, most of which were published in *Numenore*, the scholarly Internet site of the Israeli Tolkien Society. He has translated numerous articles on Tolkien from English and German into Hebrew and has given papers at several conferences on Tolkien, fantasy and science fiction, usually in Israel, but also at the 'DTG Thing' meeting in Marienthal, Germany, July 2003. He has translated the "Lay of Leithian" into Hebrew (not published yet). His main fields of interest are the Christian influences on Tolkien, Tolkien as poet and philosopher, the epic qualities of the "Lay of Leithian" and *The Lord of the Rings*, and the question of free will and determinism in Tolkien's works.

Richard Sturch

Estne Tolkien Latine Reddendus?
A Light-Hearted Look at Some of the Challenges[1]

Abstract

Four main problems are identified and discussed which arise in the task of rendering Tolkien into Latin. One is that of names (and a few other Middle-earthly words) – does one translate or simply reproduce, and in the latter case should the name be declinable or not? A second is the occasional verse: what forms should be used to translate the very different kinds of English verse that we find in Tolkien? A third is the similar variation in prose styles between the homely and the rhetorical. And a fourth, related to this last, is how to handle the "rhetorical" passages when Tolkien's style is so unlike that of the standard models for Latin prose.

About the beginning of 2002 an e-mail was passed on to me from a schoolboy named Michael Orth, who was in the early stages of learning Latin and wondered whether anyone had rendered *The Lord of the Rings* into that language. So far as I know, nobody had, or indeed has. Translations into one's own language are natural and common, and may even earn the translator a reasonable fee, but there seems little point (and even less monetary profit) in doing it into Latin! There have indeed been modern Latin translations of English texts, most notably Alexander Lenard's admirable *Winnie ille Pu*; but all those I know of have been of short and simple children's books, intended either as elementary introductions to Latin for children who might be familiar with the English originals, or simply as a jest. *The Lord of the Rings* is neither short, nor simple, nor intended for children, and a translation into Latin could hardly serve as an introduction to the language. And as for a jest – well, completed, it might easily qualify as "the greatest jest in all the history of Gondor", if by "greatest" we mean "longest". But the idea was something of a challenge, and I did in fact send Mr. Orth, in instalments, a version of the first chapter.

---

1 Many thanks are due to my brother Nicholas, classics master at the York School, Monterey, California, for corrections and improvements.

That indeed is probably the easiest part of the whole book to render into Latin. It is in simple English, and only calls for simple Latin. One can even have fun working out new terms. "Mathom", for example, cries out to be taken as a Greek borrowing, *mathoma*, plural *mathomata*, as in *diploma*. "Eleventy" is of course "undecaginta". But what is "hobbit" to be?

It is, we are assured, a worn-down version of *holbytla*, which apparently means a "hole-dweller". (Actually, Tolkien says the only English word which really influenced the invention was "hole"[2].) Very well. "Hole" would be normally rendered by *cavum* (there are other words too, but this one suggests "cave", which seems a good idea). And a hole-dweller would be a *cavicola*. I'm not sure, though, that this can easily be worn down; there are a number of words formed like this, such as *agricola* and *caelicola*, and they don't have contracted forms. A possibility would be to say "hole-*digger*" instead. Now *fossor* is the word for a digger, and "hole-digger" would be *cavifossor*; abridge it by dropping the end, as in the original; I ended up with *cafos*, genitive *cafodis*. And "Hobbiton" similarly becomes "Cafodium", with a derived adjective "Cafodiensis". (I have one slight qualm here. Might "hole-digger" suggest a nasty, wet sort of hole instead of a hobbit hole, which means comfort? But this would not be true of the abbreviated form; I think we can go on with *cafos*.)

In general, there are three, maybe four problems which face any translator of Tolkien, whatever the language he or she is using. One is the existence in the text of several different languages, and, what is more, sometimes different *levels* of language. English, which represents the Common Speech, we represent by (in this case) Latin. Names derived from English roots can be given equivalent Latin forms. The Elvish languages one simply lets stand, and the same applies to the fragments of Dwarvish and the Black Speech; this was after all Tolkien's own practice. So far, so good. But the Rohirrim spoke (at times, and among themselves) a language related to the Common Speech as Old English is to modern, and represented in the text by Old English. Not many fragments of this are given, but some are; and their names are of the same origin. But no language survives which is related in this way to Latin.[3] (A few fragments of

---

2 See *Letters*, p. 406.
3 On the problem of the relationship between the different languages in Middle-earth, see Thomas Honegger's contribution in this volume.

very archaic Latin do exist, but they are of no assistance.) As far as I can see, the only thing the Latin translator could do would be to leave the Rohirric names and fragments alone. This would give the misleading impression that their language was as unconnected with the Common Speech as, say, the Elvish languages; but that cannot be helped.

I cannot resist adding here that this problem would not arise if one were translating into Sanskrit. There we actually have a "related language" in the form of Vedic, which is older than classical Sanskrit and might be used for the Rohirrim (though perhaps it does not differ as much from the classical language as Old English does from modern). Its original users are even thought by some to have been equestrian nomads. What is more, there are also a range of languages derived from Sanskrit (the "Prakrits") which could help with the different style or levels of English which are used in *The Lord of the Rings*; in the classical Sanskrit drama they are used to represent the speech of the less educated characters. There is even one debased form, Paiśaci, which was supposed to be spoken by the Indian equivalent of goblins! Ah, well.

Levels of English. Colloquialisms are all right; there are plenty of Latin writings which use such, from Plautus to Petronius. But the world of *The Lord of the Rings* is one which has developed over millennia, languages and all, and from time to time characters (or the narrator himself) use language which verges on the archaic. I think the best way to handle this is probably to use as plain a Latin as possible for the "ordinary" passages (mediaeval Latin would be ideal, if the translator were reasonably familiar with it) and more elaborate Latin of a definitely classical style, when the English contains archaisms. We shall return to this matter later on.

Proper names pose the second (or third) problem. Tolkien can simply include names in languages other than the Common Speech as they stand. "Elrond", for example, was a foreign name in the Common Speech just as it is in English, and there is no need to alter it. But Latin is an inflected language, and actual Latin names vary in form according to what case they are in – nominative, accusative and so on. What should we do about names used in our translation? The Romans themselves often gave foreign names Latin endings. We may not be quite sure what the originals of names like "Arminius" or "Prasutagus" were, but we can be pretty sure they differed from these Latinized forms! Occasionally particularly difficult names were left indeclinable. If, for example, you look at St. Jerome's version of the genealogy which opens the Gospel of Matthew, you find both. Most of the Hebrew names there are simply left alone – "Abraham", "Isaac", "David" and so on. But some had accepted Latin forms, especially if they had endings which looked fairly like Latin or Greek ones. So "Salomon" gets the accusative "Salomonem", and most names originally ending in "-iah" take the declinable ending "-ias" (quite common in Greek, and in Latin texts using Greek names). Jerome is not quite consistent, mind you; "Abraham" is indeclinable in the genealogy, but in Luke 16:22 has a genitive "Abrahae".

So we have precedent either for adapting names or for leaving them alone and indeclinable. Let us begin by considering the names of the hobbits. Tolkien himself has used more than one way of rendering them. Some are translations, like "Proudfoot", some more or less transliterations like "Took" and "Bolger". Bilbo's real name in Middle-earth, we know, was "Bilba Labingi"[4], but the names used for him in the text are so familiar that one feels they ought to be retained. After all, there are plenty of genuine masculine names in Latin ending in "-o", like "Curio" or "Cicero" – or indeed "Otho"! "Baggins" – well, a large number of Latin words, especially present participles, end in "-ns", with a stem "-nt-"; and we can treat "Baggins" as another.

For the same reason we should not, I think, tamper with "Frodo", although his real first name was not "Froda" but "Maura"[5]. In the case of his Took companion, there was, we learn, a kind of play upon words between the names "Peregrin" ("Razanul") and "Pippin" ("Razal"), which it is impossible to reproduce. "Peregrinus" is of course actual Latin, so one wants to let it stand; but there are no obvious nicknames that are suitable and yet close to "Peregrinus". I think we had better just use "Pippinus" as the nickname. ("Pepinus", remembering the father of Charlemagne, would be tempting, but rather pointless – and not jocular enough.) But we might as well use the "real" names (or approximations) for most of the other hobbits mentioned, or translations where the names have meaning (e.g. "Cornicen" for "Hornblower", "Vermiculus" for "Grubb" and so on). "Chubb" provides a rather pleasing problem. According to my dictionary,

---

4 For these names see *The Peoples of Middle-earth*, pp. 48 ff.
5 *Ibid*.

the zoological name for "chub" (a kind of fish) is *Cyprinus* or *Leuciscus*. However, an alternative name for the chub is "chavender", and I think it would be quite a Tolkienish sort of joke to treat this form as Latin to render the name (genitive "Chavendri"). "Tucca" is a perfectly good Roman name, and will do well for "Took". Merry's real name, "Kalimac", comes out nicely as "Callimachus", the Latinized version of a Greek name. But the obvious abbreviations of this would be the Latin words "callidus" or "calidus", meaning "clever" or "fiery" respectively – neither appropriate. Probably best to say just "Calli" (another indeclinable, I fancy). His real surname was "Braldagamba", and this will do well enough in Latin without change.

Samwise and Hamfast Gamgee, we are told, were really called Banazir and Ranugad Galpsi. Translation would lead to rather clumsy forms ("Semisapiens" and "Domicola", perhaps). But it would be possible to do a mild Latinization of the original names instead, allowing us to decline the names. "Banazir" could stand (genitive "Banaziris"); "Ranugad" would probably best be "Ranugas" (genitive "Ranugadis"). Their surname could then be "Galpsius".

So, for an example of name-handling, let us take this version of part of the conversation at *The Ivy Bush*:[6]

> 'But what about this Frodo that lives with him?' asked Old Noakes of Bywater. 'Baggins is his name, but he's more than half a Brandybuck, they say. It beats me why any Baggins of Hobbiton should go looking for a wife away there in Buckland, where folks are so queer.'
>
> And no wonder they're queer,' put in Daddy Twofoot (the Gaffer's next-door neighbour), 'if they live on the wrong side of the Brandywine River, and right against the Old Forest. That's a dark bad place, if half the tales be true.'

translating as:

> "At quid dicis de hospite eius Frodone?" rogavit Noax Senior Ripulanus. "Nomine Baggins est, at maiorem partem Braldagamba tenetur. Quare Baggins ullus Cafodiensis uxorem quaerat in Gambia, demiror; alieni sunt Gambiani."
>
> "Sane alieni sunt", infit Tata Bipes (vicinus Aviti proximus) "qui trans flumen Braldahim habitent, iuxta Veterem Silvam; locum atrum et malevolum, si vel dimidium vere narratur."

---

6 *The Lord of the Rings* (*LotR*), bk. I, ch.1; there are so many editions that it seems pointless to give a page reference.

In this passage "Noakes" has simply been changed to "Noax"; "Twofoot" has been translated. *Tata* is the Latin equivalent of "Daddy", and obviously correct here. "Gaffer" is a bit more of a problem. It derives of course from "grandfather". As far as I know, there is no "familiar" form of the Latin word for "grandfather", *avus*. (There is one for "father", as noted just now – *tata*.) I have used *avitus*, "relating to a grandfather, ancestral", though admittedly it's more dignified than "gaffer" is. *Ripula* "little bank", does quite well, I think, for "Bywater"; and "Buckland" is derived from the second half of "Brandybuck", so we get *Gambia* from the second half of *Braldagamba*: I hope citizens of the modern Gambia have no objection. "Brandywine" I have had to leave in its original form *Braldahim* – another indeclinable.

"Bolger" could have been simply taken over as Latin (genitive "Bolgeri" as in *laniger*, *lanigeri*); however, as it seems the name was originally "Bolga", that had better be its Latin form. "Sackville-Baggins" is harder. "Sackville" suggests some name to do with sacking towns – but then "Sackville" is also the name of an aristocratic British family, now extinct, and probably that was what Tolkien had in mind. We need a name that would sound aristocratic to a Roman, and if possible suggest sieges and wars. I thought at one time of "Pyrrho-Baggins", recalling the warrior King Pyrrhus of Epirus who caused Rome such a lot of trouble in the third century B.C. But the nearest Roman equivalent of a British "double-barrelled" name was probably an additional name tacked on at the *end* to indicate a relationship (especially adoption). The future emperor Augustus, for instance, was born an Octavius, but after adoption by Caesar became "Gaius Iulius Caesar Octavianus". So perhaps an extra name of "Direptorianus", from *direptor*, a plunderer.

Names which are not represented by "English" (such as "Gandalf" or the names of Dwarves and Elves) can probably stand, with a slight Latinization on the same lines where needed. Might "Elrond", which we mentioned above, become "Elrons", with "Elrondis" as the genitive (as with words like "frons" in Latin)? I am inclined to think we should indeed decline it, but leave the nominative unchanged (as Jerome did with "Abraham" in Luke).

Anyway, a few more examples. By now the opening sentence of "A Long-Expected Party" (and indeed of the main part of the book),

> When Mr. Bilbo Baggins of Bag End announced that he would shortly be celebrating his eleventy-first birthday with a party of special magnificence, there was much talk and excitement in Hobbiton.

might emerge as something like:

> Nuntiato Magistrum Bilbonem Baggintem, qui Bagfinem habitaret, mox diem natalem suum undeciesimum primum convivio magnificentissimo celebraturum, rumores commotionesque Cafodium complebant.[7]

And the paragraph beginning "The fireworks were by Gandalf", which involves giving names to objects not known in the Roman world –

> They were not only brought by him but designed and made by him; and the special effects, set pieces, and flights of rockets were let off by him. But there was also a generous distribution of squibs, crackers, backarappers, sparklers, torches, dwarf-candles, elf-fountains, goblin-barkers and thunder-claps. They were all superb. The art of Gandalf improved with age.

well, more fun here:

> Haec non solum adlata sunt a Gandalfo, sed etiam creata et fabricata. Praecipua spectacula, necnon roquetas, ipse accendit; distributi autem generose erant squibae, crepacula, baccarappae, scintillatores, faces, candelae pumiliares, quendifontes, orcolatratores, et tonitratoria. Omnia praeclara erant, quia ars Gandalfi aetate maturescebat.[8]

Roqueta, *squiba* and *baccarappa* are all of course simply transferred from the English "rocket", "squib" and "backarapper"; I think they look quite convincing. ("Backarapper" is not in my dictionary; I presume it to be onomatopoeic!) The next lot are translations. *Quendi* for "Elves", as here in "*quendifontes*" for "elf-fountains", should work; it looks Latin, even though it isn't. I wish there were a more dignified-sounding word for "dwarf" in Latin, though; "pumilus", though correct, just doesn't sound right. The root "orc" had best be left alone; it seems to have been common to practically all the languages of Middle-earth.

Inventing suitable forms for the names is quite enjoyable. A more serious problem is provided by the verse. The only one I had to deal with in the translation of the first chapter for Mr. Orth was Bilbo's "Road" song.

---

7 *LotR*, bk. I, ch. 1.
8 *LotR*, bk. I, ch. 1.

This can hardly be rendered into a classical metre; most classical Latin poetry was meant to be read rather than sung. An accentual metre, then, as in much mediaeval Latin verse. Something on these lines:

The Road goes ever on and on	Ostium relinquit Via,
Down from the door where it began.	Pergit in perpetuum;
Now far ahead the Road has gone,	Via longe praecucurrit,
And I must follow, if I can,	Sequi sit propositum.
Pursuing it with eager feet,	Sequar pedibus beatis
Until it joins some larger way	Donec fit concursio
Where many paths and errands meet.	Plurimarum semitarum.
And whither then? I cannot say.	Quo me ducant? nescio.[9]

But this sort of rhythm may not do when we get to the more solemn verse. Aragorn's song about Beren and Lúthien might call for a metre like that of the *Stabat Mater* (though with eight lines per verse, not six) – more serious than that of Bilbo's road-song.

The leaves were long, the grass was green	Silvae frondibus vigebant,
The hemlock-umbels tall and fair,	Herba et conium virebant,
And in the glade a light was seen	Stellae parvae sublucebant
Of stars in shadow shimmering.	Umbratae per nemora,
Tinúviel was dancing there	Qua Tinuviel tectarum
To music of a pipe unseen,	Modis mota tibiarum
And light of stars was in her hair,	Veste reddebat stellarum
And in her raiment glimmering.	Crinibusque decora.[10]

Not easy to keep that up; but it does perhaps to some extent echo the three-syllable rhymes of the original ("glimmering", "sorrowing" and so on). *Cicuta* rather than *conium* is the classical word for "hemlock", but it doesn't fit in so well, the stress being on the second syllable.

The lament for Boromir also calls for a serious metre, but it uses much longer lines. At first I thought of something on the lines of the one Abelard used for Passiontide hymns like *Solus ad victimam procedis, Domine*; but it proved not to be long enough – only twelve syllables, whereas the English usually has fourteen. Anther possibility, the "Fourth Asclepiad", used once or twice by Horace, though it has sixteen syllables (rather longer than the English), I found very difficult to write! So I tried trochaic tetrameters, as used in the late poem

---

9 *LotR*, bk. I, ch. 1.
10 *LotR*, bk. I, ch. 11.

Pervigilium Veneris; it is a fast-moving, even tripping metre there, but perhaps it need not be. I came up with

> Trans agros et trans paludes Rohanae Favonius
> Gramine adflatu vibrato venit usque ad moenia.
> Qualia huc ex occidente, lenis aura, fers nova?
> Iam tibi Boromir procerus noctilucis visus est?
> "Lata visus est peragere septem cana flumina,
> Inque desertas pedester regiones transgredi,
> Donec in septemtrionem praeterit tenebricum;
> Inde fors aquilo sonoram bucinam perceperit."
> O Boromir desiderate, tam diu despeximus,
> Terra nec deserta nobis occidentis reddidit.

The English (which rhymes; the *Pervigilium* does not) runs

> Through Rohan over fen and field where the long grass grows
> The West Wind comes walking, and about the walls it goes.
> 'What news from the West, O wandering wind, do you bring to me tonight?
> Have you seen Boromir the Tall by moon or by starlight?'
> 'I saw him ride over seven streams, over waters wide and grey;
> I saw him walk in empty lands, until he passed away
> Into the shadows of the North. I saw him then no more.
> The North Wind may have heard the horn of the son of Denethor.'
> 'O Boromir! From the high walls westward I looked afar,
> But you came not from the empty lands where no men are.'[11]

Happily, the *Pervigilium* allows two short syllables for a long here and there, or it would be impossible to have got "Boromir" in at all.

Bilbo's chant about Earendil, though – what on earth should one do about that? I think one would have to give up any hope of suggesting the original's *tour de force* effect, and go in, not for mediaeval rhyming forms, but for classical hexameters, on the grounds that it is after all a (short) epic. (Bernard of Cluny did manage a comparable *tour de force* in the rhyming scheme of his *De Contemptu Mundi*:

> Hora novissma, tempora pessima sunt; vigilemus.
> Ecce minaciter imminet arbiter ille supremus ...

But he said he had needed divine inspiration to achieve it, and that is not available here.) Ordinary hexameters be it. But the proper names in Bilbo's chant are a nightmare. Some might be translated – "Nimbrethil" means "silver birch", so

---

[11] *LotR*, bk. III, ch. 1.

just include a reference to birches (and hope that the "e" of *betula* is short – apparently it isn't found in Latin verse, so one can't tell!). Others one would simply have to leave as they stand, probably as indeclinables, even though indeclinables are far more awkward in verse than in prose. (There is a precedent of sorts. The sixth-century epic poet Corippus cheerfully used Moorish names

> ... saevis Naffur in armis
> Silcadenitque ferus,[12]

though I cannot say it made for great verse.) So

> Eärendil was a mariner
> that tarried in Arvernien,
> he built a boat of timber felled
> in Nimbrethil to journey in;
> her sails he wove of silver fair ...[13]

becomes

> Imi qua ripas Arvernien unda rigabat
> Condidit antiquis Eärendil nauta diebus
> E betulae lignis navem, contextaque vela
> Argento splendere dedit

But this will not do. It is mere doggerel – and would anyone guess that *Arvernien* is meant to be genitive? It looks more as if it were nominative, agreeing with *unda*. I suspect that if the great work of rendering *The Lord of the Rings* into Latin were ever completed, this poem would have to be omitted altogether. But perhaps a really good Latinist would be able to cope.

Even in prose, though, the matter of what I have called "levels" of English is a serious one. In Chapter 1, as I have said, we can be simple and colloquial; but as the narrative grows darker and more serious, this becomes less appropriate. Would-be writers of Latin at school are usually given Cicero as a model. But Cicero was an orator, and there is not much occasion for oratory in *The Lord of the Rings*. Saruman's speech to Gandalf,[14] indeed, was declaimed, "as if he were making a speech long rehearsed"; it is not very Ciceronian in flavour, but does call for more rhetoric on the part of the translator than much of the book does.

---

12 *Iohannis, seu de bellis Libycis*, ii. 52-3.
13 *LotR*, bk. II, ch. 1.
14 *LotR*, bk. II, ch. 2.

> The Elder Days are gone. The Middle Days are passing. The Younger Days are beginning.

I think a Roman orator would have reversed one or other of the first two sentences (the device known as "chiasmus"):

> Praeteritis diebus antiquitatis, mediis praetereuntibus, incipiunt noviores.

Continuing:

> The time of the Elves is over, but our time is at hand; the world of Men, which we must rule. But we must have power, power to order all things as we will, for that good which only the Wise can see.

> Finito Quendorum tempore, tempus nostrum adest, tempus humanum, tempus nobis dirigendum. Imperii autem opus est, ut ad bona illa efficienda, quae nemini nisi sapientibus videnda sunt, secundum consilia nostra nos omnia regamus.

"The world of Men" – I don't think *mundus*, the obvious Latin word, will really do. Or any alternative. Best to repeat "time", I think. "Which only the Wise can see" – that could have been managed without the relative clause, but then *efficienda* and *videnda* would have looked like parallels.

> And listen, Gandalf, my old friend and helper! I said *we*, for *we* it may be, if you will join with me. A new Power is rising. Against it the old allies and policies will not avail us at all. There is no help in Elves or in dying Númenor. This then is one choice before you, before us. We may join with that Power. It would be wise, Gandalf. There is hope that way. Its victory is at hand; and there will be rich reward for those that aided it. As the Power grows, its proved friends will also grow; and the Wise, such as you and I, may with patience come at last to direct its courses, to control it. We may bide our time, we can keep our thoughts in our hearts, deploring maybe evils done by the way, but approving the high and ultimate purpose: Knowledge, Rule, Order; all the things that we have so far striven in vain to accomplish, hindered rather than helped by our weak or idle friends. There need not be, there would not be, any real change in our designs, only in our means.

> Ausculta ergo, Gandalfe, tam diu mihi amice, tam diu adiutor. "Nobis" et "nostra" dixi, recte quidem si mihi coniungeris. Potestas nova emergit, contra quam socii consiliaque obsoleti omnino inutiles fiunt. Neque a Quendis neque a Numenore moribundo auxilium superest ullum. Hoc bonae spei eligi potest, ab hoc potestate stare; quod prudentium esset, Gandalfe. Victoria eius imminens adiutoribus praemia ditissima praebebit, non solum potestati crescenti sed etiam fidis amicis famam atque imperium. Quorum sapientes, quales et tu et ego, perseverantia tandem consilia potestatis dirigere poterimus et gubernare.

> Opperiri possibile erit absconditis in corde sententiis, dum facta deploramus incommoda, altum autem finem et honestum probamus – prudentiam, regimen, disciplinam, quas adhuc omnes efficere frustra conati sumus, ab infirmis aut inertibus amicis magis impediti quam adiuvati. Non quae petimus, sed quibus petenda efficimus mutare necesse esset.

Definitely "Ciceronian" language we are unlikely to find much of. Tolkien does have his purple passages, but he builds them up with "ands" and "buts" rather than with elaborate structures and periods. Look, for example, at the paragraph which describes what happened when Frodo put on the ring in the Sammath Naur. There are eight "ands" and a "but", and only two subordinate clauses. The next paragraph is similar – seven "ands" and only one subordinate clause.[15]

> And far away, as Frodo put on the Ring and claimed it for his own, the Power in Barad-dûr was shaken, and the Dark Tower trembled from its foundations to its proud and bitter crown. The Dark Lord was suddenly aware of him, and his Eye piercing all shadows looked across the plain to the door that he had made; and the magnitude of his own folly was revealed to him in a blinding flash, and all the devices of his enemies were at last laid bare. Then his wrath blazed in consuming flame, but his fear rose like a vast black smoke to choke him. For he knew his deadly peril and the thread upon which his doom now hung.
>
> From all his policies and webs of fear and treachery, from all his stratagems and wars his mind shook free; and throughout his realm a tremor ran, his slaves quailed, and his armies halted, and his captains, suddenly steerless, bereft of will, wavered and despaired. For they were forgotten. The whole mind and purpose of the Power that wielded them was now bent with overwhelming force upon the Mountain. At his summons, wheeling with a rending cry, in a last desperate race there flew, faster than the winds, the Nazgûl, the Ringwraiths, and with a storm of wings they hurtled southwards to Mount Doom.

A translator might of course choose to overrule this style, so to speak, on the grounds that it simply does not achieve the same effect in Latin; but he or she would be ill advised to try and turn it into periods. It might be better, actually, to follow the same pattern but reduce the number of "ands".

> Ut procul Frodo Annulum indutum sibi asseruit, etiam in Cellis Igneis, intimo in Sauronis regno, tremuit Potentia Barad-dûri, et Arx Tenebrarum a fundamentis quassata est usque ad acerbam verticem superbiae suae.

---

15 *LotR*, bk. VI, ch. 3.

I have, with some hesitation, translated "Sammath Naur". There is a bit of a problem over "Dark Lord" and "Dark Tower". No Latin word seems to have quite the overtones of the English "dark". *Ater* comes closest; but for the Tower I think we want an allusion to the veils of shadow which Sauron spun about it, so *Arx Tenebrarum*, "Citadel of Shadows". *Sauronis* I have used for "his", lest it look as if the events were taking place at the heart of Frodo's realm . The singular I think would be *Sauron*, as in the English; Greek names ending in "-on", like "Platon" or "Antiphon" dropped the final "-n" when taken over into Latin, but "Sauron" is not Greek.[16] Saruman spoke of the rising Power as *potestas*, which is generally a favourable word; but here I have used the less favourable *potentia*.

> Subito Frodonem sensit Dominus Ater, et Oculus suus trans campum perque omnes caligines ad ianuam a seipso factam perspexit. Quasi fulgure inlustratus simul immanem suam stultitiam intellexit et consilia hostium tandem patefacta.

I felt that "blinding" (of the flash, *fulgur*) had to go; Sauron is not blind but seeing the awful truth for the first time! It is a standard expression in English, but not in Latin, where it would just confuse.

> Inde furens irae flamma conflagravit, timor autem eum fumi ingentis instar et nigerrimi strangulavit. Periculum enim imminens sensit, et quanto in discrimine fatum staret suum. Cuncta terroris insidia, cunctas doli perfidias, cuncta bella consiliaque mens excussit. Per omne regnum suum tremor cucurrit, pavere servi, constitere legiones, et sine animi gubernatione duces incerti desperaverunt, quia ex attentu Domini exciderant; quae enim Potentia eos rexerat nunc vi ingentissima totius mentis ad Montem animum attendebat. Arcessitu eius, acerrimo clamore conversi, cursum angustum et extremum vento celeriores Nazgûles, Annuli Daemones, alis tumultuosis, ad Montem Fati se proripuerunt.

Animum attendebat does not really do "mind and purpose ... bent" justice, but it's the best I could manage. And there is no way that I can see to get the effect of "with a storm of wings they hurtled southward"; in fact, to keep "southward", *meridionem versus*, would slow down and weaken the whole effect. And there does not seem to be any Latin word with quite the connotations of "wraith"; "demons of the Ring" will have to do. (*daemon* is not classical Latin; Christian writers borrowed it from the Greek; but we have used late Latin forms of verse, and why not late Latin words as well?)

---

16 The late Greek borrowing *daemon* kept the "-n"; so did Jerome's *Salomon*.

Well, I hope I have given some idea of what would be involved in rendering The Lord of the Rings into Latin. In my day-dreams I can envisage the final result, "wall upon wall, battlement upon battlement, black," (well, perhaps not that, except in ink) "immeasurably strong", drawing on Cicero, Adam of St. Victor and Tacitus, Terence, Vergil and the *Carmina Burana* as needed. My one sorrow is that I fear it is unlikely ever to become actual.

About the author

Richard Sturch is a retired Anglican priest and former lecturer. He is Secretary of the Charles Williams Society and author of (among other things) *Four Christian Fantasists* (Walking Tree Publishers, 2001). His main research interests are in apologetics and the philosophy of religion.

Mark T. Hooker

Dutch *Samizdat*: The Mensink – van Warmelo Translation of *The Lord of the Rings*

Abstract

This article takes a first look at a recently discovered Dutch *samizdat* translation of *The Lord of the Rings* and compares it with the two published Dutch translations of the *LotR* (Schuchart 1958 and 1996).

Samizdat is not a very Dutch concept, but it is nevertheless the one that first came to mind when a Russian Tolkienist sent me a file containing the Mensink- van Warmelo Dutch Translation of *The Lord of the Rings* (*LotR*). All the major elements of *samizdat* are there. The interesting thing was that the language of the translation is Dutch and not Russian.

Samizdat is Russian for 'self-publishing'. In the West, the term *self-publishing* is normally associated with the vanity press, where authors pay to have their own works published. In the Soviet Union, however, *samizdat* was another story. In the Soviet Union, *samizdat* is the term for illicit, underground publishing. To paraphrase Tolkien: In a typescript underground there lived a Hobbit.

Samizdat is one of the things that makes the Russian translations of *LotR* so interesting, and it is part of the reason that there are nine of them in print, and quite a few more in unpublished typescripts lying around in desk drawers. Russian Tolkien *samizdat* traces its origins to the period of the Cold War, when Tolkien was banned in the Soviet Union. The prohibition on the official publication of Tolkien in the Soviet Union did not stop Russian translations from circulating, however. Tolkien just went into *samizdat*.

Samizdat was the opposite of the centralized Soviet-controlled publishing system. It was not a system at all, but rather a number of isolated groups of individuals who shared works of literature that were otherwise not available. The *samizdat* translations of *LotR* were done by translators, whose imagination was captured by Tolkien's vision and who wished to share it with friends and family.

The extent to which they were captivated by Tolkien's vision is made evident by the amount of effort and resolve needed to produce a *samizdat* book. *Samizdat* books were written out by hand or laboriously typed six copies at a time. Copying machines were controlled items and computers were undreamed of at that time. The *samizdat* translators were neither paid nor encouraged to do so. In fact, they placed themselves at risk by producing the translations. A *samizdat* author could be fired or go to jail.

To avoid that risk, some *samizdat* authors did not allow their works to circulate, but wrote 'for the desk drawer', as the Russians say. That phrase stands out very starkly in the foreword to the Mensink-van Warmelo translation of *LotR*. In the late-1970s, Mrs. E.J. Mensink-van Warmelo prepared her own translation of *LotR*, because she did not like the translation by Max Schuchart. This is a very Russian reaction. Russians are doing the same thing, not only with Tolkien, but also with Harry Potter. Mrs. Mensink-van Warmelo was clearly as captivated by Tolkien as were the Russian *samizdat* translators. Her translation ran to over 1200 pages typed on a typewriter, which is a lot of work, as anyone who has ever typed that much text will tell you. The translation itself was the challenge for her, says the foreword, and her translation would have disappeared into a drawer ("dreigden ... in een la te verdwijnen"), were it not for her son (Wouter Mensink). He had the translation bound for her, just as many a Russian *samizdat* translation was also bound. He also had it scanned into a file, which was the form in which the translation reached me via – of all people – a Russian Tolkienist.

Max Schuchart received the Nijhoff Prize for his translation of *LotR*, in 1958. This translation was revised by Mr. Schuchart in 1996. Up until now, if you had seen one Dutch translation, you had seen the Schuchart. The Mensink-van Warmelo translation offers something other than the original to compare Schuchart to. It was harder to find translation mistakes in the three Dutch translations than in the nine Russian translations, but it was not impossible. The focus on mistakes is to make this article interesting. If all the translations were perfect, there would not be any point in talking about them, and Mrs. Mensink-van Warmelo would not have felt the need to do her own. The goal of this paper is an initial evaluation of the worth of Mrs. Mensink-van Warmelo's efforts.

During the coronation of Aragorn in Chapter Five of Book VI ('The Steward and the King'), Gandalf says: "Now come the days of the King, and may they be blessed while the thrones of the Valar endure." (R. 304) The last seven words are missing in the first Schuchart edition. "Nu zijn de dagen van de Koning aangebroken, en mogen zij gezegend zijn." (Schuchart 1967, p. 1266)

The missing words were reinserted in the Mensink-van Warmelo and in the second Schuchart edition. "Nu komen de dagen van de Koning en mogen ze gezegend zijn zolang de tronen van de Valar standhouden!" (Mensink-van Warmelo 1977, p. 206) "Nu zijn de dagen van de Koning aangebroken, en mogen zij gezegend zijn zolang de tronen van de Valar blijven bestaan!" (Schuchart 1997, III p. 1170) The two complete sentences differ only in nuances of style and shades of meaning. The Mensink-van Warmelo is more literal. The Schuchart is more literary. (1)[1]

Chapter One of Book II ('Many Meetings') finds Frodo recovering in Rivendell. The narrator offers the reader Gandalf's evaluation of Frodo's condition. There seemed to be little wrong with Frodo, "but to the wizard's eye there was a faint change, just a hint as it were of transparency, about him, and especially about the left hand that lay outside upon the coverlet." (F. 294-5) Neither the first nor the second edition by Schuchart says which hand it was that was laying on the coverlet (Schuchart 1967, p. 287; 1997, p. 276). It is a small detail, but it sets the stage for the scene in Chapter Four of Book VI ('The Field of Cormallen'), in which the reader again finds Frodo recovering in bed, with "one hand behind his head and the other resting upon the coverlet. It was the right hand, and the third finger was missing." (R. 282) In this scene, Schuchart does say which hand it was (Schuchart 1967, p. 1244; 1997, p. 1151). Mensink-van Warmelo specified which hand it was in both scenes (I p. 202; III P. 192). (2)

Mensink-van Warmelo's translation of *coverlet* as (3) *sprei* is closer to the original, but Schuchart's rendition of *hint of transparency* ["zweem van doorzichtigheid"] (4) is the better of the two.

> Schuchart (1967): Maar voor het oog van de tovenaar was er een flauwe verandering; als het ware omgaf hem een zweem van doorzichtigheid; vooral de hand, die op de deken lag. (p. 287)

---

[1] See the end of this article for a listing of the 'scorings'.

> Schuchart (1997): Maar voor het oog van de tovenaar was er een flauwe verandering; een zweem van doorzichtigheid omgaf hem, als het ware; vooral de hand, die op de deken lag. (p. 276)

> Mensink-van Warmelo (1977): Maar voor het oog van de tovenaar was er toch een lichte verandering in hem, als het ware iets doorschijnends, en vooral in de linkerhand die boven op de sprei lag. (I p. 202)

Mensink-van Warmelo and Schuchart also have a disagreement about which finger of the right hand was missing in the scene from Chapter Four of Book VI. Schuchart says that it was *the third finger* ("de derde vinger"). Mensink-van Warmelo says that it was *the middle-finger* ("de middelvinger"). The third finger of the hand is the definition given by the *Oxford English Dictionary* (*OED*) for the *ring-finger*. The *Van Dale* Dutch defining dictionary describes the *ringvinger* as the finger next to the little-finger (pink).

For the Dutch reader, the definition 'the third finger' is unclear. Mensink-van Warmelo's translation is one indication of that. Another is a quick poll taken among Dutch native speakers. When asked in Dutch which finger of the hand was the third finger, all the respondents agreed with Mensink-van Warmelo. Neither of the translators, therefore, had the correct formulation. In English, the fingers are numbered first to fourth, starting with the finger next to the thumb. The middle finger is, therefore, the second finger in English (see *OED*: 'finger', 'middle finger').

Tolkien's circumlocution avoided saying ring-finger explicitly, but identified the ring-finger implicitly through its description. The successful translation should do so as well. The best approach would appear to be to take the description from the Van Dale definition: "de vinger naast de pink." (5) Two of the nine Russian translators got it right, as did one of the three Polish translators and the Bulgarian.

In Chapter Nine of Book VI ('The Gray Havens'), Sam explains that Rosie Cotton was not pleased that he left, but she could not say anything to keep him from going. Tolkien gave a reason that she could not say anything, but Schuchart missed the point in both versions. She did not have a right to, because Sam had not proposed to her yet. If Sam had already proposed to her, given her forthright categorization of the year that he was away with Frodo on the quest to destroy the Ring as "wasted", she would undoubtedly not have hesitated to tell Sam not to go with Frodo.

Mensink-van Warmelo makes Tolkien's circumlocution around Sam's proposal of marriage much more understandable to modern readers for whom 'speaking with a girl' is not clearly synonymous with proposing marriage anymore. The first example of this usage in the *OED* is from *Othello* act 1, scene 3. "She thank'd me, And bade me, if I had a Friend that lov'd her, I should but teach him how to tell my story, And that would woo her. Upon this hint I spake." To give Schuchart his due, only one of the nine Russian translators got it right, too. (6)

> JRRT: "It's Rosie, Rose Cotton", said Sam. "It seems she didn't like my going abroad at all, poor lass; but as I hadn't spoken, she couldn't say so. And I didn't speak, because I had a job to do first. But now I have spoken, and she says: 'Well, you've wasted a year, so why wait longer?' 'Wasted?' I says. 'I wouldn't call it that.' Still I see what she means." (R. 376)

> Schuchart (1967): 'Het is Roosje, Roosje Katoen', zei Sam. 'Het schijnt dat ze het helemaal niet prettig heeft gevonden dat ik weg ben gegaan, arme meid; maar omdat ik niets had verteld kon ze het niet zeggen. En ik heb niets gezegd, omdat ik eerst een karwei had op te knappen. Maar nu heb ik het 'er verteld en ze zei: ...' (p. 1338)

> Schuchart (1997): 'Het is Roosje, Roosje Katoen', zei Sam. 'Het schijnt dat ze het helemaal niet prettig vond toen ik wegging, de arme meid; maar omdat ik niets had gezegd kon ze dat niet zeggen. En ik had niets gezegd, omdat ik eerst een karwei te doen had. Maar nu heb ik het haar gezegd en ze zei: ...' (p. 1237)

> Mensink-van Warmelo (1977): 'Het is Roosje, Roos Katoen', zei Sam. 'Het schijnt dat ze het helemaal niet prettig vond dat ik op reis ging, de arme meid; maar omdat ik haar niet gevraagd had, kon ze dat niet zeggen. En ik heb haar niet gevraagd omdat ik eerst werk te doen had. Maar nou heb ik haar gevraagd en ze zegt: ...' (p. 253-4)

In Chapter Two of Book I ('The Shadow of the Past'), Gandalf explains how the Ring came into Frodo's possession. He says that "Bilbo was *meant* to find the Ring, and *not* by its maker. In which case you were also *meant* to have it." (F. 88) This was a difficult passage for both translators.

The first edition Schuchart and the Mensink-van Warmelo both have typographical errors. (7) In Schuchart, the pronoun *you* was replaced by the pronoun *he*, which in Dutch differ by only one letter *jij/hij* [you/he]. "In welk geval hij ook was *voorbestemd* on hem te bezitten." This was corrected in the second edition. In Mensink-van Warmelo, the pronoun *it* [the Ring] was repeated unnecessarily: "... was dat jij hem zou hem krijgen."

Schuchart's rendition of Tolkien's repeated *meant* as *voorbestemd* [predestined] is much closer to the mark than Mensink-van Warmelo's rendition, but perhaps a bit overstated (1967, p. 76; 1997, p. 81). Her version is much too literal. She said *de bedoeling was* [it was intended] (I p. 67). This is what you say when there has been a mistake, and something did not work out right. (8) You got roses, but you were supposed to get tulips.

The third problem in this passage was the phrase with *not* [and *not* by its maker]. Schuchart's version was the better of the two. He included the *its* in *its maker* [de Maker ervan], while Mensink-van Warmelo left out *its* [de maker]. (9) Standing alone without the *its* [i.e. the Ring's], *the maker* can be misinterpreted to mean God.

A brief look at some of the names offers a few interesting comparisons as well.

Farmer Cotton is a name that Tolkien specifically stated had nothing to do with the material cotton. He instead pointed to its origin as a place name, derived from cottage (TC 174).[2] Both translators, however, had the same poor solution based on the material cotton. In both versions, Farmer Cotton is known as Boer Katoen. (10) To have the effect Tolkien wanted, Farmer Cotton should have been known as Boer Huizinga, a relatively common name in Holland. The element *huizen* [houses] is common in Dutch toponyms in such places as Huizinge (Groningen), Den Huizen (Overijssel) and Huizen (Noord-Holland).

Robin Smallburrow is a meaningful Hobbit name that Tolkien wanted translated by sense (TC 187). Both translators have interesting renditions. Schuchart calls him Robbie Lutjeburg. This is the toponymic origin that Tolkien wanted Farmer Cotton to have. It changes *burrow* to a *castle*, but successfully keeps the sense of *small/little* with the element *lutje*, which can be found in place names like Lutjebroek (Noord-Holland) [small swamp], Lutjewinkel (Noord-Holland) [small settlement – a suburb – near the larger town of Winkel], Luttenberg (Overijssel) [a settlement on the smaller – in comparison to the near-by Lemelerberg – of two hills]. Schuchart uses a commonly found Dutch

---

2 J.R.R. Tolkien, 1975, 'Guide to the Names in *The Lord of the Rings*', in Lobdell, Jared (ed.), 1975, *A Tolkien Compass*, New York: Ballantine Books, (reprinted 1980), pp. 168-216. Abbreviated as TC.

version of Robin, but Mensink-van Warmelo decided on a name that was even more Dutch: Klaas. Her version is Klaas Kleinhol. The alliteration gives it an interesting effect. Her last name is exactly what Tolkien wanted, a sense translation, or a calque. The element *klein* means *small*, and the element *hol* is the word that comes from the opening line of *The Hobbit*: "In een hol onder de grond woonde een hobbit." (11)

Crickhollow was Frodo's destination when he left Hobbiton at the start of his quest. Tolkien's instruction for the translator was that the name is made up of two elements. The first element – *crick* – is an obsolete element that is to be retained in the target language. The second element – *hollow* – is meant to be recognizable, and should be translated (TC 194). Schuchart followed Tolkien's instructions to a T. His rendition of *Crickhollow* is *Krikhol*. In Dutch toponymy, the element *hol* is found in a number of place names like Schiphol [ship's hollow], Boerenhol (Zeeland) [farm in a valley], and Kolhol (Groningen) [a cold hollow]. Mensink-van Warmelo, however, looked a little too far into the dictionary and found that a *crick in the neck* (back) is called *spit* in Dutch, and made her name *Spithol*. (12)

To give Mensink-van Warmelo her due, one of the Russian translators also had trouble interpreting *crick*. He turned it into *Cricket Hollow* [Sverchkovaya Loshchina], following his English-Russian dictionary rather than looking in a toponymic dictionary to find the real meaning of *crick*.

The first meaning of *crug* [pronounced crick] in the Great Welsh-English dictionary is encountered much more often in place names. It is *hill, hillock*. This meaning is found in place names like Cricklas [green hill], Yr Wyddgrug [the conspicuous hill] (with lination of the 'C' to 'G' as is common in Welsh compound names), Cricieth [the hill of the captives], and in the tautology Creech Hill: *cruc* (Old Welsh) + *hill* (English). Tolkien would have undoubtedly been aware of this meaning as well, but he did not give a meaning for *crick* in his instructions to translators. He only indicated that it was an obsolete element. Given Tolkien's love of linguistic jests, it is not unreasonable to assume that he saw a pun in Crickhollow, and did not want to "spoil the joke," as Bilbo put it. The combination of *crug* (Welsh: *hill*) and *hollow* (English: *depression*) is a bilingual oxymoron.

Tolkien has a lot of other exotic vocabulary to challenge the translator. The Tolkienism *eleventy-one* is a challenge because it is a made-up word. Schuchart turned it into *elftigeneen*, which is literally 'eleventy and one'. This is a very English word order. The normal Dutch word order for compound numbers is 'one and twenty' [eenentwintig], or 'seven and sixty' [zevenenzestig]. Mensink-van Warmelo captures this feeling much better with her *eenentelftig*. This is literally 'one and eleventy'. The addition of the letter 'T' before the word *eleventy* is based on the construction of Dutch compound numbers in the eighties. The Dutch word *eight* is *acht*, but *eighty* is *tachtig*. *Eighty-one* is *eenentachtig* in Dutch. (13)

In Chapter One of Book I ('A Long-expected Party'), one of the guests comments on Bilbo's disappearance with "But why worry? He hasn't taken the vittles with him" (F. 56). The word *vittles* is a marked variant of *victuals*. Its use helps to describe the speaker to the reader. For the American reader, the image is that of Jed Clampett of *The Beverly Hillbillies*. Schuchart's party guest said that Bilbo had not taken the *bikkesement* [grub] with him. Mensink-van Warmelo's party guest said that Bilbo had not taken the victuals [proviand] with him. She missed the stylistic marker. (14)

In Chapter Three of Book I ('Three is Company'), where Frodo and company meet the elves, Gildor warns the elves not to say anything that should be kept secret, because "Here is a scholar in the *Ancient Tongue*" (F. 119, emphasis added). The whole sentence is full of elevated stylistic markers. Schuchart has a pedestrian *de Oude Taal* [the Old Language] (Schuchart 1997, I p. 119; 1967, I p. 108). Mensink-van Warmelo's version, however, has a much older, fairy-tale air about it. She says that Frodo is a scholar in *de Aloude Taal* [the Ancient Language] (p. 88).

This is just a short comparison of the Schuchart and the Mensink-van Warmelo translations, but it is enough to develop an idea of their relative merit. From the reference points examined in this paper, Schuchart got 6.5 plus points and 5.5 minus points. Mensink-van Warmelo got 6.5 plus points and 6 minus points. That gives Schuchart a slight edge on points. In any event, the continued comparison of the two translations appears to be a worthwhile project.

About the author

Mark T. Hooker is a visiting scholar at Indiana University's Russian and East European Institute (REEI). In 2003, he spoke at *MythCon XXXIV* and at *Nimbus-2003*. At *MythCon XXXIV*, he presented a paper entitled 'Ten Rings for Russian Men', which examines the ten translations of J.R.R. Tolkien's masterwork, and gave a slide show of Russian illustrations of J.R.R. Tolkien's *The Hobbit*. At *Nimbus-2003*, the first annual international Harry Potter Symposium, he presented a paper entitled 'Tanya Grotter: A Harry Potter Knock-off or Parody?' His articles on Tolkien have been published in English in *Beyond Bree*, *Tolkien in Translation* (Cormarë Series No. 4), *Tolkien Studies*, and *Lothelanor* (Journal of the Belgian Tolkien Society); in Dutch in *Lembas* (the journal of the Dutch Tolkien Society) and in Russian in *Palantir* (the journal of the St. Petersburg Tolkien Society). His monograph entitled *Tolkien Through Russian Eyes*, was published in 2003, simultaneously both in English (Walking Tree Publishers, Cormarë Series No. 5) and in Russian (*Tolkienistica Rossica Magna*, Moscow: TTT, Saint Petersburg: TO).

Editions used

TOLKIEN, J.R.R., *In de ban van de Ring* (in 3 delen, vijfde druk), Utrecht/Antwerpen: Prisma-Boeken, 1967.

In de ban van de Ring (herziene vertaling in 1 boek, vijfde druk), Utrecht: Het Spectrum, 1997.

Scoring

(1) Schuchart loses half a point for leaving out the last seven words in his first edition, but putting them in the second.
Mensink-van Warmelo gets a whole point for including them the first time.

(2) Schuchart loses one point for leaving out which hand it was.
Mensink-van Warmelo gets a point for including this detail.

(3) Mensink-van Warmelo gets half a point for *coverlet*.

(4) Schuchart gets a whole point for *transparency*.

(5) Both translators lose one point for *the third finger*.

(6) Schuchart loses one point for getting the words right but not the meaning, and Mensink-van Warmelo gets one point for getting the meaning right.

(7) Both translators lose half a point for a typographical error.

(8) Schuchart gets a point for *voorbestemd* [predestined].
Mensink-van Warmelo loses a point for *de bedoeling was* [it was intended].

(9) Schuchart gets a point for *its maker*.
Mensink-van Warmelo loses a point, because *de maker* can be understood literally as God.

(10) Both translators lose one point for translating Farmer Cotton as the cloth and not as a place name.

(11) Schuchart loses half a point for changing *burrow* to *castle*, but gets half a point for his creative translation of *small* as *lutje*.
Mensink-van Warmelo gets a whole point for doing exactly what Tolkien wanted.

(12) Schuchart gets a whole point for doing exactly what Tolkien wanted.
Mensink-van Warmelo loses a whole point for looking too far into the dictionary.

(13) Schuchart gets half a point for getting the meaning right without creating a neologism.
Mensink-van Warmelo gets a whole point for an imaginative neologism.

(14) Schuchart gets a whole point for getting the word and the stylistic marker right.
Mensink-van Warmelo loses half a point for missing the stylistic marker.

(15) Schuchart gets half a point for getting the word right without the stylistic marker.
Mensink-van Warmelo gets a whole point for getting both the word and the stylistic marker right.

Rainer Nagel

The Treatment of Proper Names in the German Edition(s) of *The Lord of the Rings* as an Example of Norms in Translation Practice

Abstract

The translation of proper names in literature has always been regarded as a problem area both by translators and linguists, especially when an author uses telling names to illustrate particular plot aspects. In most cases, translators are left to their own devices as to capture the exact meaning of such a term and find a suitable equivalent in the target language. While *The Lord of the Rings* is basically no exception in this field, in this case the aspiring translator might benefit from help by the author himself, in that J.R.R. Tolkien had prepared an extensive glossary of translation hints, explaining not only the concepts behind the names, but also giving suggestions (or, in terms of translation theory, norms) for the major European languages. This article looks at these norms in the light of means of translation involved, and will also enter into the ramifications of German Tolkien translations based on and beyond this material.

1. Introduction

The treatment of proper names has always been an area of concern not only in actual translation, but also in linguistic translation theory.[1] The central issue can be fitted nicely into a concept as translation as part of a larger process of text production and text reception:[2]

The translator occupies an intermediary position between a text producer and a text recipient in that he forms a bridge between speakers of two different languages. This basically means that first he has to process and understand (and interpret) the source language text before he can go on to produce a derived version of that text in the target language. This makes the translator's task a lot more difficult, for not only does he have to satisfy his own "threshold of termination" in the words of Beaugrande/Dressler (1981:43), but also has to

---

1 For instance, see Newmark (1988:214-6) and, from the multitude of German studies on this subject, Gläser (1989), Kalverkämper (1978:85-88), Rühling (1992), and Snell-Hornby et al. (1998:297f.).
2 Basically adapted from Reiß/Vermeer (1984) and Wilss (1996) as regards the role of the translator and Beaugrande/Dressler (1981) as regards the text-linguistic approach.

anticipate the readers'. Part of this anticipation is not only a thorough knowledge of both the source language and the target language (with knowledge of the target language being the more important one[3]), but also substantial inferential knowledge about the target language's culture, in order to be able to properly translate the text without confusing the target reader with concepts strange or even alien to his culture.[4]

Before we go on further, a simple example from a role-playing game translation (not exactly literature, but actually a special language, albeit one with a lot of literary and standard-language influences[5]) may serve to illustrate this, *viz.* the 2001 German translation of the *Dungeons and Dragons Player's Handbook*. One of the magic spells mentioned in this rulebook has the name of, "bull's strength". Its game function is to make the spell's recipient stronger. In German culture, strength (constructive strength, that is), however, is not usually connotated with bulls, but much more often with bears. Thus, instead of using the literal translation *Stierstärke*, the German translators opted for the culturally more fitting *Bärenstärke*.[6]

2. General Remarks on the Translation of Literary Names

Literary names often tread a fine line between being exotic monickers to convey atmosphere and being vehicles to carry the story along, or to serve as the author's vehicle to comment upon certain parts of the story. Fantasy or historical novels add a further complexity by using older and/or archaic forms, often in the form of obscured compounds.[7]

---

3 Cf. especially Hönig/Kußmaul (19964: passim) and Lang (1992).
4 For purposes of this article, I will not go into the problem of possible misinterpretations on the part of the translator when processing the source language text. Due to the extensive glossary provided by Tolkien it is next to negligible with the main topic of this paper, the German version of *The Lord of the Rings*, anyway (some problems of the 'new' German translation notwithstanding, into which I delve elsewhere in this book).
5 Cf. Nagel (1993) for a more detailed substantiation of this claim.
6 Of course, such examples could also be taken from other fields of language – just think of the difficulties of rendering in English the German *Gemütlichkeit* or *Schadenfreude* without using explanatory phrases, or about the problems in correctly representing *jihad* when asked to explain the term's meaning. Fairy tales have provided us with problems dealing with range of meaning between, say, English *hag* and *witch* versus German *Vettel* and *Hexe*, and so on.
7 I.e., words that, historically speaking, were once compounds, but the individual parts of which can no longer be seen as such by modern speakers, for instance the names for the days of the week in both English and German (cf. also Faiß [1978]).

The translator's basic choice here is still the one outlined as early as Kalverkämper (1978:86f.): direct translation (i.e., complete integration into the target language) or keeping of the original form (i.e., retention of the foreign term amidst the target language text, creating a stand-out linguistic sign drawing the reader's attention). Especially the latter course of action might result in a problem if the untranslated name draws the reader's attention much more than would be appropriate given the name's original function in the text, thus shifting the reader's focus and unduly influencing text reception.

Classical examples of necessary adaptations include the following names from Ben Johnson's *Bartholomew Market* (German as *Batholomäus-Markt*), as listed in Gläser (1989:71f.), all of which are telling names identifying their bearer's function in the story: "Dame Overdo" → "Frau Übermaß"; "Dame Purecraft" → "Madam Listig" (notice the change from *Frau* zu *Madam* to subtly shift the semantic level); "Winwife" → "Mitgiftjäger". In the last example, the German translation focuses even stronger than the English original on this particular character's textual function.[8]

Getting closer to the realm of fantasy literature, a brief survey of the translation of personal names in the fantasy novel *Dragons of Autumn Twilight*, by Margaret Weis and Tracy Hickman, will show a more varied choice between translation, retention, and mixing of the two forms:

A map at the fore of the book shows the following place names (grouped by me for reasons explained after the listing):

(1)   Pax Tharkas, Qualinesti, Que-kiri, Que-shu, Xak Tsaroth
(2a) Darken Wood, Gateway, Newport
(2b) Crystalmir Lake
(2c) Haven, Solace

---

8 An interesting problem can be made out while looking at one particular feature of the English translation of the German science fiction series *Perry Rhodan* (treated in more detail in Nagel [1995], a somewhat shorter precursor to the present article). Some of the earlier German issues deal with a planet called "Gray Beast". Since *Perry Rhodan* was pretty anglocentric at that time (around 1962), use of an English name is no great wonder, and German readers didn't give English names a second look back then (rather, they somehow expected them). The American translator, however, decided to treat this as a linguistic sign requiring special attention, leading to the bewildering fact that the English version of the novel has the German translation of *Gray Beast*, "Grautier". What seemed like a good idea at first came off highly confusing for the American audience, since most American readers, as opposed to the majority of German ones, were not able to make out the term's meaning, thus unduly shifting attention and emphasis.

All entries under (1) are clearly identifiable as fantasy names without a foundation on existing languages (which even applies to "Pax Tharkas," despite the obviously Latin root of its first part, which turns out to be pure coincidence) and, thus are impossible to translate. They are meant to serve as landmarks of the imaginary culture(s) as described in the novel, and are accordingly treated as such in the translation.

Things get more interesting with the entries grouped under (2a) through (2c). All of these are 'telling names' that have a function in the story, but the translator's treatment of them varies, as can be seen from the respective translations:

(2a) Düsterwald[9], Torweg-Pass, Neuhafen
(2b) Krystalmirsee
(2c) Haven, Solace

The terms in (2a) have been translated fully and, thus, integrated into the target language. *Crystalmir Lake*, on the other hand, is described as a lake with crystal-clear water, created in the form of an obscured compound by shortening an etymologically proposed *Crystal Mirror (Lake)* to *Crystalmir* by way of 'historical' elision of unstressed syllables (much along the same lines as Old English *hlǣf-dige*, which became *lady*). *Krystalmirsee*, although trying to adapt the spelling to German conventions and giving a partial translation, fails to capture the more complex etymology of the source word. "Haven" and "Solace", names for towns, are left untranslated, although both have textual functions closely mirroring their given names, an analogy now totally lost to a German reader without knowledge of the source language, English.

3. Regarding Tolkien's Proper Names: An Introduction

Tolkien's meticulous attention to even such details as possible translations of his novel helps the translator to avoid much of the pitfalls mentioned above, since Tolkien himself gives ample hints on how to view the imaginary world he has created, and how to interpret its lexical components. While reading his

---

9 I like to claim a Tolkien influence on the German translator with this word, with *Düsterwald* being taken from the translation of *The Lord of the Rings*, where it represents not something like *Darken Wood*, but the more complex *Mirkwood*, *mirk* being an older form of *murk*.

respective notes (published posthumously as Tolkien [1980][10]) is interesting from the point of view of the historical linguist in any case, it is with the practical applicability to translation (and translation theory, as regards norming) that I am concerned here.

When I talk about 'translation norms', I do so using the definition in Hermanns (1991:163): "[W]e could say that 'translational norms' are the social reality of concepts of translational correctness; this social reality secures the coordination concerning form and use of translational means in a socio-cultural community."

3.1 The Development of Tolkien's Norms

The first non-English versions of the *Lord of the Rings* were published in 1956 (Dutch) and 1959 (Swedish), respectively. Tolkien had always kept an eye out for translations of his work, and his thorough knowledge of quite a number of European languages allowed him to keep up with many of the problems involved in the translation of his invented names. We know a lot about his attitude to translations from his correspondence (as published posthumously in 1981, hereafter referred to as *Letters*). A letter written on 3 July 1956, dealing with place name translation in the Dutch translation that was being prepared at that time, best sums up his attitude (*Letters* 250f.; italics are Tolkien's):

> The translator has (on internal evidence) glanced at but not used the Appendices. He seems incidentally quite unaware of difficulties he is creating for himself later. The 'Anglo-Saxon' of the Rohirrim is not much like Dutch. In fact he is pulling to bits with very clumsy fingers a web that he has made only a slight attempt to understand [...]
>
> The essential point missed, of course, is: even where a place-name is fully analysable by speakers of the language (usually not the case) this is not as a rule done. If in an imaginary land *real* place-names are used, or ones that are carefully constructed to fall into familiar patterns, these become integral names, 'sound real,' and translating them by their analysed senses is quite insufficient. This Dutchman's Dutch names should sound real Dutch [...]
>
> I enclose in justification of my strictures a detailed commentary on the lists.

---

10 And no longer included in subsequent editions of this book.

However, he also cared about translation problems that had nothing do with proper names, as evidenced by one of his remarks on the Swedish translation in a letter from 24 January 1961 (*Letters* 304f.):

> Dr. Ohlmarks, for instance, though he is reported to me to be clever and ingenious, can produce such things as this. In translating vol. i p. 12, 'they seldom wore shoes, since their feet had long leathery soles and were clad in a thick curling hair, much like the hair of their heads', he read the text as 'their feet had thick *fea*thery soles, and they were clad in a thick curling hair [...]' and so produces in his Introduction a picture of hobbits whose outdoor garb was of matted hair, while under their feet they had solid feather-cushion treads! This is made doubly absurd, since it occurs in a passage where he is suggesting that the hobbits are modelled on the inhabitants of the idyllic suburb of Headington.

These and similar problems (*Letters* 304-307; cf. also Carpenter [1977:300]) led Tolkien to devise a glossary of what he regarded as the most important proper names (the above-mentioned Tolkien [1980]), which had to be used by all subsequent translators (Polish edition in 1961, Danish edition in 1968, German edition in 1969, and so on). As Tolkien himself summed up his view in a letter of 24 January 1961 (regarding the problems on the Swedish translation): "The original is my only protection against the translators" (*Letters* 304). This shows how acutely Tolkien's "concept of translational correctness" (to use Hermann's term) was developed.

3.2 Tolkien's Basic Positions as Evidenced in his Glossary

In his glossary, Tolkien is not only acutely aware of the existence of the translator, but addresses him directly with strong as well as strict norms.[11] This is almost a one-of-a-kind phenomenon in the history of literary translation (most translations never go beyond a bilingual list of terms compiled by an editor without much – if any – explanation) which falls outside the scope of what most translation studies and textbooks have to offer on the position of the author in the translation process.

---

11 He would have wholeheartedly agreed with the view put forth in Hermanns (1991:164f.): "To put this more clearly still in terms of translational behaviour: norms allow the translator who is faced with a contingent, unpredictable and potentially destabilizing input – the Source Text – to reduce the number of potential solutions for this array of translational problems by adopting only those solutions suggested by the norm as being likely to result in a Target Text that accords with a given model, and thus with a certain notion of correctness, and hence with the values and attitudes that lie behind these models and correctness notions."

Tolkien's rather strict views on norming in translation can be given in his own words (Tolkien [1980:155]; italics are Tolkien's):

> All names not in this list should be left *entirely* unchanged in any language used in translation, except that inflectional *-s, -es* should be rendered according to the grammar of the language.
>
> It is desirable that the translator should read Appendix F in Volume III of *The Lord of the Rings* and follow the theory there set out. In the original English text English represents the Common Speech of the supposed period. Names that are given in modern English therefore represent names in the Common Speech, often but not always being translations of older names in other languages, specially Sindarin (Grey-elven). The language of translation now replaces English as the equivalent of the Common Speech; the names in English form should therefore be translated into the other language *according to their meaning* (as closely as possible).

Most translation theories allow for the translator's shifting of the meaning of parts of the source text if the needs of the target language require such (for instance, see Reiss/Vermeer [1984:§4] as regards "Skoposfestlegung"). Tolkien strictly forbids this, explicitly stating that adaptations to the target culture may only be made if a word's original meaning is not lost in doing so: "But of course the translator is free to devise a name in the other language that is suitable in sense and/or topography [...]" (Tolkien [1980:156]). Should this not be possible, Tolkien clearly prefers unchanged retention (even risking reader alienation and resulting gaps in the flow of reading due to linguistic signs perceived as standing out in Kalverkämper's sense) to culture-specific modification. Such ideas are actually in stark contrast to one of the basic tenets of modern translation theory, as exemplified in Reiss/Vermeer (1984:100): "Es ist wichtiger, dass ein gegebener Translat(ions)zweck erreicht wird, als dass eine Translation in einer bestimmten Weise durchgeführt wird."[12]

A case in point is the entry concerning one of Tolkien's minor characters, the innkeeper "Barliman Butterbur" (Tolkien [1980:162]):

> So far as I know, not found as a name in England, though *Butter* is so used, as well as combinations (in original place-names) such as *Butterfield*. These have in the tale been modified, to fit the generally botanical names of Bree, to the plant-name 'butterbur' (*Petasites vulgaris*). If the popular name for this

---

12 "It is more important to achieve a given purpose of translation than to translate in a certain way." (My translation.)

contains an equivalent of 'butter', so much the better. Otherwise use another plant-name containing 'butter' (as German *Butterblume, Butterbaum*, Dutch *boterbloeme*) or referring to a fat thick plant. The butterbur is a fleshy plant with a heavy flower-head on a thick stalk, and very large leaves.

Butterbur's first name *Barliman* is simply an altered spelling of 'barley' and 'man' (suitable to an innkeeper and ale-brewer) and should be translated.

The original German translator, Margaret Carroux, working after the publication of this glossary, adhered strictly to Tolkien's norm (as she did in most cases) and opted for "Gerstenmann Butterblume" as the German name. It is interesting to note, though, that when Wolfgang Krege did his controversial re-translation of the *Lord of the Rings* in the late nineties, he re-translated *butterbur* as "Butterblüm", using the mutated form to move the name away from its plant root and rather into the realm of slightly obscured plant-derived surnames, despite the fact that there is no such thing as a German plant called *Butterblüm*.

To come back to the question of obscured compounds as raised in §2, Tolkien's views on this subject become clear in the next passage (Tolkien [1980:167f.]; the German translator, by the way, opted for the, at the time, more regular "Harfuß"):

> *Harfoots* (plural): meant to be intelligible (in its context) and recognized as an altered form of an old name = 'hairfoot', that is 'one with hairy feet'. It is supposed to represent archaic English *hǣrfot*, later *herfoot*, with the usual change of *er* to *ar* in English. Modern English *hair*, though related, is not a direct descendant of Old English *hǣr, hēr* = German *Haar*. German *Harfuss* would adequately represent the form, meaning, and slight change of spelling in an old proper name.

As regards what I would like to call 're-etymologisation', Tolkien indeed treads a fine line here, coming close to a tendency mocked by Kalverkämper (1978:88): "sonst wird aus *Churchill* ein *Kirchberg*, aus *Casanova* ein *Neuhaus*, aus *Johann Sebastian Bach* ein *Jean Sébastien Rousseau*, aus *La Fontaine* ein *Der Brunnen* oder aus *Shakespeare* ein *Schwingespeer*."[13]

---

13 "Otherwise, *Churchill* would turn into *Kirchhügel* ['church-hill'], *Casanova* into *Neuhaus* ['new house'], *Johann Sebastian Bach* into *Jean Sébastien Rousseau* ['John Sebastian Brook'], *La Fontaine* into *Der Brunnen* ['The Well'], or *Shakespeare* into *Schwingespeer* ['Shake (a) Spear']." (My translation.)

The Treatment of Proper Names   97

I would like to end this part of my paper with one instance of successful adaptation of a rather complex name into German: the treatment of *Shelob*. Tolkien (1980:173) provides the translator with the following normative information:

> Though it sounds (I think) a suitable name for the Spider, in some foreign (orkish) tongue, it is actually composed of *she* and *lob* (a dialectal English word meaning 'spider'; see Bilbo's song in chapter VIII of *The Hobbit*). The Dutch version retains *Shelob*, but the Swedish has the rather feeble *Honmonstret*.

The problem here is in translating gender-indicating *she* while at the same time conveying the notion of a fearsome, spider-like monster.[14] Margaret Carroux solved this problem by basing her translation on the old German term *Kanker* "spider" (cf. Kluge [1975²¹:346]), adding the suffix -*a* which indicates female gender, resulting in *Kankra* – a word not existing in German and only 'retroactively' analysable by someone with a thorough knowledge of the history of German, almost on the same footing as the similarly less-known English term.

4. A Taxonomy of Translation Methods on the Basis of German-Edition Personal Names

The typology I am going to use here is based on the one presented in Rühling (1992). It consists of three broad groups: translation (with various sub-groups; see below); elimination (further subdivided into total elision and paraphrasing); and adoption (directly, or with orthographic alterations). Since Tolkien's word-by-word glossary is very strict in its treatment of terms, the second procedure is not really an option for the translator.[15]

4.1 Translation

Due to Tolkien's extensive norming, direct, literal translation is the most commonly used procedure. It is most often applied with morphologically complex

---

14 To the best of my knowledge, *lob* for spider is last recorded in standard (non-dialectal) English in 1676. Most of the time, the word is used with religious connotations, which is quite apt with reference to *Shelob* as a dire peril for Frodo's quest.
15 There are, however, a few instances in which Margaret Carroux comes close to paraphrasing. For instance, the race of "Half-orcs" is not translated as "Halborks", as one might expect, but almost gives a paraphrase with "diese halben Orks" ("these beings who are part orcs"). This is rare, though.

names and works by translating each component individually to form a new, German compound:

Barrow-downs	Hügelgräber-Höhen
Goldberry	Goldbeere
Grey Pilgrim	Grauer Pilger[16]
Middle-earth	Mittelerde
Mirrormere	Spiegelsee
Ring-wraiths	Ringgeister
Silverlode	Silberlauf
Treebeard	Baumbart
Underhill	Unterberg
Weathertop	Wetterspitze
Wormtongue	Schlangenzunge

Of these, *Mirrormere* and *Silverlode* should occupy a more distinct sub-category, since *mere* is nowadays only used poetically for "lake," while the "road, run" meaning of "lode" is regarded as obsolete (see *OED*).

Related to direct translation (or, rather, a subgroup of it) is substitution of native forms, mostly used with personal names:

Bill Ferny	Lutz Farning
Hob	Hinz
Nob	Kunz

Sometimes, this use of native forms works on a rather deep level in the German translation, as already evidenced with the *Shelob – Kankra* equivalency. Other examples include "Swanfleet" ("Schwanenfleet" in German, using the old North German term for "moor") and "Goblin-men", which is translated as "Bilwißmenschen". *Bilwiß* is an old German term, mainly used in southern Germany, to indicate "witch", "sorcerer", or "goblin" (in the original sense of German "Kobold"), a term nowadays not usually known to most speakers of German.[17]

This brings us back to the treatment of obscured forms, already entered into when talking about *Harfoots* in §3.2. In the taxonomy adopted here, such trans-

---

16 Since this is a name for Gandalf and, thus, has additional meaning beyond its components, I treat it as a compound, although it may look like a syntactic group of adjective + noun.
17 See Kluge (1975²¹:78), where the word is given as *Bilwis*, the name of a corn demon, the etymology of which is unclear.

lation figures as "etymologising translation", defined by Rühling (1992:155) as: "Auf der Ebene des Transfers wird durch solche Übertragung ein die Ökokultur der Ausgangsseite identifizierendes Kennzeichen getilgt, nämlich der Code, der [...] keinen Hinweis auf den sprachlichen Ursprung mehr enthält."[18] This means that a name which can no longer be morphologically analysed into its component parts, is translated into components that may still be analysed by speakers of the target language (an etymological simplification by translation, if you will).

Thus, "Dwarrowdelf" (see below) is turned into "Zwergenbinge", "Greyhame" (*grey* + Old English *hama* "garment, clothing") into "Graumantel", "Rivendell" (*riven* = "cleft, cloven"; see *OED*) into "Bruchtal", and the horse name "Shadowfax" (from Old English *sceadu* "shadow" and Old English *feax* "hide"[19]; the compound as such is not documented in Old English literature) into "Schattenfell".

Dwarrowdelf is of special interest, in that Tolkien developed its determinant *dwarrow* out of Old English *dweorg* "dwarf", which Tolkien used as the basis for the plural form *dwarves*[20] coined by him (*RtK* 518f.):

> It is to mark this that I have ventured to use the form *dwarves* [...] *Dwarrows* would have been better, but I have used that form only in the name *Dwarrowdelf*. [...] For that meant 'Dwarf-delving' and yet was already a word of antique form.

Despite all her meticulous attention to such matters, Carroux fails in at least one prominent example, *viz.* the town of "Michel Delving".[21] This name, Margaret Carroux translates as "Michelbinge", obviously unsure what to do with *Michel* but correctly translating *delving* ("a place where people delve into the earth") as *Binge*. What she does not notice, though, is that *Michel* reflects an unrounded form of Old English *mycel* "much", a form that was pretty common in Late Old English as well as Middle English and only gave way to *much* in Early Modern English. It is highly interesting to note that *Michel Delving* is among those few

---

18 "On the level of transfer, such translations eliminate a linguistic sign identifying part of the source text's eco-culture, i.e., the code which [...] no longer contains any hint at its linguistic origin." (My translation.)
19 Tolkien (1980:172) gives the paraphrase "having shadow-grey mane (and coat)".
20 As opposed to *dwarfs*, which was the common norm in the mid-20th century; cf. also Nagel (1993:265).
21 I am indebted to Alexandra Velten of Johannes Gutenberg University, Mainz, for bringing this to my attention.

place names *not* listed in Tolkien's prescriptive glossary, subtly re-emphasising the need for such an extensive guideline for translators not as well versed in the history of the English language as Tolkien was.[22]

Albeit not so intended by the translator, *Michelbinge* leads to the last sub-group of direct translation as given in Rühling's taxonomy: hybrid translation, mixing elements from more than one national language into one complex term. Retaining this hybrid factor might be said to be the opposite of Rühling's "etymologising translation", since it does not even try to make the word's motivation clear to the reader.

Hybrid formations are common occurrences in *The Lord of the Rings* in various ways: Combinations such as "Ithilstone" (*Ithil*[23] = name of a city) pair an English word with one of Tolkien's invented languages, while others combine English words with words from other real-world languages, such as "Bree-hill"[24] and "Bree-land" (with the town name *Bree* actually being the Celtic word for "hill") or "Chetwood" (with *chet* being Celtic for "wood", literally meaning "Hill-hill" or "Wood-wood", which has to be regarded as a private pun on Tolkien's part). The German versions act accordingly, by pairing a German word with the untranslated second (or, structurally speaking, first) element: "Ithilstein", "Breeberg", "Breeland", and "Chetwald". A similar phenomenon occurs when Tolkien mixes Old or Middle English words with Modern English ones: The Old English word "Ent" (meaning "giant", but here applied to living trees) is used in combinations such as "Entmoot" and "Entwives", which are turned into German "Entthing" and "Entfrauen", respectively. "Isenmouthe" (from Old English *īsen* "iron" becomes "Isenmünde", while "Eastemnet" (from Old English *emnett*, "level ground, plain") becomes "Ostemnet".

Doing so is actually in accordance with Tolkien's wishes, as evidenced in his respective entries. To quote just two, in his notes on *Bree* Tolkien (1980:180) says: "retain, since it was an old name, of obsolete meaning in an older lan-

---

22 Also, there is no etymological basis for *Michel* in German, except as a proper name (which is ultimately of Hebrew origin, anyway); Kluge (197521) has no corresponding entry. As regards the translation, the fact that there is also a "Little Delving" might have been a hint.
23 *Ithil* is the Sindarin term for "moon", and the "Common Speech" translation "City of the Moon" appears infrequently in the text.
24 "Bree-hill" is a tautology common on the map of England, the result of the migration of different language groups across the face of the map. For a more detailed discussion, see Hooker (2002).

guage[.]" As for *Isenmouthe* (and *Isengard*, which we will visit later on), Tolkien (1980:187f.) states:

> These names were intended to represent translations into the Common Speech of the Elvish names *Angrenost* and *Carach Angren*, but ones made at so early a date that at the period of the tale they had become archaic in form and their original meanings were obscured. They can therefore be left unchanged, though translation (of one or both elements in either name) would be suitable, and I think desirable when the language of translation is Germanic, possessing related elements.
>
> *Isen* is an old variant form in English of *iron*; *gard* a Germanic word meaning 'enclosure', especially one round a dwelling or group of buildings; and *mouthe* a derivative of *mouth*, representing Old English *mūða* (from *mūð* 'mouth') 'opening', especially used of the mouths of rivers, but also applied to other openings (not parts of a body). *Isengard* 'the Iron-court' was so called because of the great hardness of stone in that place and especially in the central tower. The *Isenmouthe* was so called because of the great fence of pointed iron posts that closed the gap leading into Udûn, like teeth in jaws (see III 197, 209).

Tolkien goes on to list the translations of these names in the Dutch and Swedish editions, and to give advice on which words to use in German, Danish, and Swedish (since he is not satisfied with the existing Swedish versions).[25]

> *Shire*, Old English *scīr*, seems very early to have replaced the ancient German word for a district, found in its oldest form in Gothic *gawi*, surviving now in Dutch *gouw*, German *Gau*. [...] The Dutch version used *Gouw*; *Gau* seems to me suitable in German, unless its recent use in regional reorganisation under Hitler has spoilt this very old word.

Margaret Carroux not only shared Tolkien's views on the "spoiling" of *Gau* but, being German, felt the need for not using this word even more urgently. She opted for the name "Auenland", explaining her choice in the German version of the Appendix (*Anh.* 124): "Für Auenland steht im Englischen *shire*, dem das deutsche *Gau* am nächsten käme, wenn es nicht so pervertiert worden wäre."[26]

---

25 It is highly interesting that, given such meticulous normative advice, Carroux translates *Eastemnet* as *Ostemnet*, ignoring Tolkien's (1980:183) remark: "Rohan; retain it (though it contains *east* it is not a Common Speech name, but Rohan for 'east-plain')."
26 "For Auenland ["meadow-land"], the English text has *shire*, which would be most closely resembled by German *Gau*, had this not been so perverted." (My translation.)

4.2 Adoption

We find both sub-groups (direct = unchanged adoption and adoption with adaptation(s) to the target language) in the German translation of *The Lord of the Rings*.

Direct adoption usually occurs in monomorphemic names not of (Modern) English origin, such as "Ent", "Hobbit" or all names of supposedly Elvish origin (even if morphologically complex within the Elvish tongues).[27] A similar example is "Smial" as developed (hypothetically, but following established historical sound laws of English) from (documented) Old English *smygel* "hole" as a term for a Hobbit's dwelling-hole, assuming smoothing of /yj/ to /ij/ to /i:/ and then change to /aɪ/ as per Great Vowel Shift.[28]

Adapting a loan-word to the target language is sub-divided into "transcription" and "other alterations" in Rühling (1992), which, however, does not allow for sufficient diversification. Instead, I propose the sub-groups of "phonological alteration" (meaning retaining the source language's spelling, but adapting it to the source language's pronunciation) and "graphemic alteration" (adapting the source language's spelling to the target language's phonology).[29]

Phonological alteration does not merit too closely a discussion. To take just a brief look at the two main heroes of the novel, the difference between the English "Frodo" /frəʊdəʊ/ and the German /fro:do:/ is as negligible as the differences in /sæm/ (English) and /sam/ (German) for "Sam."

Graphemic alteration usually entails changing a grapheme, or a sequence of graphemes, uncommon to the target language into more suitable ones, while trying to retain the original pronunciation as closely as possible. Thus, Sam's surname "Gamgee" becomes "Gamdschie"; "orc" is turned into "Ork"; "Oliphaunt" is rendered as "Olifant"; and the surname "Took" becomes "Tûk". The place-name *Isengard*, as mentioned earlier, is a similar case when Margaret Carroux

---

27 With these, their Common Speech versions are subject to standard translatorial treatment, though: while the river "Baranduin" is taken over into German exactly as is, its Common Speech equivalent "Brandywine" is turned into "Brandywein", and the river "Lhûn" (Elvish "Lune") is turned into "Luhn".
28 Cf. *RtK* 518 for more on this word's etymology; for the description of a *smial*, see Foster (1978:361f.).
29 In a sense, this is a re-use of the notion of "phonologische Kalkierung" as introduced by Gläser (1989:69), but with more tightly defined categories.

stresses the relation to "Garten" as an enclosed space (making the translation of the place's later transformation into "Treegarth" as "Baumgarten" even more naturally-looking than the English version) by altering it to "Isengart" (which may also involve a slight nod to the customary hardening of word-final consonants in German).

Some translations are as onomatopoetically-minded as their originals. Thus, a *Neekerbreeker* (an insect identified by making the sound "neek-breek") becomes "Kirperzirper" (retaining both the insect-sound notion and the internal rhyming structure; see also Nagel [1993:134]), whereas with the translation of the nickname "Sharkey" as "Scharrer", the name's original meaning ("This is supposed to be a nickname […], based on orkish *sharkû* 'old man'." – Tolkien [1980:173]) gives way to trying to stay close to the original's phonology ("Scharrer" basically translates as "someone who scratches").

5. A Digression: Secondary Translation on the Basis of an Already-Established Norm

Translation norms can be especially interesting when the work created on their basis becomes the foundation for another, derived work. I will now briefly concentrate on the *Lord of the Rings Role-Playing Game*, as published 2002 by Decipher Games. The game as such is, of course, based on Tolkien's book and, thus, needs to conform to the terminology created by Tolkien himself. When translating this game, the German version of the novel had to be adhered to as closely as possible. This means that the team of translators had to work on what could be called a "secondary norm", since not only the translation of those terms normed by Tolkien, but also all other parts of the book referred to in the game rules had to be followed.

An example of this is the translation of two abilities aimed at giving game characters advantages during game play (called "Edges" within the framework of the rules), "Valour" and "Valiant". Now, to avoid ambiguity in role-playing rules as befits the needs of a special language (cf. Nagel [1993:§1.2.3]), we would like these terms (the game functions of which are quite distinct), although etymologically related in English, to be clearly distinguishable in German (such as, "Tapferkeit" and "Mutig"). However, since both entries in the rule-book are introduced by quotes from *The Lord of the Rings*, translatorial preference had to take a back seat to adherence to the original. In this case, it meant that the head translator *had* to decide to follow the usage in the Carroux translation,[30] which uses "Tapferkeit" and "Tapfer", respectively. As one of the translators later – quite rightly – commented, this distinction has the potential for reader confusion, but given the primary source text (of which the role-playing game, even in its English original, is in the end no more than a derived text), no other solution was possible.

Another area where a terminological problem was finally solved by consulting the German translations has to do with one of the types of characters players are allowed to represent: the "Minstrel". Add to this "sub-classes" such as the "Rohirric Bard" and the "Tribal Chanter" and the need for clear-cut translational distinctions becomes obvious. The problem is compounded by the fact that, in Tolkien's novel, the culture of the Rohirrim is based on that of the Anglo-Saxons, whose culture did not know the (Irish) bard, but rather the (Anglo-Saxon) *scop*. To remedy this fact, the first draft of the master glossary for the individual translations (in fact, a sort of "tertiary norm" after Tolkien's and Carroux's) gave "Minstrel" as "Barde" and "Bard" as "Skald".[31] "Sänger" could then have been used for "Chanter".

However, the term "minstrel" is mentioned several times in *The Lord of the Rings* (whereas the term "bard" is not), and the passage "a minstrel of Gondor stood forth" towards the end of the book has the translation "trat [...] ein Sänger von Gondor vor", forcing an entire re-thinking of the newly-created distinctions. With "Sänger" now referring to the basic class, it was decided to retain "Barde" for "Bard" to keep closer contact to the original text; the "Tribal

---

30 It was a deliberate decision not to use the newer translation by Wolfgang Krege, since in many cases, as exemplary mentioned in §3.2, Krege moves away from Tolkien's intentions rather than toward them. This is especially problematic in his treatment of Sam addressing his master Frodo with "sir" or "master", which Krege, allegedly following current trends in German usage, turns into "Chef" ["boss"], which is out of synch with the original text's relation between the two persons and also shifts the stylistic level of the text precariously; as regards the use of language in *The Lord of the Rings*, see also Einhaus (1986:§2.3.3) and Chance (2001).
31 The decision to use the North Germanic term instead of the West Germanic *scop* was made on the knowledge that skalds are a well-known concept in role-playing games, while most readers of the intended target audience had never heard of *scops*. Since there was some kind of relation between the Anglo-Saxon and the Norse cultures, this seemed to be the easiest way to solve the problem.

Chanter" became "Stammessänger", the German compound making it easier to distinguish it from the more general "Sänger".

Sometimes, however, the team of translators had to consciously violate Carroux's preceding work. One of these cases is "Half-orc" (cf. footnote 13). Carroux's "halber Ork" did not lend itself well to being used as a distinct categorial term for beings grouped together for purposes of having the same game statistics, which is why the translators finally opted for the more compact "Halbork", which, after all, has become a staple of fantasy role-playing games.

6. Conclusion

To sum up, norms can indeed be a great help in translating proper names, especially if these are morphologically complex or generally meaningful. However, to have the best possible effect and to result in a translation really equivalent to the original, three criteria need to be met:

1. The author of the source language text must have an active interest in seeing his or her personal names retained as closely as possible.
2. In the case of complex or even obscured names, the author of the source text needs to have the linguistic competence to make his or her creations transparent to the translator (i.e., explain their morphological or etymological motivations, however obscured they may be).
3. The translator needs to accept the norms as set by the original author, regarding them, in the terms of Beaugrande/Dressler (1981:129) as a "cohesive and coherent text capable of utilization."

For various reasons (usually time constraints on the author's – or the translator's – part, but very often the simple fact that authors do not write with the prospect of translation in mind, let alone are interested in it), these criteria can only rarely be met, resulting in hasty and/or inadequate translations.[32]

---

[32] My favourite example in this regard is the German version of Clive Cussler's novel *Raise the Titanic*. The German version is only two-thirds the length of the original, since the translator decided unilaterally that a huge part of the story (how the American President, who has lost interest in almost anything, gets a new lease on life by having a love affair) would simply be uninteresting for his readers. Come to think of it, *Hebt die Titanic!* is a very good case study for looking at 'translations gone bad', i.e., translations that violate most of the tenets put forth in translation textbooks. Hönig/Kußmaul [1996[4]:ch. X] have a closer look at the translation of this novel, which is highly recommended for both translators and researchers in translation theory.

In view of this, *The Lord of the Rings* may be seen as an exemplary case, since Tolkien felt very strongly about his story, resulting in extensive notes as to its translation; also, he had the linguistic competence to make sensible suggestions regarding most European languages he expected his novel to be translated into. Another factor contributing to the successful use of the norm was that translator Margaret Carroux adhered to them in most cases, resulting in a German translation that almost always captures the spirit of the original, in some cases (see *Isengart – Baumgarten*) even slightly improving it.

About the author

Rainer Nagel holds a PhD in English Linguistics from Johannes-Gutenberg University, Mainz. His PhD thesis was on word-formation in special languages. His research subjects are morphology/word-formation, historical linguistics, translation studies, and ESL studies. He currently teaches at Johannes Gutenberg-University, Mainz.

References

Anh. = *Der Herr der Ringe. Anhänge*, (second edition, first edition 1969), Stuttgart: Klett-Cotta, 1979.

BEAUGRANDE, Robert de & Wolfgang DRESSLER, *Introduction to Text Linguistics*, London & New York: Longman, 1981.

CARPENTER, Humphrey, *J.R.R. Tolkien: A Biography*, London: Allen & Unwin, 1977.

CHANCE, Jane, *Lord of the Rings: The Mythology of Power*, Lexington: University Press of Kentucky, 2001.

EINHAUS, Barbara, *The Lord of the Rings: Logik der kreativen Imagination*, München: tuduv, 1986.

FAISS, Klaus, *Verdunkelte Compounds im Englischen. Ein Beitrag zu Theorie und Praxis der Wortbildung*, Tübingen: Narr, 1978.

FOSTER, Robert, *The Complete Guide to Middle-Earth. An A-Z guide to the names and events in the fantasy world of J.R.R. Tolkien from The Hobbit to The Silmarillion*, London: Unwin, 1978.

GLÄSER, Rosemarie, 'Zur Übersetzung von Eigennamen', In: Friedhelm Debus and Wilfried Seibicke (eds.), *Reader zur Namenkunde. Band I: Namentheorie*, Hildesheim, Zürich, New York: Olms, 1989, pp. 67-78.

HERMANNS, Theo, 'Translational Norms and Correct Translation', In: Kitty van Leuven-Zwart & Ton Naaijkens (eds.), *Translation Studies: The State of the*

Art. Proceedings of the First James S. Holmes Symposium on Translation Studies, Amsterdam & Atlanta: Rodopi, 1991, pp. 155-69.

HÖNIG, Hans G. & Paul Kussmaul, *Strategie der Übersetzung. Ein Arbeits- und Lehrbuch*, (fourth edition, first edition 1982), Tübingen: Narr, 1996.

KALVERKÄMPER, Hartwig, *Textlinguistik der Eigennamen*, Stuttgart: Klett-Cotta, 1978.

KLUGE, Friedrich, *Etymologisches Wörterbuch der deutschen Sprache*, (twenty-first edition, first edition 1883), Berlin & New York: de Gruyter, 1975.

LANG, Margaret, 'The problem of mother tongue competence in the training of translators', In: Mary Snell-Hornby et al. (eds.), *Translation Studies. An Interdiscipline*, Amsterdam & Philadelphia: Benjamins, 1992, pp. 395-99.

Letters = The Letters of J.R.R. Tolkien, Humphrey Carpenter and Christopher Tolkien (eds.), London, Boston & Sydney: Allen & Unwin, 1981.

NAGEL, Rainer, *Fachsprache der Fantasy-Rollenspiele. Wortbildungselemente und -prozesse*, Frankfurt: Lang, 1993.

'Normenvorgabe in der literarischen Übersetzung. Illustriert an den Eigennamen in J.R.R. Tolkiens *The Lord of the Rings*', In: *Zeitschrift für Anglistik und Amerikanistik* 43, (1995), pp. 1-10.

NEWMARK, Peter, *A Textbook of Translation*, New York: Prentice Hall, 1988.

OED = The Oxford English Dictionary, Oxford: Oxford University Press, (second edition, first edition 1929ff.), 1989.

REISS, Katharina & Hans J. Vermeer, *Grundlegung einer allgemeinen Translationstheorie*, Tübingen: Niemeyer, 1984.

RtK = The Return of the King. Being the third part of the Lord of the Rings, New York: Ballantine, 1965.

RÜHLING, Lutz, 'Fremde Landschaft. Zum Problem der geographischen Eigennamen in den Übersetzungen von Strindbergs naturalistischen Romanen *Röda Rummet, Hemsöborna* und *I Havsbandet*', In: Fred Lönker (ed.), *Die literarische Übersetzung als Medium der Fremderfahrung*, Berlin: Schmidt, 1992, pp. 144-72.

SNELL-HORNBY, Mary et al. (eds.), *Handbuch Translation*, Tübingen: Stauffenburg, 1998.

TOLKIEN, J.R.R., 'Guide to the Names in the *Lord of the Rings*', In: Jared Lobdell (ed.), *A Tolkien Compass*, New York: Ballantine, 1980, pp. 153-201.

WILSS, Wolfram, *Knowledge and Skills in Translator Behavior*, Amsterdam & Philadelphia: Benjamins, 1996.

Beregond, Anders Stenström

Tolkien in Swedish Translation: From *Hompen* to *Ringarnas herre*

Abstract

Hompen, 1947, was the first published translation of *The Hobbit*, and indeed of any Tolkien text. This article presents the story of Swedish Tolkien translation, to which a number of translators have contributed over the decades, ending with the new translation of *The Lord of the Rings* that is currently being prepared.

Publication of Tolkien's texts in Sweden has a long history. His article (with S.R.T.O. d'Ardenne) 'MS Bodley 34. A re-collation of a collation' was published in the Swedish semestrial *Studia Neophilologica* in 1948.[1] Even more notable is the appearance in the previous year of *Hompen*, by a wide margin the first published foreign translation of *The Hobbit*, and so of any of Tolkien's texts. I have seen no record of what bright eye at the publishers, Kooperativa Förbundets Bokförlag, spotted the book, but it was translated by Tore Zetterholm, and illustrated by his younger brother Torbjörn Zetterholm (cover and maps were by Charles Sjöblom). Both the Zetterholms were talented people, at the start of long careers as writer and as artist, respectively.[2]

Apart from being the first, the translation is now perhaps best known because of Tolkien's disapproval of Tore Zetterholm's change of *hobbit* to *hompe*,[3] a choice that however was not wholly without reason. The form of the word *hobbit* has no close parallels in Swedish other than the loanword *gambit*, while the invented *hompe* sounds plausibly indigenous. Even more notable, and far less reasonable, is the change of *Bilbo* to *Bimbo*.

---

1 *Studia Neophilologica* vol. XX, issues 1–2. The article is on pp. [65]–72.
2 Tore Zetterholm, 1915–2001. Author of 28 titles of fiction published 1940–1995; also books on China, Tibet, Buddhism, literary history; literary anthologies; apart from *The Hobbit* translated works by Arthur Koestler and others (including one collection of Chesterton's Father Brown stories). Sometime chairman of the Swedish dramatists' association.
Torbjörn Zetterholm, 1921– (younger brother of Tore). Artist in various techniques, especially woodcuts; typical subjects are landscapes, animals and plants. He has participated in art exhibitions worldwide. Apart from *The Hobbit*, he has illustrated H.C. Andersen and others.
3 See Letter 190:8. In Letter 188:2 there is a more sweeping criticism.

The treatment of *elf* and *goblin* is also interesting. The direct cognate of *elf* was lost from Swedish; what survived in our folklore was a formally feminine derivative, of which the modern form is *älva*. The beings referred to are indeed mostly thought of as females, but it is quite possible to speak of Oberon as an *älvkung*, for instance. Thus, Tolkien's elves are *älvor* in Zetterholm's translation, somewhat unfortunately: the etymological relation is there, but in connotation *älva* is close to English *fairy*. English *goblin*, on the other hand, has no obvious Swedish counterpart, either as word or as notion. Zetterholm rendered it *svartalf*; the real cognate of *elf* was long ago reintroduced, as a literary loan from Old Norse, in the shape of *alf*, and terms from Icelandic mythology like *ljusalf* and *svartalf* ('light-elf' and 'black-elf') became established in Swedish nineteenth-century poetry. To complicate the matter, the loanword developed two versions: one with naturalized pronunciation, nowadays accordingly spelt *alv*, and one with the *f* pronounced at face value, thus remaining *alf* in modern spelling. A *svartalv* or *svartalf* is a malign underground being, which explains Zetterholm's choice.

There seems to have been no reprint of *Hompen*, and the book has become rare and valuable. Five of the illustrations are reprinted in *The Annotated Hobbit*.

It was a different publishing house, Gebers Förlag, that tried its fortune with *The Lord of the Rings*. In this case Swedish was, after Dutch, the second language into which the work was translated, and the three volumes appeared in 1959, 1960 and 1961. The prime mover in this was Disa Törngren, an editor at Gebers. As translator she chose Åke Ohlmarks, who had previously (among other things) translated *Edda* texts. He could therefore be expected to do justice to the 'Germanic' elements in Tolkien's text.[4]

Once again, the translation's claim to international fame rests on Tolkien's documented criticism, and his exasperation with the picture Ohlmarks gave of him in the introduction to the book. "Ohlmarks is a very vain man (as I discovered in our correspondence) preferring his own fancy to facts, and very

---

4 Åke Ohlmarks, 1911–1984. Translator of many titles: Old Norse literature, classic religious texts, Nostradamus, Shakespeare, and, of course, Tolkien. Author of popular books of history and biography, history of religion, divination and other subjects.

ready to pretend to knowledge which he does not possess" (Letter 228:6), Tolkien accurately observed; the examples in Letter 229 prove his point.

In some instances, however, Ohlmarks' familiarity with Old Norse terms and their literary or obsolete counterparts in Swedish served well. For *elf* he used *alv*, thus bringing this word out of the little-known company of *van* and *dis* into modern currency. The choice may seem obvious in hindsight, but we could see above that it was not obvious to Zetterholm. It was a bold stroke (as Tolkien's use of *elf* in a way was[5]) and perfectly fitting – the recorded use of the word showed connotations very similar to those of English *elf*. Similarly, for *Westron* Ohlmarks used *väströna*, modelled on a rare old word *norröna* (referring to the language community around the North Sea in the days of the Norse heroic literature), which, it is safe to say, very few of the readers had ever heard or seen; again a well-founded choice that might have been felt as too quaint, but that proved to work excellently.

In other cases, however, Ohlmarks did not recognize relationships that should have been obvious. As Tolkien noted in 'Guide to the Names in *The Lord of the Rings*',[6] the element *harrow* in *Dunharrow* was translated as the farm implement, and not with Swedish *harg*, which is the formal cognate and a place-name element. *Trollshaws*, a name occurring on the map, was translated *Trollbergen* ('troll mountains'), despite the map showing it as a wood and *shaw* nicely corresponding to Swedish *skog* (though a more archaic synonym would be preferable to translate the archaic shaw).

The word *hobbit* was not spared this time either. In Swedish nouns, the inflexional stem usually ends on a stressed syllable; if the lexical form ends on an unstressed syllable, this usually falls into one of certain recognizable patterns: some kinds of unstressed ends are dropped, others lose their vowel, others are merely retained, and still others acquire stress in inflected forms. A word that is not well known and does not fit a common pattern may cause consternation. As indicated above, the only existing noun that ended on unstressed *-it* and could set a pattern for *hobbit* was the unusual word *gambit*.[7] Ohlmarks

---

5 See his doubts about its success in Letter 151:2.
6 In Jared Lobdell (ed.), *A Tolkien Compass*, La Salle, Ill.: Open Court, 1975, pp. [153]–201.
7 *Kredit* is also a trochee when used as an accountancy heading, but is then indeclinable.

seems to have taken for granted that *hobbit* simply did not fit Swedish speaking habits; he argued that it would be assimilated with the many words ending on stressed *-it* (the Greek and Neo-Latin suffix that appears as *-ite* in English), forgetting that the choice of plural form could easily block that assimilation. His radical solution of the problem was to drop the end of the word, turning it into *hob*. Pronounced [hu:b], it has a nice round sound, but that is the only merit I will grant it.

In fact, Ohlmarks greatly exaggerated the problems with *hobbit*. There are comparable words, like *fänrik* and most notably *robot* (in Swedish that word has a short first o, making it a near-rhyme on *hobbit*); nobody has ever felt the need to truncate the latter into *rob.

Characteristic of Ohlmarks' text is his propensity for embroidering every description. Not only are Bilbo's riches, in the opening of the tale, a legend (as in the original), but his travels are *sägenomsusade* ('legendary') as well. People not only began to call him *well-preserved*, but began to 'emphasize' that he was. So it goes on all the way through; I will just present a random example from each following volume. In the chapter 'The King of the Golden Hall' the original says: "His voice rang clear as he chanted in the tongue of Rohan a call to arms". Ohlmarks renders this as "Hans stämma klang klar som en stormklocka när han på Rohans språk högtidligt framsjöng det gamla vapenropet" ('His voice sounded clear like a stormbell as he in the language of Rohan solemnly chanted the old call to arms'). In 'The Tower of Cirith Ungol' Tolkien's straightforward "Then he heard the hideous voice speaking again" becomes "... och så kom det en en hest morrande, vidrig orcherstämma" ('and then there came a hoarsely growling, hideous orc-voice'). The last example also shows another of this translation's quirks, the turning of *orc* into *orch* (rather than *ork*, which would be a regular Swedish spelling).

Ohlmarks frequently misinterpreted the original. Sometimes he simply misread. In 'The Ride of the Rohirrim', for example, when the Riders had "no sight or sound" of the enemy, the translation says "varken suck eller läte" ('neither sigh nor sound'). The difference between *dead* and *death* would be overlooked: *the Paths of the Dead* became *Dödens stig* ('the path of Death'), and in 'The Siege of Gondor', Pippin, coming down to the city gate as Gandalf confronts the

Lord of the Nazgûl, "stopped dead", of which Ohlmarks made "hade hejdat döden" ('had stopped death'). Funny examples like that have given Swedish Tolkien fandom much to laugh at. The favourite one is at the end of 'The Riders of Rohan', where Aragorn speaks of the ancient forests, where "the Firstborn roamed". Ohlmarks here tells us that "den Förstfödde bölade" ('the Firstborn [singular] bellowed'), comically associating the verb *roam* with Swedish *råma* ('moo, low'). When reading this as a child, I was intrigued by the quasi-mithraistic notion of some primordial bull.

Annoyingly, Ohlmarks is very often inconsistent in his translation of names. *Isengard*, for instance, appears first as *Isengard*, reappears three sentences later as *Isendor*, soon afterwards is *Isendal*, reverts to *Isengard* and remains so for the rest of the first volume; it is only in the next one that it finds its final form as *Isengård*.

The name of the book itself fared badly. The first volume is titled *Sagan om Ringen*[8] ('the (fairy-)story of the ring') with no title given for the work as a whole. In the synopsis at the beginning of the second volume, the work was referred to as *Ringarnas Ring* ('the Ring of rings'). In the synopsis of the third volume, the title of the work became *Härskarringen* ('the ruler-ring'), and this is now the publishers' official name for it. But most Swedish readers actually use *Sagan om Ringen* for both the first volume and the work as a whole.

And there are very many Swedish readers. Despite all the shortcomings of the translation, the work — whatever its title is supposed to be — has had enormous success in Sweden, and is said to have sold 2 million copies (in a country with a population of 9 million in 4,5 million households).

The work was in fact successful from the beginning; there were enthusiastic reviews (along with some negative ones, naturally), and the sales, though not sufficient to prompt a reprint for some years, were enough to give the publishers the confidence to issue a translation (also by Ohlmarks) of *Farmer Giles of Ham* — its Swedish title is *Gillis Bonde från Ham* — in the same year as the third volume of *Härskarringen*.

---

8 It actually says *Sagan om ringen* on the titlepage of the first edition, but at least on covers (I have not looked at the various title-pages) the publishers have also used *Sagan om Ringen*, which I regard as the 'normal' form.

It was presumably this success that prompted the re-translation of *The Hobbit*, made by Britt G. Hallqvist and published by Rabén & Sjögren (a publishing house linked back to the former KF Bokförlag) under the title *Bilbo: en hobbits äventyr* in 1962. As is seen, the word *hobbit* was left intact this time, as well as the name *Bilbo*.

Britt G. Hallqvist was a well-known author and translator.[9] The first edition of *Bilbo* was illustrated by Tove Jansson, the Finnish artist and author who created the Moomin-trolls. Jansson's pictures for *Bilbo* are sometimes idiosyncratic (the barrel-dumping wood-elves have horns like cattle), but in general highly atmospheric, and Hallqvist's text captures the shifting moods of the original very well, I think.

Ohlmarks later averred that it was Tolkien who had demanded of Rabén & Sjögren that *hobbit* be used, and that it bothered them much. It is not impossible that Tolkien did ask this, or even demand it, but it is certainly also possible that Hallqvist simply found *hob* indefensible.

More often than not, however, Hallqvist adopted names and terms from Ohlmarks' translation. *Mörkmården* for *Mirkwood* is one instance, of which it may be noted that the author's criticism in 'Guide to the Names' is not quite fair: besides meaning 'marten', *mård* is actually a place-name element meaning 'hard ground', a rare one, but prominent in the name of the forest *Kolmården*, once notorious for its bands of highwaymen. So *Mörkmården* is in fact a plausible, and perhaps suitably ominous, name for a dark wood, and the archaic *mården* makes up for the fact that Swedish *mörk* 'dark' (adj.) is an everyday word, as opposed to the archaic English *mirk*. What is lost in this translation is that *Mirkwood* specifically reflects an ancient Germanic expression (of which the regular Swedish counterpart is *Mörkveden*[10]).

---

9 1914–1997. More than 40 children's books; poetry; hymns. Apart from *The Hobbit* and (as we shall see) *Smith of Wootton Major* she translated works by Richard Adams, H.C. Andersen, T.S. Eliot, Goethe, the Grimm brothers, Kipling, Jean de la Fontaine, Edward Lear, C.S. Lewis (*The Magician's Nephew*), A.A. Milne, Nesbit, Mary Norton, Beatrix Potter, Shakespeare, Pamela Travers, Peter Weiss, Oscar Wilde, Laura Ingalls Wilder and others. She was a member of a liturgical commission, and an Honorary Doctor of Theology.
As a curious coincidence, Tore Zetterholm was one of the recipients of the annual literary award of the national newspaper *Svenska Dagbladet* in 1950, and Britt G. Hallqvist was the children's author recipient in the same year.
10 It may, however, be noted that Ohlmarks was consistent here, in that he regularly used *Mörkmården* to render *myrkvifr* in his translations of Old Norse literature.

Other instances are *Dimmiga bergen* for the *Misty Mountains*, and *Ensamma berget* for the *Lonely Mountain* (though in the latter case Hallqvist is consistent, while Ohlmarks alternatively used *Ensliga bergen* — yes, plural), and she also used his *Bagger* for *Baggins*. But rather than adopting Ohlmarks' *Hobsala*, Hallqvist kept *Hobbiton* unchanged, presumably because she did not use his *hob*. She also left *Sackville* and, very notably, *Rivendell* unchanged; Ohlmarks had turned that name into *Vattnadal*, which, as Tolkien noted in 'Guide to the Names', clearly "suggests that the translator thought that *Riven-* was related to *river*". It would have been interesting to see what Hallqvist would have come up with if she had tried to make Swedish versions of those names.

Also, happily, Hallqvist agreed with Ohlmarks in rendering *elf* with *alv*. For the difficult *goblin* she chose *vätte*, in Swedish folklore a word for a more or less uncanny creature, and as good a solution as may be found.

As all around the world, the interest in Tolkien increased markedly at the end of the '60s. The first paperback edition of *Härskarringen* came in 1967, and sales started to soar. The opening '70s saw the birth of organized Tolkien fandom in Sweden. The rising interest also led to a new wave of translations. Of the appendices of *The Lord of the Rings* only 'The Tale of Aragorn and Arwen' and Appendix D were included in *Härskarringen*. In 1971 a volume called *Ringens värld* was published, containing all the appendices (though the section on runes was only summarized), translated by Ohlmarks. (I got the book for Christmas; happiness on earth could not be greater.)

The next year saw no less than three new translations: Geber's publishing house and Ohlmarks produced *Tom Bombadills äventyr* (*The Adventures of Tom Bombadil*; the form *Bombadill* is another of the translator's eccentricities — he must have wanted the name to be stressed on its last syllable), and *Träd och Blad* (*Tree and Leaf*), while Rabén & Sjögren and Hallqvist presented us with *Sagan om Smeden och stjärnan* (*Smith of Wootton Major*), with Pauline Baynes' illustrations.

A few more of Tolkien's works were given Swedish versions by Åke Ohlmarks. *Om Beowulfsagan* (1975) contains translations of three of Tolkien's scholarly texts: *Beowulf: The Monsters and the Critics*, 'Prefatory Remarks on Prose

Translation of *Beowulf*, and 'English and Welsh'. A translation of *The Father Christmas Letters*, titled *Breven från jultomten*, appeared in the same year as the original (1976). But Ohlmarks also translated books on Tolkien by Paul H. Kocher and Randel Helms, and published a general presentation, *Sagan om Tolkien* (1972), and a reference work, *Tolkien-lexikon med allt från Alvhem till Örtplyte* (1976), under his own name, before his fall-out with Christopher Tolkien changed the course of things.

Ohlmarks' story about this is that he wished to anticipate *The Silmarillion* by publishing an account of its contents, based on information that Christopher Tolkien had given him on a visit to England at the end of 1974, and with an introductory description of Christopher Tolkien himself, his house and family; when he received a letter of disapproval, he felt so hurt that he never answered it. Perhaps this was the reason, or perhaps it was simply that the shortcomings of his translations had been noted. In any case Gebers, where now Erland Törngren, son of Disa, was in charge of Tolkien-publishing, could get the Swedish translation rights for *The Silmarillion* only on condition that they found another translator for it than Ohlmarks.[11]

The choice fell on Roland Adlerberth, a translator with long experience.[12] His *Silmarillion* was published in 1979, and the Tolkien books that have appeared in Swedish after that are translated by him: *Sagor från Midgård* (*Unfinished Tales*), 1982; *Herr Salig* (*Mr. Bliss*), 1983; and *De förlorade sagornas bok* (*The Book of Lost Tales*), vol. 1 1986 and vol. 2 1988. All of these were ably treated and read smoothly. Or so I have been told: I have in fact not read these translations myself.

It is interesting to note that in *De förlorade sagornas bok* the word *älva* was taken into service again, this time to represent *fairy* (for which it fits). Adlerberth

---

11 This was not quite the end of Ohlmarks' career as a Tolkien translator: he was engaged to translate the poetry by Tolkien quoted in Carpenter's biography, and a new edition of *Ringens värld* in 1980 included (beside the Appendices, and the two translations by Ohlmarks first published separately in 1972) his translation 'Beorhtnoths hemkomst'. In the same year his translation of David Day's *A Tolkien Bestiary* was published. But he increasingly devoted himself to maligning Tolkien and those connected with him; from his tract against Christopher Tolkien, *Tolkiens arv*, in 1977, to his outlash against the Swedish Tolkien societies, *Tolkien och den svarta magin*, in 1982 (see my article 'Tolkien in Sweden' in *Inklings* 1984). In 1980 I heard him lecture on the theory that J.R.R. Tolkien had not written *The Lord of the Rings*, but only reworked a manuscript inherited from E.V. Gordon.

12 1923–1993. Translator of books by dozens of authors (i.a. Alexandre Dumas, Joseph Conrad, Michael Ende, Robert Heinlein, V.S. Naipaul, Jules Verne): mainly crime stories, science fiction, fantasy and nature books.

generally used Ohlmarks' names and terms, like *alv* and *orch*, and also kept Hallqvist's *vätte*; for *fay* he chose *fé*, quite suitably.

Except for *Herr Salig*, Adlerberth's translations were published with impressive cover pictures painted by Inger Edelfeldt.[13] She also in those years made cover art for new editions of *Härskarringen* (three different sets), *Ringens värld*, and *Gillis Bonde från Ham*. Twelve of her paintings were chosen for the 1985 Tolkien Calendar from Allen & Unwin.

The list of Adlerberth's translations rightly suggests that Tolkien did command a large readership throughout the '80s. He still does. In view of this, it is curious that the publishers have never thought it worthwhile to have his *Letters* translated.

Gebers was merged into the large firm Norstedts in the beginning of the '90s, and a decade later Rabén & Sjörgen became a part of the same publishing group.

As this article is being prepared for print, in 2004, so is the first volume of a new Swedish translation of *The Lord of the Rings*. This time the prose is to be done by Erik Andersson,[14] and the poetry by Lotta Olsson.[15] Neither has entered the Tolkien field before, but Andersson is a well-established translator, and Olsson an accomplished poet. This time, there will be no *hob* and no *Vattnadal*, that much is already clear. Ever since the enterprise was announced, early in 2003, it has aroused expectations among the Swedish Tolkien fans. The general public is indeed also interested, and newspapers, radio and television have paid their tribute by reporting about the project.

A few of the solutions that Andersson is considering for names in the book have become public. So, the last we heard, he plans to render *Baggins* with *Secker* (close to *Sækker*, the choice in the Danish translation of *The Lord of the Rings*, and *Sekker* in the first Norwegian translation). Many readers have an affection for *Bagger*, but the crux is to translate *Bag End* with a related name

---

13 1956–. Illustrator of various books. Author of some twenty titles: novels, short stories, comic books, children's books, poetry. Recipient of several literary awards.
14 1962–. Translator of 37 titles, mainly science fiction and crime stories; author of short stories, essays and three novels.
15 1973–. Collections of poetry, children's books, a couple of translations.

of appropriate meaning (Ohlmarks substituted *Baggershus*, roughly 'Baggins' manor', for *Bag End*, and Hallqvist followed him), which will be more feasible with something like *Secker*. Andersson's willingness to discard an ingrained name in order to be true to the text bodes well.[16] The advice of some long-time students of Tolkien's works (including myself) has also been sought on matters of fact and nomenclature.

The new translation by Andersson and Olsson will have a new title, *Ringarnas herre* ('The lord of the rings'), and the first volume will be called *Ringens brödraskap* ('The brotherhood of the ring'). A host of fans and general readers is waiting for it.

About the author

Beregond, Anders Stenström, has been a Tolkien devotee since 1967, and carries the byname Beregond since the beginning of 1976, when he was admitted into the Forodrim Tolkien Society. He has researched diverse aspects of Tolkien's works, and his articles have appeared in many publications, not least in Arda, and his contribution to the J.R.R. Tolkien Centenary Conference is found in the published proceedings. With Kristina Valinger, he is responsible for the Swedish subtitling of Peter Jackson's film version of The Lord of the Rings. He lives in Uppsala, Sweden, and he works as a verger.

---

16 Still, we hear that Andersson plans to employ Ohlmarks' translation of *the Shire* as *Fylke*, disregarding an essential feature of the original name: its grammatically definite form. Also, *fylke* primarily refers to Norwegian shires, which makes it an odd choice in a Swedish translation. But to many readers it is no doubt simply a nice-sounding name of obscure meaning.

Vincent Ferré

Tolkien, our Judge of Peter Jackson

Translated by Daniel Lauzon

Abstract

This article discusses J.R.R. Tolkien's judgement upon cinema and the adaptability of *The Lord of the Rings* (as exposed in his *Letters*), then confronts his criteria and judgement with the story-line submitted to Tolkien in 1957-1958, and with Ralph Bakshi's and Peter Jackson's achievements, 'The Lord of the Rings' and 'The Fellowship of the Ring'.[1]

Peter Jackson's 'Fellowship of the Ring' is a fair adaptation of *The Fellowship of the Ring*, chiefly owing to its visual qualities and to the believable representation of a universe it offers the viewer. It may please both types of audiences: firstly, the readers of Tolkien, because our memories of the book overlap the movie and are superimposed on it, restoring some density to a film which otherwise would seem all too frantic and too 'flat'; it can also please those who are not familiar with Tolkien, and most of all trigger an interest in reading the book, for in the film these viewers are given a glimpse of a rich and believable world. Indeed, a dramatic increase in book sales has been observed since the movie entered the popular mindset, which is undoubtedly one of its chief virtues, so seldom it is that mainstream cinema leads to literature.

This is a film which holds no major misinterpretations – the viewer quickly comes to the realization that 'The Fellowship of the Rings' is not primarily geared towards children, unlike 'Harry Potter'; that it is no science-fiction; that there is no trace of racism in Tolkien's work, etc. – and a film which, most importantly, paves the way of the newcomer towards the book: could we, prior to its release, have expected the movie to meet such demands, given the high costs and obvious commercial constraints tied to its making?

---

1 NB: It is understood that *The Lord of the Rings/The Fellowship of the Ring* refers to the work by J.R.R. Tolkien, whereas 'The Lord of the Rings'/'The Fellowship of the Ring' designates the film adaptations. In the case of Peter Jackson, this article (written at the beginning of 2002) is concerned with 'The Fellowship of the Ring'.

More simply, could anyone have even considered adapting a book of such importance into an art house movie? We, the public, certainly cannot appreciate the constraints Peter Jackson had to deal with, even though they can be inferred from his public declarations: without the determination of this director (and his close collaborators), no doubt the adaptation would have strayed a lot farther from J.R.R. Tolkien's *The Lord of the Rings*.

Moreover, to enumerate such differences as exist between the movie and the text is probably mistaken: even though some websites, well before the release of the movie, listed the changes found in the script (or what was held as such), one must not forget that a work of film is in essence much more than that; to judge Peter Jackson's movie based on his scriptwriting only would be to show serious disregard for the specificities of cinema. To cite an example drawn from my own experience, working on the dialogues as a consultant for the French dub has not allowed me – even with the images available on numerous websites – to *visualize* the film, because the sole addition of these elements (script + dialogues + screenshots) is a far cry from an edited movie. Surely that is what those viewers have overlooked who went to see the film with (favourable or unfavourable) prejudices, which the first true experience of the movie could not alter.

Before turning specifically to the film by Peter Jackson, I believe it is important to widen the scope of the discussion. One of the issues that frequently turn up is that of the adaptability of *The Lord of the Rings* to the screen. All has been said of this matter, but Tolkien's own opinion has not been sought often enough. Now his *Letters* prove once more to be of special interest, since there emerges a difference between his (nuanced) stance of principle, and his severe (and well-founded) judgment of a project submitted to him in 1957-58.

We are well aware of the importance of the visual element in Tolkien's works: he illustrated them (as publications – *Pictures by J.R.R. Tolkien* and *J.R.R. Tolkien: Artist and Illustrator*[2] – have reminded us), and "visualize[d] with great clarity" the landscapes of Middle-earth.[3] It is no wonder, then, that the author, when consulted, looks favourably upon a project he hopes will be better than

---

[2] *Pictures by J.R.R. Tolkien*, London, HarperCollins, 1992 (revised edition), 112 p.; W.G. Hammond, C. Scull, *J.R.R. Tolkien: Artist and Illustrator*, London, HarperCollins, 1995, 208 p.
[3] *The Letters of J.R.R. Tolkien: A Selection*, edited by H. Carpenter, London, Allen&Unwin, 1981, p. 280 (abridged as *L*).

the BBC adaptation – a failure, in his opinion.[4] He does not show great interest: this reserve, devoid of hostility, constitutes his stance of principle, which may be interpreted merely as a sign that, in his eyes, the literary work comes first, the cinematographic transposition having little to do with this but being potentially "good for publicity".[5]

He is however aware of the difficulties entailed ("the risk of vulgarization"[6]) and admits the necessity to *reduce*: "an *abridgement* by selection with some good picture-work would be pleasant [...]".[7] Here there emerges one of the first criteria to his judgment of an animation film project presented to him by an American producer, Forrest J. Ackerman: the *images* (mountains and deserts) hold his attention because they seem well-suited to his work.[8] This interest in the visual aspect is confirmed a little later on, as Tolkien explains that sets and scenery could constitute the main interest of the screen adaptation that is submitted to him.[9]

Thus, Tolkien is not going to reject *any* adaptation, but one in particular, the 1958 'story-line'; and even where he is most critical of it, he still submits solutions that take heed of the specificities of cinema, pondering ways to convey in images the difficulties of the quest, or proposing to light the scene at Weathertop by using a fire.[10]

For the 1958 story-line proves to be catastrophic; what is known of it comes solely from Tolkien's own description, but that is sufficiently long and precise to inform us on the essential points: names are erroneously transcribed, dialogues are calamitous, the narrative structure is disrupted – episodes are displaced or condensed, the interlacement (intertwining of plots) is ill-treated –, additions (fairy castle, immoderate use of magic) and cuts deface the plot, which moreover comes off as incoherent; some characters are altered (Gandalf, Bombadil, and the Orc, endowed with feathers and beaks).

---

4 "[...] the sillification achieved by the B.B.C." (letter of May 1957 to Rayner Unwin, *L*, p. 257; cf. pp. 228-29).
5 Letter of September 1957 to Rayner Unwin (*L*, p. 261).
6 *L*, p. 257.
7 *L*, p. 261.
8 "[...] this Mr Ackerman brought some really astonishingly good pictures (Rackham rather than Disney) and some remarkable colour photographs" (letter of September 1957 to Christopher Tolkien, *L*, p. 261).
9 Letter (probably of June 1958) to Forrest J. Ackerman (*L*, p. 274).
10 *L*, p. 274.

Amongst all this evidence of infidelity, this confusion, three things stand out: excessive simplification, the undermining of the story's believability – so fundamental as it is to Tolkien – and, in the author's own terms, a "pull-back towards more conventional 'fairy-stories'".[11] He does not argue against the necessity of selecting scenes: I have already mentioned the possibility of 'abridgement', and further on, Tolkien states anew that a "reduction or selection of the scenes and events" is necessary; but he clearly disagrees with what he is being given to read, which seems to him like a "*contraction*"[12] or "*compression*".[13] Evidently irritated and hurt, he does not mince words in his critique of the puerile cartoon project, considering that the important moments are forgotten – Frodo's mission "has been murdered"[14] – to allow for fight scenes, and the screenwriter (whom, with respect to decency, we will name 'Z', after Tolkien's fashion[15]), according to him, is blatantly guilty of "extreme silliness and incompetence".[16]

The purpose of this short reminder is to provide a few indications on what might have been Tolkien's own judgment regarding the subsequent adaptations.

Let us start with a few words on Ralph Bakshi's 1978 effort filming a script written by C. Conkling and P.S. Beagle. A few quick words, though, for most of what has been reproached to Z, unfortunately, can also be found in Bakshi, except that *that* movie has ultimately seen the light of day. One could say, to make a long story short, that Bakshi's 'Lord of the Rings' is somewhat akin to *Bored of the Rings*[17] by Henry N. Beard and Douglas C. Kennedy, the *Lord of the Rings* spoof published in 1969 by Harvard lampoonists, but that, in the case of Bakshi, the parody was unintentional.

The storytelling is incoherent: the director retains disparate elements without linking them together, performs a few too many ill-chosen ellipses, and makes

---

11 *L*, p. 261.
12 "*Contraction* of this kind is not the same thing as the necessary reduction or selection of the scenes and events that are to be visually represented" (*L*, p. 272).
13 *L*, p. 261
14 "[...] he has made no serious attempt to represent the heart of the tale adequately: the journey of the Ringbearers. The last and most important part of this has, and it is not too strong a word, simply been murdered" (*L*, p. 271).
15 *L*, p. 270ff.
16 Letter of April 1958 to Rayner Unwin (*L*, p. 267).
17 Henry N. Beard and Douglas C. Kennedy, *Bored of the Rings: A Parody of J.R.R. Tolkien's The Lord of the Rings*, New York, New American Library, 2001, 160 p.

reference to facts not included in the film – in such a scene, Sam evokes the Elves as he does (at the same point) in Tolkien's book, but these have not yet been mentioned in the movie. Relationship between characters are illogical: thus Butterbur, who initially is being critical of Strider, begs him for protection and then returns to criticizing him again, these changes of heart occurring in the space of a few moments. And there is, of course, the moment when the film comes to its sudden and unexpected end at middle course in the book, after the battle at Helm's Deep (III, 7) and before Frodo and Sam make it to Shelob's Lair (IV, 9). Making an animated film out of this story was an audacious and problematic choice, hence the need to avoid childishness with all the more precautions;[18] yet the Orcs are totally ridiculous, the facial expressions silly. Most notable is the sojourn in Lórien, where the screenwriters have felt the need to invent some novel activities, such as the picking of flowers, which seems incongruous to say the least.

Here we see all that Peter Jackson has successfully avoided, and achieved in his 'Fellowship of the Ring'. In many ways, he follows closely the spirit of *The Lord of the Rings*, if not the letter. So it is with coherence and believability, two essential qualities of the adult 'fairy-story' as outlined by Tolkien in his essay: Jackson wished for the suspension of the viewer's disbelief – to resort to the famous phrase by Coleridge, picked up by Tolkien –, and the representation the director proposes, especially with the collaboration of renowned illustrators John Howe and Alan Lee as conceptual artists, seems convincing, inviting the viewer to 'penetrate' the secondary world even more forcefully, perhaps, than a tale could.

Jackson is also successful with compensation and displacement: it is probable that the extensive use of Elvish – indeed greater than in *The Lord of the Rings* – is not aimed at producing some cheap effect, but is a case of using the proper resources of cinema in an attempt to counterbalance the loss of other elements pertaining to Middle-earth. Attention to linguistic portrayal is also sparklingly reflected in the (relative) faithfulness to Tolkien's own dialogues, to the beauty

---

18 Another important problem is the change of times: filmgoers of twenty-five years ago were soaked in the atmosphere of the seventies and could perceive what in his 'Lord of the Rings' pertains to Bakshi, director of the celebrated 'Fritz the Cat' (1971), something moviegoers of today arguably cannot relate to.

of his writing: from that point of view, the original English version, which features a variety of different accents, is an immense pleasure, all the more so because the actors generally offer good and believable performances in the first film, sometimes even uncovering aspects of the book often overlooked – such is the case for Boromir, who comes off with a lot more nuance than the character readers of the book typically remember. Finally, this same complexity can be found in the careful depiction of Frodo's relationship with the Ring, where the ever-growing fascination of the hobbit is made evident, even though some of the simplifications are only too regrettable: so it is that the meaningfulness of a familiar scene, where the Black Rider is drawing near the four hobbits hidden under a tree, is thwarted by Jackson. In the film, it is Sam who prevents Frodo from slipping on the Ring, whereas in Tolkien's original version,[19] the Rider leaves at the very moment Frodo is about to succumb: this is the first telltale sign of a major issue that develops as the story is told, that of chance and of fate. We can appreciate the loss suffered by the film in this apparently insignificant transformation.

What is unfortunate is that this is not the only one; I will now turn successively to the question of focalization and to that of the representation of evil, before touching on Tolkien's play on a 'fiction of authenticity,' so as to emphasize what fundamentally separates film from book.

In *The Lord of the Rings*, Tolkien chooses to present the story from a hobbit point of view, a story in which Sam and Frodo are established as the main characters. This is clearly seen, for example, in his decision to limit the importance of Aragorn, to postpone the telling of his love story with Arwen until the Appendices, etc. Now Jackson profoundly alters this equilibrium, putting Gandalf and Aragorn to the forefront as the true heroes of the film: one may think of the role assumed by Aragorn at the Council of Elrond or of his help and words of encouragement to the fleeing Frodo at the Breaking of the Fellowship – best left unmentioned is the kitschy scene involving a moonlight kiss between Aragorn and Arwen. Yet we should not be too quick to judge Jackson's aesthetic predilections, and some effects can be attributed to his credit: if the white-haloed apparition of the Elves may seem naïve, it effectively renders the

---

19 *The Lord of the Rings*, London, HarperCollins, 1995, p. 73.

slightly ingenuous wonderment of the hobbits at the sight of these beings out of what they considered to be legend.

More problematic is the representation of Evil. The in-frame appearance of Sauron during the Prologue allows the viewer to make a better assessment of what is at stake in the 'Quest' of the Ring, but this faithful depiction of an episode from the *Silmarillion* is at odds with an essential trait of *The Lord of the Rings*, where the past is evoked on numerous occasions (tales of Eärendil, Beren and Lúthien, etc.) but never actually shown, and where the incarnation of Evil is never seen. That the title character of the book (the 'Lord of the Rings') remains invisible is indeed a *coup de force*! Aside from achieving indisputable narrative success, Tolkien is here pondering the relationship between man and 'monster', his enemy, in a kind of brilliant rewriting of *Beowulf* – he has studied the poem in this perspective –, thereby escaping Manichean dichotomies by suggesting (to put it simply) that 'evil' does not lie so much in one character than in all of them at once, most of whom experience moments of weakness, sometimes irremediably so: one may think of Gollum, Boromir and Denethor, but also of Frodo, Gandalf and Galadriel. Unfortunately, Peter Jackson trips a second time and founders in Manichean over-simplification by making too much out of Saruman, that is a mere replica of Sauron who is seen mustering his armies and making use of magic (whereas magic, on the contrary, has a complex status in Tolkien's works) to prevent the Company from crossing the Caradhras, or to fight it out with Gandalf in an extremely questionable scene.

Finally, it is important to note that Tolkien's play on a 'fiction of authenticity' has completely vanished from the first film, as it was originally released and seen by millions of viewers. While *The Lord of the Rings* underlines the believability and historical aspect of the tale, it also clearly states its own nature as a book by emphasizing the writing of the Red Book (as 'the book within the book', *a mise en abyme*) and providing numerous hints that characterize the tale as a *history*. I have cited elsewhere[20] as an example the passage in the Prologue ('Concerning Pipe-weed') reproducing one of Merry's texts on the origins of tobacco in the Shire, a text 'quoted' by Merry himself hundreds of pages after

---

20 Vincent Ferré, *Tolkien. Sur les rivages de la Terre du Milieu*, Paris, Christian Bourgois Éditeur, 2001, p. 106.

(during the meeting with Théoden in Isengard): "It was Tobold Hornblower, of Longbottom in the Southfarthing, who first grew the true pipe-weed in his gardens, about the year 1070 [...]".[21] This sentence, appearing in the midst of the tale, has been encountered before by the reader, but it will not actually be set to paper (by Merry) until much later! Now the deletion of the Prologue (and that, now forthcoming, of the Appendices?), in which the narrator introduces the readers to the hobbits' universe, was far from inevitable, on the contrary; the choice of replacing it with an *account* of the battle against Sauron is significant, insofar as Peter Jackson sacrifices an essential element of the literary *device* for the sake of a narrative passage – it is a good thing that the 'extended version' of the first film, on dvd, corrects this awkward choice.

I might as well speak of the most unengaging aspect of this movie, and that is the music by Howard Shore: sometimes it is so jarringly emphatic that the whole scene is dragged down into pomposity and slushiness. It is also regrettable that a book in which a slow pace and a contemplative quality are essential should be transformed into an action movie (compared to a video game in certain quarters for its succession of unexpected turns) where all that does not directly forward the main plot is set aside, for there is more to *The Lord of the Rings* than its *story*; it is regrettable that more cannot be present (or felt) of the more enigmatic side of this work, constantly hinting at a world wider than the characters can see, at a past only guessed at, and leaving a trail of unanswered questions (Bombadil, the fate of our heroes after the tale has ended), masterfully suggesting the passage of time and a sense of historical depth. But 'suggestion' is probably incompatible with the choice of cinematographic means such as those available to Peter Jackson.

In the end, the fairest 'adaptation' of *The Lord of the Rings* may be a quasi-contemporary film, which admittedly has nothing to do objectively with J.R.R. Tolkien's work. This film tells the story of a man on the verge of death who may try to elude this fate; a man who must *choose* to act or to resign himself to it, as his companions did; who must clear-mindedly choose the moment and course of action. The film poses essential questions: must what befalls us necessarily happen to us? Can we alter what seems to be our 'fate'? Must rebellion

---

21 *The Lord of the Rings*, p. 544.

be solitary, or can we rely on someone else's support (without which, in the end, we would not succeed)? This detour serves to highlight what thematically (the question of courage, of death) and technically (focalization, duration) are weak points in Jackson's work.

The name of this film? 'A Man Escaped' ('The Wind Bloweth Where It Listeth') by Robert Bresson, 1957.

About the author

Vincent Ferré teaches Comparative Literature at the Université de Caen, near Paris. His chief area of interest is the modern novel (1910-1950), especially Proust, Broch and Dos Passos. On J.R.R. Tolkien, he has published articles and *Sur les Rivages de la Terre du Milieu* (2001), an analysis of *The Lord of the Rings* which focuses on the theme of death, and he is currently editing a collection of articles (to be published in 2004). He has also been an advisor on the French translation of Peter Jackson's 'The Fellowship of the Ring' and is in charge of translations of Tolkien's works for Christian Bourgois Editeur – he is working on many projects, most of them with the collaboration of Daniel Lauzon, who translated this article, and David Riggs.

Anthony S. Burdge & Jessica Burke

Humiliated Heroes: Peter Jackson's Interpretation of *The Lord of the Rings*

Abstract

Tolkien in writing *The Lord of the Rings* and even *The Hobbit* has almost single-handedly resurrected images of the hero. Inspired by heroic motifs from Beowulf to King Arthur, Tolkien wished to reintroduce such heroism to a world robbed of such wealth, a world corrupted by mechanized visions of greed and power rather than a world sustained by honor, virtue, and Yeats' sanctified earth. Tolkien's heroes are so remarkable, so applicable and so universal because of their adherence to Frye's fictional modes. Tolkien doesn't merely write of one hero in one mode alone. Tolkien has heroes and anti-heroes in virtually all the modes. Since the publication of *The Lord of the Rings* there have been scores of would-be usurpers who have attempted to interpret the epic tale into other media – from graphic novels to fan fiction to radio drama to film. There has been one interpretation that will stand alone and for many it will be the 'quintessential' interpretation: this is, of course, Peter Jackson's film adaptations of *The Lord of the Rings* (2001-2003). In these works Jackson endeavors to preserve Tolkien's heroes, however, he fails miserably. One of his chief failures is his and his screenwriters' inability (or unwillingness) to understand how each of Tolkien's heroes incorporated one of Frye's fictional modes. In his haste to bring *The Lord of the Rings* to the mainstream, Jackson has succeeded in demoralizing not only Tolkien's heroes, but his anti-heroes as well. This articles endeavors to show this demoralization.

> Tolkien's protagonists are heroes not because of their successes, which are often limited, but because of their tenacity in trying. (Garth 2003:303)

By defying modern history and breathing the ancient air of saga and medieval romance, Tolkien almost single-handedly reconstructs heroic narrative for the 20th century in his masterpiece of epic fantasy *The Lord of the Rings*.[1] The heroes of his sprawling trilogy, and its villains, reflect the myths and ancient lore, from *Beowulf* to the Icelandic *Eddas*, medieval romances to the Finnish *Kalevala*. Courage, honor, strength, and leadership are traits Tolkien and his colleagues

---

[1] For simplicity's sake we will refer to *The Lord of the Rings* (both book and film) henceforth as *LotR*, *Fellowship of the Ring* as *FotR*, *The Two Towers* as *TTT*, and *The Return of the King* as *RotK*.

possessed in times of war, similar to antiquated heroes who excelled on the fields of battle. Inspired by these gallant traits, Tolkien wished to reintroduce such heroism to a world robbed of such wealth, a world corrupted by mechanized visions of greed and power rather than a world sustained by honor, virtue, and Yeats' sanctified earth.[2] Such qualities helped him "restore the hero to modern fiction" (Reilly 1968:1). Tolkien's heroes are so remarkable, so applicable and so universal because of their adherence to Frye's fictional modes.[3] Tolkien doesn't merely write of one hero in one mode alone. Tolkien has heroes in all the modes. Tolkien's protagonists, primarily the Fellowship – the nine walkers set against unspeakable odds in the face of utter extinction – become heroes for the welfare of their people. They all have their doubts and their faults, just as Tolkien and his WWI fellows did, yet they keep trying, they continue to 'soldier on' in the face of Galadriel's "long defeat" and they continue to touch each of us who journeys along with them (Tolkien 1994:348). Since the publication of *LotR* there have been scores of would-be usurpers who have attempted to interpret the epic tale into other media – from artwork to graphic novels, from to fan fiction to radio drama, and now to a live-action feature film. In the 1970's *The Hobbit* and *LotR* were translated to animated films, but there has been only one cinematic interpretation that will stand-alone, and for many it will be the 'quintessential' interpretation of *LotR*: this is, of course, Peter Jackson's film trilogy *LotR*, released successively from December 2000 to December 2003. In these works Jackson and his screenwriting team consisting of Philippa Boyens and Fran Walsh,[4] endeavor to preserve Tolkien's heroes, however, he fails miserably. One of his chief failures is his and his screenwriters' inability (or unwillingness) to understand how each of Tolkien's heroes incorporated one of Frye's fictional modes, or how many of Tolkien's protagonists shift amongst the modes. In his haste to bring *LotR* to the mainstream, Jackson has succeeded in flattening Tolkien's heroes into one mode, thereby demoralizing and humiliating Tolkien's

---

2 In *The Cutting of an Agate*, when discussing Edmund Spenser, Yeats points out the shift that took place from 'Merry England' to 'Modern England'. For Yeats, this 'Modern' world was born when Bunyan wrote "the other great English allegory …". Yeats says: "Religion had denied the sacredness of an earth that commerce was about to corrupt and ravish, but Spenser had still its sheltering sacredness" (Yeats 1919:213-55). In our opinion, Tolkien was writing in an attempt to resurrect this 'sacredness' and bring it to a world so corrupted.

3 Frye discusses these modes or forms of literature, in his essay 'Historical Criticism: Theory of Modes' which appeared in *Anatomy of Criticism* in 1957 (Frye 2000:33-67).

4 For simplicity, we will refer to the entire screenwriting team – Jackson, Boyens, and Walsh – as Jackson et al.

creation. The writers of this article can admire the audacity of such a work, but the interpretation on behalf of the screenwriters[5] is where the delineation occurs. While Tolkien himself wrote across the modes of fiction, dealing with heroes of every scope of the imagination, Jackson, Boyens, and Walsh sought to limit all of Tolkien's characters.

In an attempt to detract the mainstream from its admiration of *LotR* trilogy, Edmund Wilson wrote a severe and unforgiving critique of Tolkien's work, "Ooo, Those Awful Orcs", published in *The Nation* in 1956. Wilson chastises Tolkien for the simple fact that an Oxford don shouldn't be 'wasting' his time with such "hypertrophic" drivel. In Wilson's mind, *LotR* is "essentially … a children's book which has somehow got out of hand …"[6] Wilson does identify, however unwittingly, the essence of why Tolkien and why *LotR* has touched the primordial vein in each of us:

> In the *Saturday Review of Literature*, a Mr. Louis J. Halle, author of a book on *Civilization and Foreign Policy* answers as follows a lady who … has inquired what he finds in Tolkien: "What, dear lady, does this invented world have to do with our own? You ask for its meaning – as you would for the meaning of the *Odyssey*, of *Genesis*, of *Faust* – in a word? It makes our own world, once more heroic. What higher meaning than this is to be found in any literature?" (Becker 1989:51)

Wilson goes on to rebuke and censure the world of fantasy because, in his opinion works of such scope, whether as masterful as Tolkien's or not, beyond the confines of 'proper' literature and therefore an utter waste of anyone's time: he was insulted at having to review it at all. Yet, in his condemnation of *LotR*, Wilson touches on precisely what Tolkien's creation provides the world—heroism. In addition to creating a secondary world perhaps more believable than this primary one we are all born into, Tolkien provides heroes that stretch across every mode of fiction and gives us all a believable hope our world sorely lacks.

---

5 We would like to note that we hold an utmost respect for the creative team behind the films – the actors involved, the geniuses who hold ground in the forges of WETA, and the artists who gave Tolkien's Middle-earth scope. We also have a measure of respect for Peter Jackson himself who took on the task, and without whom the project would have never seen fruition. Yet, our 'issues' remain largely with the interpretations of Boyens and Walsh, and the attitudes of Boyens in particular (as seen in many documentaries and interviews concerning her work on the films) which will be discussed in this article.
6 Becker (1989:50-51).

Tom Shippey harkens to the Edmund Wilson's rejection of *The Hobbit* and *LotR* as he discusses the reality that Tolkien was writing in a form unfamiliar to and uncomfortable for the reading public (Shippey 1983:160-61). *LotR* was published in the same decade as *Waiting for Godot* and many other hallmarks of the post-modern movement founded on the denunciation of Tolkien's epic ideals and romantic ideology. In the decades prior to Tolkien, the public were familiar with heroes written in the *low mimetic* or ironic style, thanks in large part to Dickens, Thackeray, and the scores of Victorian authors reveling in the 'penny dreadfuls'. What was Tolkien to do? Write across the modes. And it is the quality and the exceptionality of Tolkien's creation that Peter Jackson and his screenwriting team have found particularly difficult to translate to film. Within the first act of Jackson's film, Frodo is willing to take on the quest, yet fails to stand up for himself when faced with battle – both on Weathertop and at the Ford of Bruinen. Gandalf is exposed as a clumsy old fool. Aragorn is a reluctant heir, but he is a fierce action hero comparable to the legions of brooding action stars that have been spawned in our infant millennium. Merry and Pippin serve as the comic relief, until Gimli joins the fray with dwarf jokes and wry glances. Faramir is turned from an honorable vestige of the race of Númenor, a shining ray of hope for mere mortal readers and for Frodo in the wilds of despair, into a corrupt display of mechanical greed and everything Tolkien was writing against. Jackson *et al.* have created a film where Tolkien's heroes have less choice, less free will, and less strength united against their common enemy. This interpretation allows the enemy more 'intelligence', turning it into an all-encompassing entity, which strikes fear into every heart of the Free Peoples of Middle-earth.

Tolkien never states that the end of Sauron or the One Ring is the end of evil, however, Jackson represents the One Ring as *the* symbol of evil, the ultimate symbol of power and corruption with whomever it comes in contact with. Since the One Ring is now established as evil incarnate, the end of evil is synonymous with the destruction of the Ring, and in so doing, Jackson has managed to turn Tolkien's melodic fugue of fictional modes into a monotone landscape written primarily in one mode alone, thereby flattening and humiliating each character in turn. Jackson has challenged Tolkien's heroes of romance, myth, and *high mimesis*, into heroes of the *low mimetic* or ironic modes only. Jackson has compartmentalized Tolkien's language as well as the characters of Middle-earth into colloquialisms of limited mentality. Jackson and the screenwriters also display their inability to understand the nuances and profundity of Tolkien's creation.

Barely three years after the publication of the first volume of *LotR*, Northrop Frye published a fundamental handbook for any student of myth, literature, or the written word: *Anatomy of Criticism*. Dense and insightful Frye picks up where Aristotle left off, discussing literature, its form and function. Frye describes the hierarchy of fictional modes, listing five, which range from myth to irony (Frye 2000:33-67). Rarely, however, can an author create a work that so adeptly moves between the modes as flawlessly as a fish moves through a mountain stream. Shakespeare is the first who comes to mind, Tolkien the second with his ability to write "with a thousand voices" (Campbell 1976:321). The first of Frye's modes deals with myth:

> 1. If superior in *kind* both to other men and to the environment of other men, the hero is a divine being, and the story about him will be a *myth* in the common sense of a story about a god. Such stories have an important place in literature, but are as a rule found outside the normal literary categories ... (Frye 2000:33).

Tolkien scholar Tom Shippey discusses Frye and *LotR*'s ability to fit into the fictional modes in *The Road to Middle-earth* (1983) and *J.R.R Tolkien: Author of the Century* (2000). In his earlier book, Shippey doesn't place Gandalf or *LotR* as a whole into the mode of myth. While we agree that *LotR* is not a mythic tale, as was *The Odyssey*, *The Aeneid*, or other classics of Greco-Roman literature which deal with the trials and tribulations of gods and monsters, Gandalf is certainly superior to mortal man, and superior in both 'kind' and 'degree' to Aragorn and the race of Númenor. Shippey doesn't classify Gandalf as belonging to the realm of myth because he "can feel fear and cold" (Shippey 1983:159). If memory serves, fear was an emotion the classical gods were capable of feeling. Prometheus cast fear into the heart of Mount Olympus itself for his gift to mankind, hence his punishment. Gandalf is a member of the *Istari*, or 'Wizard', and therefore a *Maiar*, or a member of Tolkien's pantheon, so it can be argued that Frye's first mode applies to Gandalf since he can be classified as a 'god' of sorts, and this mode deals with the divine. In his *Letters*, Tolkien explains the *Istari* as "guardian Angels" but not infallible creatures:

> It appears finally that they were as one might say the near equivalent in the mode of these tales of Angels, guardian Angels. Their powers are directed primarily to the encouragement of the enemies of evil, to cause them to use own wits and valour, to unite and endure. They appear always as old men and sages, and though (sent by the powers of the True West) in the world they suffer themselves, their age and grey hairs increase slowly. Gandalf whose function is especially to watch human affairs (Men and Hobbits) goes on through all the tales. (*Letters* 159)⁷

This quality of suffering, the ability to have fault, and to fall as Saruman fell cause some, like Shippey to classify the *Istari* in modes other than myth. Yet, the gods of Greece and Rome were capable of very human emotions, were capable of suffering, and were capable of many falls from grace.

Though brilliantly portrayed by Sir Ian McKellan, the diminishing of Gandalf's character begins almost immediately in the first film. When Bilbo slips on the Ring and disappears at the Birthday Party, Gandalf is as surprised as the other attendees are. It may seem a minor change, but Gandalf is robbed of knowledge, consequently being ignorant of Bilbo's trick (Tolkien 1994:25). This deteriorates the trust in the relationship of Bilbo and Gandalf, and eliminates Gandalf's initial knowledge of the Ring. From Gandalf's reaction in the film, it's unclear whether his surprise stemmed from Bilbo's disappearance, or had the hobbit had the means to disappear, intrinsically changing *The Hobbit*'s plot as well. When Jackson's Gandalf is speaking with Saruman, Gandalf states "All these long years, it has been in the Shire, under my very nose" – again implying ignorance which then humiliates Gandalf's role from divine messenger to ironic twit. Saruman's accusation of Gandalf's "love" of the "halfling's leaf" which has slowed Gandalf's mind, allows Jackson's Gandalf the Grey to be seen as a bumbling ignoramus under the effects of a drug. The implications of marijuana are obvious. Jackson's idea of Gandalf as a drug-induced fool is an insult and a degradation of character from myth to irony. Mere mortals would be wary of divinity, yet would identify with and pity a substance abuser. Tolkien continues to establish Gandalf's divinity in letter 156:

> There are naturally no precise modern terms to say what he was. I wd. Venture to say that he was an *incarnate* 'angel' – strictly an αγγελοζ⁸: that is, with the other *Istari*, wizards, 'those who know', an emissary from the Lords of the West,

---

7 References are to the edition by Carpenter 2000.
8 Greek for 'messenger' (*Letters* 445).

sent to Middle-earth, as the great crisis of Sauron loomed on the horizon. By 'incarnate' I mean they were embodied in physical bodies capable of pain, and weariness, and of afflicting the spirit with physical fear, and of being 'killed', though supported by the angelic spirit they might endure long, and only show slowly the wearing of care and labour. (*Letters* 202)

We know Gandalf has limits: that he can be wearied, frightened, and stumped (Tolkien 1994:280-82; 297-305; 315-23). Tolkien discusses Gandalf's return from death after the physical fall from the Bridge of Khazad-Dûm and the battle with the Balrog (Tolkien 1994:321-23). But, his return has a singular purpose: to complete the task he set upon, to end the Shadow, and to aid those mortals he was sent to aid (Tolkien 1994:484-93). The task of the *Istari* when arriving in Middle-earth ca. 1000 in the Third Age is to guide, protect and assist the people of Middle-earth in the fight against the rise of the Shadow. In Valinor, Gandalf (which is but one of his many names) is known as Olórin, wisest of the Maiar (Petty 2003:59). Jackson's version of Gandalf flattens him onto a more 'attainable' rung – the *low mimetic* – alongside men where he is not the chief in all matters concerning Saruman or the Ring: this absolutely opposes Tolkien (Tolkien 1994:243). The knowledge that Gandalf possesses is glossed over or relegated to other characters in the films tapering the presence the wizard commands. The *Istari* are capable of fault, as Gandalf admits he was lulled by the words of Saruman, but Elrond defers to the work Gandalf accomplished against the Shadow: "'We were all at fault,' said Elrond, 'and but for your vigilance the Darkness, maybe, would already be upon us …'" (Tolkien 1994:244). Elrond informs the Council of Gandalf's knowledge of the Ring: "But Gandalf has revealed to us that we cannot destroy it by any craft that we here possess" (Tolkien 1994:259). By changing these instances, Gandalf's role as the chief motivator behind matters concerning Saruman and the Ring is undermined. It is Gandalf's role in these matters that Aragorn acknowledges in Tolkien's original, when the crown is to be placed upon Aragorn's head at the coronation: "… let Mithrandir set it upon my head, if he will; for he has been the mover of all that has been accomplished, and this is his victory" (Tolkien 1994:946).

By placing Gandalf on an equal plane with men rather than presenting him as the exalted and wise wizard he is, Jackson *et al.* have the latitude to manipulate the character to suit the needs of their interpretation. In *TTT* and more so in the *RotK* this revisioned Gandalf breaks a prime *Istari* law: not to dominate the free will of the creatures of Middle-earth. "Saruman's flaw that leads him down the path of shadow is that he chooses to ignore the primal edict of the *Istari* – to guide the creatures of Middle-earth, but not directly take over for them, and especially not to force them against their will" (Petty 2003:147). Applying Petty's thoughts to the films, this Gandalf is as guilty as Saruman. In *TTT* Théoden is possessed by a spell of Saruman's. Gandalf strikes him upon the head by means of exorcism. Compare this scene of violence and humiliation with Tolkien's Gandalf who escorts King Théoden to a porch to see the fields of Rohan and breathe the free air, which releases him from the spell of Wormtongue's words (Tolkien 1994:504).

The greatest digression from Tolkien, however, concerns the dealings with Denethor. When Gandalf and Denethor interact for the first time, Pippin "saw a likeness between the two, and he felt a strain between them, almost as if he saw a line of smouldering fire, drawn from eye to eye that might suddenly burst into flame" (Tolkien 1994:740). We see the two duel from the instant Gandalf and Pippin arrive: "For a moment the eyes of Denethor glowed again as he faced Gandalf and Pippin felt once more the strain between their wills; but now almost it seemed as if their glances were like blades from eye to eye, flickering as they fenced" (Tolkien 1994:796). Jackson *et al.* unbalance the characters further by allowing Gandalf the White to be more dominant and Denethor the weaker. This film Denethor abandons his city's defense, refusing to call for aid by lighting the beacons. In the book, these beacons are already lit as Gandalf rides through the land into Gondor (Tolkien 1994:731). Tolkien's Denethor doesn't send his army home, as Jackson depicts when the host of Mordor is upon the city. Denethor knows "Much must be risked in war ... Cair Andros is manned, and no more can be sent so far. But I will not yield the River and the Pellenor unfought ..." (Tolkien 1994:798).

Saruman is the clear anti-hero in the first two films: the strengths that Gandalf the Grey possessed, the screenwriters gave to Saruman. Yet for the scenes here, Gandalf the White must have a will of his own, a character bolstered from somewhere. And, since his will has been transmuted to Saruman, Jackson *et al.* have now heighten this flattened Gandalf by bestowing him with qualities possessed by Tolkien's Denethor. It is unclear whether Denethor is distraught by the death of his son Boromir or by the use of the Palantír, which isn't revealed in the theatrical version of *RotK*. As Tolkien writes, we are given a clear indication when Denethor finally snaps and Gandalf wins the battle of wills in default. As Faramir lies wounded, we witness through Pippin's eyes: "As he watched, it seemed to him that Denethor grew old before his eyes, as if something had snapped in his proud will and his stern mind was overthrown" (Tolkien 1994:805). It is only after this that Gandalf then takes charge of the last defense of the City (Tolkien 1994:806), without having to physically assault Denethor in order to do so, as Jackson *et al.* depict.

The carefully balanced framework that Tolkien creates for his characters is one of opposing forces, Saruman and Gandalf, wizards who represent two sides of the same hero type, one who falls and one who ascends. Gandalf ascends taking Saruman's place at the head of his order as Gandalf the White, but then dominates the will of Denethor who is frenzied from the moment we meet him in the film. By excluding Elrond's regard for Gandalf and by creating this domination of Denethor by Gandalf, Jackson denies his audience the fact that Gandalf is the fulcrum, the balance-point between Middle-earth, and encroaching Darkness. It is the path of wisdom that Gandalf follows: a path that Saruman abandoned by heeding Sauron's call and changing his White robes for those of Many Colors (Tolkien 1994:252). By suggesting that Saruman is wiser than Gandalf the Grey, and not showing the true Fall from Grace as represented in breaking the White light or by properly depicting Saruman's physical end, Jackson *et al.* displace Tolkien's hierarchy of modes and Gandalf's distinguished role within it. Likewise, by creating a pathetic need for tension between Denethor and Gandalf, which sets Gandalf in the position of power, Jackson *et al.* have created a lesser character untrue to Tolkien.

Frye's modes continue beyond the first mode of myth to include romance:

> 2. If superior in *degree* to other men and to his environment, the hero is the typical hero of *romance*, whose actions are marvellous but who is himself identified as a human being. The hero of romance moves in a world in which the ordinary laws of nature are slightly suspended: prodigies of courage and endurance, unnatural to us, are natural to him, and enchanted weapons, talking animals, terrifying ogres and witches, and talismans of miraculous power violate no rule of probability once the postulates of romance have been established. Here we have moved from myth, properly so called, into legend, folk tale, *märchen*, and their literary affiliates and derivatives. (Frye 2000:33)

This 'superior in degree' applies to Aragorn, but so too to Frodo, for even though a hobbit and by Deborah Rogers' definition an ironic hero of Frye, Frodo is more than the other hobbits (Lobdell 1980:75-76). In *The Hobbit*, Tolkien sets up the Bagginses as slightly different than other hobbits: they had fairy blood (Tolkien 1997:2-3) and, by association Frodo has this 'otherness', this marginality about him (Tolkien 1994:22) seen by Faramir in Ithilien (Tolkien 1994:653). These are not everyday hobbits. Yet the "prodigies of courage" Frye speaks of are more natural to Frodo than to us. He has no fault, nor any question of conversing with dwarves, wizards, Elves, or appreciating Wizard magic – and all before the quest at hand is embarked upon (Tolkien 1994:24-25; 38-40). Yet, enchanted weaponry is not natural to him; Sting is not a common hobbit trifle, nor is the Ruling Ring something to scoff at. But Frodo is merely the tip of the proverbial iceberg. Aragorn and Faramir also belong to this mode of romance as well, and just as Gandalf was disgraced, so too were they.

Frye's modes go on into the merely mortal and less than mortal:

> 3. If superior in degree to other men but not to his natural environment, the hero is a leader. He has authority, passions, and powers of expression far greater than ours, but what he does is subject to both social criticism and to the order of nature. This is the hero of the *high mimetic* mode, of most epic and tragedy, and is primarily the kind of hero that Aristotle had in mind.
>
> 4. If superior neither to other men nor to his environment, the hero is one of us: we respond to a sense of his common humanity, and demand from the poet the same canons of probability that we find in our own experience. This gives us the hero of the *low mimetic* mode, of most comedy and of realistic fiction. "High" and "low" have no connotations of comparative value, but are purely diagrammatic, as they are when they refer to Biblical critics or Anglicans …
>
> 5. If inferior in power or intelligence to ourselves, so that we have the sense of looking down on a scene of bondage, frustration, or absurdity, the hero belongs to the *ironic* mode. This is still true when the reader feels that he is or might be in the same situation, as the situation is being judged by the norms of a greater freedom (Frye 2000:34).

Théoden and Éowyn fall under the category of *high mimesis*, as do a good majority of Tolkien's secondary characters. Another character often overlooked when dealing with those of the *high mimetic* mode is Sam. Deborah Rogers in her article "Everyclod and Everyhero" classifies Sam, in particular in the ironic mode, as does Shippey. But Sam bridges the final three modes, as do many of Tolkien's characters, easily shifting between them. When Sam resists the powers of the Ring, he has certain strengths that even Gandalf didn't have, which don't put Sam above Gandalf, but certainly elevate this crudely spoken hobbit beyond the level of the Gaffer, and even of Merry and Pippin – although they too can elevate themselves beyond the ironic into *high mimesis*. Gandalf barely wants to touch the Ring, as taken to the extreme by Peter Jackson in his films – Jackson never has Gandalf actually pick up the Ring. In "The Tower of Cirith Ungol" Sam not only touches the Ring, but he becomes a Ringbearer for a time, yet he can still overcome the Ring, and when asked to physically give it back to Frodo, he does so without a second thought (Tolkien 1994:716-19; 879-91). Sam exemplifies much of Tolkien's style: his ability to move amongst the modes, just as Frodo functions between the modes, shifting from *high mimetic* to the romantic mode.

Peter Jackson *et al.* restructure Tolkien's characters, lessening one trait and elevating another, thereby creating an unbalanced, unstructured film. The Nine Walkers, the Fellowship, are grouped together because there are the Nine, the Black Riders pursuing Frodo and the Ring. Elrond states what we as readers already know, being with Frodo on his flight from Bag End, being with Fatty Bolger as Crickhollow was attacked, and, of course, being with Frodo at the Ford of Bruinen: "The Company of the Ring shall be Nine; and the Nine Walkers shall be set against the Nine Riders that are evil. With you and your faithful servant, Gandalf will go. ... For the rest, they shall represent the other Free Peoples of the World ..." (Tolkien 1994:268). The film version of the Fellowship equals nine companions not because of this dichotomy set forth by Elrond, nor because of the holy meaning behind the number nine, but because Merry, Pippin, and Sam intrude upon the Council and force themselves upon Elrond. The three hobbits aren't included because of their abilities, nor as a representation of their own "Free Peoples" – the hobbits. Perhaps Jackson is referring, in his own part, to Deborah Rogers' 'EveryClod' that at their heart every hobbit is provincial, boorish, cloddish, and not of a heroic nature:

> Hobbits are ... easy for the reader to identify with. ... We are all in some way small, provincial, and comfort-loving – and we see ourselves as such. At first we like to imagine ourselves as heroes, but experience makes us sceptical; we become convinced that, in fairness, we are not heroes. Maybe as Lords of the Jungle we broke into our neighbor's shadetree, and got spanked. Maybe our

> term in the army ended, but the war kept on for years. Maybe 'our' leading man married another leading lady. We become wary of admitting even to ourselves that we like to see ourselves as heroic. One of the notable features of twentieth century literature is the antihero; Northrop Frye's ironic literary mode has taken over our everyday lives. Everyclod is at the center of our vision, which has become cloddish. ... But this is not Tolkien's mode. One of the reasons he is likable and unusual among contemporary authors is that he does not focus on the cloddish, though he does focus on the hobbits. Bilbo, Frodo, Sam, Merry, and Pippin are all to a greater or lesser extent billed as Everyclod at the beginnings of their stories, but as we know, each of them becomes a hero. (Rogers 1980:75-76)

But, even Rogers admits that each in their own turn, the hobbits all become heroes. This intrusion of the hobbits from their "cloddish" way of living into the depths of heroism may be Jackson and the screenwriters' fundamental belief that the hobbits belong to the ironic mode alone and cannot grow beyond it. When speaking of Tolkien's heroes, in *Tolkien and the Great War*, John Garth echoes Rogers' view of the hobbits, yet he doesn't limit himself to one species of Middle-earth inhabitant alone; Garth broadens his view to include all denizens of Tolkien's world:

> His characters set out more often than not, from a point something like Frye's 'ironic' mode, in bondage, frustrations, or absurdity, but they break free of those conditions, and so become heroes. They achieve greater power of action than ourselves, and so reach the condition of characters in the older modes identified by Northrop Frye in his cyclical view of literary history: myth, romance, and epic. (Garth 2003:305)

Tolkien's heroes ascend to higher states of heroism, climbing the ladder of Frye's modes to achieve greater heroic status than when they first set out. The film heroes are reluctant to break free of their own bondage and levels of frustration. Frodo, in the film, draws his sword on Weathertop against the Ringwraiths yet drops it in fear followed by a stab wound which weakens him far quicker and is unable to defend himself at all when he reaches the Ford. He is lured more and more into the depths of the Ring's corruptible nature with the help from Gollum. Throughout the film he is continuously fawning over and fondling the Ring as opposed to his original reaction to it in Rivendell when asked by Gandalf (not Elrond) to "Bring out the Ring":

> There was a hush, and all turned their eyes on Frodo. He was shaken by a sudden shame and fear; and he felt a great reluctance to reveal the Ring and a loathing

of its touch. He wished he was far away. The Ring gleamed and flickered as he held it up before them in his trembling hand. (Tolkien 1994:241)

Jackson depicts Frodo and most of the council as having fallen under the Ring's 'spell'. While the Council argues as to what the Ring's fate will be Frodo states that he will take the Ring to Mordor. It is unclear whether he chooses to do so to stop the bickering or to bring the Ring straight to Sauron while under its spell. Perhaps Jackson's failure to have Frodo defend himself on Weathertop – an internal desire to cease the external pressure of the Ring or an internal acquiescence to an internal desire to take the Ring to its maker – is a harkening to two schools of thought discussed in *The Road to Middle-earth*. On the one hand lies the belief that evil is an external force which coaxes the individual to action, on the other is the philosophy that evil is internal and part of the individuals mind.

> Tolkien's way of presenting this philosophical duality was through the Ring. It seems in several ways inconsistent. For one thing it is notoriously elastic, and not entirely passive. It 'betrayed' Isildur to the arrows of the orcs; it 'abandoned' Gollum, says Gandalf, in response to the 'dark thought from Mirkwood' of its master; it all but betrays Frodo in the *Prancing Pony* when it slips on his finger and proves his invisibility to the spies for the Nazgûl then present. ... For all that it remains an object which cannot move itself or save itself from destruction. It has to work through agency of its possessors, and especially by picking out weak points of their characters – possessiveness in Bilbo, fear in Frodo, patriotism in Boromir, pity in Gandalf. When Frodo passes it to Gandalf so that its identity can be confirmed, 'It felt suddenly very heavy, as if *either it or Frodo himself* was in some way reluctant for Gandalf to touch it' (I, 58, my italics). Maybe the Ring is magically conscious of Gandalf's power: maybe, though, Frodo is already afraid that he will lose it. These two possible views are kept up throughout the three volumes: sentient creature, or psychic amplifier. (Shippey 1983:108)

Tolkien describes a more rational decision by his Ringbearer, "Only after hearing the debate and realizing the nature of the quest did Frodo accept the burden of his mission" (*Letters* 241). Jackson *et al.* not only want us to believe the Ring has more power than Tolkien imagined it did,[9] but they also wish us to believe Frodo is fouler and possesses a higher degree of internal evil than

---

9 The Ring 'speaks' as Gandalf discusses, over tea, its history with Frodo in the "Shadow of the Past" scene in *Fellowship of the Ring* and it speaks again the lines in the Black Speech that Gandalf spoke in the book during the "Council of Elrond scene". By transferring these lines partly from Gandalf to the Ring, Jackson *et al.* equate the Ring as an equal to Gandalf.

Tolkien wanted us to think, thereby making him not a hero of romance, but a hero of a lower mode. Only in the end does Frodo realize his failure, his remedy is to heave Gollum into the fire at Mount Doom. The film's rendering of Frodo's actions is the opposite of Tolkien's original, where at least he has some "tenacity in trying" (Garth 2003:303). Jackson' depiction of Frodo also lessens the hobbit's free will against annihilation. Frodo chose to grasp Galadriel's phial and not the Ring (Tolkien 1994:691). In the film version of this scene, the phial is forgotten, and when Frodo is physically reaching for the Ring at the behest of the Ringwraith during the Dead Marshes scene, Sam takes Frodo's hand, physically preventing Frodo from touching the Ring thereby removing Frodo's free will. Tolkien exemplifies Frodo as the leader amongst the hobbits. Though weakened by the wound he suffered from the Morgul blade, he still summons the courage to face the enemy head on. He invokes divinity on Weathertop, as Strider later tells the hobbits "... more deadly to him was the name of Elbereth" (Tolkien 1994:193). The decision to not include the invocation of a divine representation of Middle-earth diminishes the aspect of Providence in Tolkien's world and strips the protagonists of this 'final' ray of hope. The heroes can only harm their enemies via direct action throughout the course of the film. Passivity seems to have no place in a blockbuster feature film, yet Jackson's Frodo is far more passive than intended and the shift we all feel is a taming of Frodo from a true hero of romance, to a lesser hero of a lower mode.

Tolkien's presentation of Frodo harkens to the officers with whom Tolkien was himself familiar with in the army. His fellow officers were all learned men. Their academic prowess earned them the position officer. In Jackson's film we rarely see such prowess in relation to Frodo, or indeed any of the hobbits. If Jackson had included the hobbits encounter with Gildor just outside the Shire, it may have hampered the film's progression of the story, however it would have reflected the knowledge the hobbit possessed and would have placed Frodo in a higher mimetic mode as a leader. There are only minor occasions where Frodo's knowledge, and the wisdom passed to him from Bilbo are referenced in the film. Frodo understands portions of Aragorn's song, in the extended version of *FotR*, he guesses the password to enter Moria. As the hobbits arrive on the outskirts of the Shire they hear "singing in the fair elven tongue, of which Frodo knew only a little and the others knew nothing" (Tolkien 1994:78). The hobbits knew the travelers upon the road were elves, but it was Frodo who knew the particulars. Tolkien describes the other hobbits, especially Merry and Pippin who possess no knowledge outside the Shire, in a fashion similar to those who joined the army, those not as fortunate in education as he was. Tolkien has a "deep sympathy for the 'Tommy', especially the plain soldier from the agricultural counties" (Garth 2003:95). This is not to say that the other hobbits were not learned in their own right, but were not as privileged as Frodo. Gildor supports this after Frodo is the only one of the hobbits to greet him in the high-elven speech:

> *'Elen síla lúmenn' omentielvo*, a star shines upon the hour of our meeting,' he added in the high-elven speech.
>
> 'Be careful, friends!' cried Gildor laughing 'Speak no secrets! Here is a scholar in the Ancient Tongue. Bilbo was a good master. Hail Elf-friend!' ... (Tolkien 1994:79)

Brian Sibley[10] relates the link of Frodo and Sam to that as "an archetypal English thing and it is the relationship between an officer in the army and his batman, the person who is of much lower order in society and rank ..." Frodo's actions on Weathertop, his calling upon the aid of Elbereth, are typical reactions from an army officer facing danger in the midst of injury and weakness, summoning strength from character and status. The screenwriters render these scenes in opposition to the books where Merry, Pippin, and Sam all draw their swords. Yet in the film, it is Frodo who fails to confront his enemy. Boyens states, concerning Frodo and Sam's officer to batman relationship

> ... that's great for Sam's character to understand where that came from, but you don't necessarily want to cast Frodo in the light of one of those pampered officers who has someone running around shining their shoes. It is not so much that we moved Sam away from his roots, as we tried not to give the impression that Frodo was in any way his superior, because I don't think, at all believe, Frodo feels that.

Tolkien doesn't necessarily reveal how Frodo feels of the structure of his relationship with Sam. Though grateful to have him there on the journey, it is through Frodo and Sam's interaction and experiences that exemplify the officer and batman bond. Sibley comments that "*The Lord of the Rings* has many complexities

---

10 Subsequent references to commentary from Sibley, Boyens, and Wenham are from the documentary "From Book to Script: Finding the Story" released as part of *TTT* extended edition DVD.

in its narrative and units, but its heart is the relationship of Frodo and Sam." The officer leads in turmoil, he sets an example, the batman tends to the officer's needs and takes care of him, but faces just as much danger as the officer does in battle. Tolkien's own experience in WWI (which these motifs draw from) shows he is anything but pampered. It is also through this officer and batman dichotomy that we see Frodo placed in the romantic or high mimetic mode, above Sam, at certain points in the trilogy. Boyens' desire to depict Sam and Frodo on "equal footing" reflects the flattening of the modes. Frye discusses this technique with regard to low mimetic tragedy:

> The best word for low mimetic or domestic tragedy is, perhaps, pathos, and pathos has close relation to the sensational reflex of tears. Pathos presents its hero as isolated by weakness, which appeals to our sympathy because it is on our own level of experience. (Frye 2000:38)

By removing Frodo's knowledge base, and putting Sam and Frodo on the same ground, Boyens has firmly placed Frodo in the *low mimetic* mode because of a desire (on the part of the screenwriters) for pathos. The strengths Tolkien gives Frodo are stripped away. He is left with only weakness, which causes him to refuse his own defense on Weathertop and tell Sam to 'go home' on the stairs of Cirith Ungol. Drawing his sword on Sam in Osgiliath and rejecting Sam's loyalty at Cirith Ungol betrays the officer/batman dynamic, and their friendship. Frodo appears physically fragile when he becomes easily ensnared in Shelob's web, and allows Gollum to physically beat him before Shelob's attack. This progresses to Jackson's interpretation of the events at Mount Doom when Frodo claims the Ring. The impact of Frodo claiming the Ring in the film is lessened by the exclusion of Frodo's full statement at the critical moment:

> I have come ... But I do not choose now to do what I came to do. I will not do this deed. The Ring is mine! (Tolkien 1994:981)

Jackson *et al.* have stated that the Ring is of utmost evil and power. Yet Frodo is able to resist it enough to push Gollum into the fire after their struggle thereby taking the Ring from Frodo forever. This action contradicts everything the screenwriters have sought to establish when concerning the Ring. Why tamper with Tolkien's original, which has Gollum dancing wildy and slipping over the edge (Tolkien 1994:982). Jackson *et al.* make Frodo passive when Tolkien has him active (on Weathertop and at the Ford of Bruinen), yet have him active when he should have no action left. Tolkien discusses Frodo's failure and claiming of the Ring:

> If you re-read all the passages dealing with Frodo and the Ring, I think that you will see that not only was it *quite impossible* for him to surrender the Ring, in act or will, especially at its point of maximum power, but that this failure was adumbrated from far back. He was honoured because he had accepted the burden voluntarily, and had then done all that was within his utmost physical and mental strength to do. He (and the Cause) were saved by Mercy: by the supreme value and efficacy of Pity and forgiveness of injury ... No, Frodo 'failed' ... But one must face the fact: the power of Evil in the world is *not* finally resistible by incarnate creatures, however 'good'. (*Letters* 251-52)

In the following letter, written the next day, Tolkien points out what so many, Jackson *et al.* included, have chosen to disregard: Frodo failed as a hero, not because he was weak but he had no strength left to fight:

> I have just had another letter regarding the failure of Frodo. Very few seem to have observed it. But following the logic of the plot, it was clearly inevitable, as an event. And surely it is more significant a real event than a mere 'fairy-story' ending in which the hero is indomitable? It is possible for the good, even the saintly, to be subjected to a power of evil which is too great for them to over come – in themselves. In this case the cause (not the 'hero') was triumphant, because by the exercise of pity, mercy and forgiveness of injury a situation was produced in which all was redressed and disaster averted. (*Letters* 252-53)

The Ring as Tolkien states is "*not* finally resistible by incarnate creatures, however 'good'." This acknowledges that although, as Shippey pointed out, there may be a struggle within Frodo with concern to the Ring (Shippey 1983:108), yet Frodo is good. He is our hero of romance, because he struggles with the weight of the world, as he knows it – this struggle, whether prompted by internal or external catalysts – is slightly beyond the everyday struggles we as mere mortals face. A hero of romance doesn't have to worry about bill collectors or irritating in-laws. A hero of romance is concerned with universal struggles between Good and Evil, Sacred Quests, the pursuit of Truth, heroic ideals, and magical Rings. Yet Frodo is also a common 'man'. He is identifiable through his struggle, and we all wonder what we would do if faced with such a task. Would we have pity for Gollum? Would we have the strength to destroy the Ring? Would we *go* in the first place? This 'applicability' places Frodo in the *high mimetic* and, from time to time, in the *low mimetic*[11] modes. During the progression of the film, Frodo exhibits qualities that are less than 'good'. His treatment of Sam, his alliance with Gollum, and his actions at Mount Doom reflect wickedness inherent inside Frodo. In both letters Tolkien addresses the aspects of mercy, pity, and forgiveness, values which Bilbo showed Gollum in *The Hobbit*. After Frodo claims he cannot feel any pity for Gollum, Gandalf foreshadows Gollum's role: "My heart tells me that he has some part to play yet, for good or ill, before then end; and when that comes, the pity of Bilbo may rule the fate of many" (Tolkien 1994:58). Jackson *et al.* allow Frodo to have pity upon Gollum throughout the films, which betrays the pity of Bilbo, and undermines Tolkien's original where Frodo only looked upon Gollum with true mercy after speaking with Faramir. Frodo knew he couldn't succeed in his quest without Gollum, and reminds Sam: "But do you remember Gandalf's words: *Even Gollum may have something yet to do*? But for him, Sam I could not have destroyed the Ring" (Tolkien 1994:926). R.J. Reilly states in his article 'Tolkien and the Fairy Story' that "Frodo becomes increasingly tempted to keep the Ring for himself, and in the end it is really against his own will that the Ring is destroyed." Jackson reveals Frodo wilfully shoving Gollum into the fire, essentially murdering him and destroying the Ring simultaneously thereby succeeding in what he set out to do. By acting in this fashion Gollum has no active role to play as implied by Gandalf thus lessening the mercy of Bilbo.

These events at the end of the third film don't follow the logic of Tolkien's plot and nullify the element of mercy set forward in Jackson's initial plot in *FotR*. Throughout Jackson's trilogy, Frodo fails to exert any free will of his own. Reilly, when discussing various opposing views to the hallmark 'critique' – or castigation – of *LotR*: Edmund Wilson's aforementioned article reveals the "ethical character of the trilogy" and its relevance to the everyday world. When speaking of the hobbits, Reilly quotes critic Patricia Meyers: "Frodo and Sam ... are clearly endowed with free will, and free will implies a structured universe." How are we to view Frodo in the film and the universal structure Jackson builds? For Jackson *et al.* there is no free will. In a 1963 letter Tolkien writes about Frodo claiming the Ring and his 'failure':

---

11 Frodo's place in the *low mimetic* mode seems to be confined to the beginning of the book. Once he sets out, he has passed beyond the borders of his land – both literally and figuratively.

> It is a very important point ... the events on Mt. Doom proceed simply from the logic of the tale up to that time ... it became at last quite clear that Frodo after all that had happened would be incapable of voluntarily destroying the Ring ... indeed Frodo 'failed' as a hero. (*Letters* 325-26)

Following the logic of Jackson's sequence of events does Frodo's pushing Gollum into the fire show his incompetence at completing the Quest? This interpretation of Frodo has him tempted early on to use the Ring, in *FotR* when the hobbits are hiding from the Black Riders, which contradicts Tolkien's Frodo, who reproaches himself for his weakness of will after putting it on at Weathertop (Tolkien 1994:194). Perhaps moviegoers, unfamiliar with Tolkien's unadulterated text, view Frodo as hero, but after all of Gollum's manipulations and temptations would Frodo really be able to destroy the Ring and become the hero Jackson wants him to be? Jackson *et al.* undermine the intelligence of their audience, disregard the intelligence of Tolkien's readers, and succeed only in flattening Frodo from an extraordinary hero capable of being both a true hero of romance and a hero of the high mimetic mode into a monotone character of irony and pathos.

The anonymous author of the 13th century Icelandic prose epic *The Saga of the Volsungs* based his stories on ancient Norse heroic material. Tolkien was inspired by these tales, especially those concerning Sigurd the Dragon Slayer, the Goths, Huns, and Burgundians, amongst other ancient cultures. These ancient narratives serve as models and guideposts to heroic motif and lives. Tolkien's characters encounter problems on the social, political and spiritual levels and some play roles from lost king to divine messenger. The heroes of Middle-earth don't doubt their path, and aren't limited by its boundaries. Frodo knows danger, and faces it unwaveringly at Weathertop, and the Ford of Bruinen. Gandalf is the divine messenger sent to Middle-earth to guide the Free Peoples against the growing darkness. These characters and their companions all exhibit the wisdom of Sigurd and display their ability to survive in heroic modes far above our stations in life. Their actions also exhibit their active roles in their own fate and their ability to understand that such fate may not be all glory and roses. "When men come to battle, a fearless heart serves a man better than a sharp sword" (Byock 1990:65). Such a symbol of destiny is the sword.[12] Aragorn carries the shards of Narsil as a reminder of his destiny and his role as the heir of Isilidur. The broken sword

---

12 Petty (2003:274).

motif is seen throughout many ancient sagas and in the high romance of the Middle Ages.[13] With this symbol of destiny it is easier for Aragorn to embrace his future role as king of Gondor, whose heart is fearless. Some may say, however, carrying the shards, of a broken sword is not logical. The future king of Gondor in Jackson's trilogy is without his symbol of destiny or identity. Speaking with Arwen in Rivendell in *FotR*, the screenwriters give lines originally spoken by Aragorn in the novel to Arwen, thereby changing his role as an awaiting heir to a reluctant Ranger. "I am but the heir of Isildur, not Isildur himself" (Tolkien 1994:241) states Tolkien's Aragorn to Boromir, which changes to "You are Isildur's heir, not Isildur himself." Perhaps, by altering this it wouldn't giveaway the plot of *RotK* to an unfamiliar audience, but this reinterpreted Aragorn not only rejects his role, showing reluctance to take on the mantle as a hero of high romance, but reflects him as a hero craving the pathos of *low mimetic* mode. Arwen regurgitates Aragorn's lines as he places Narsil's broken hilt back on its shrine after Boromir allowed it to carelessly clatter to the floor. This particular scene is glaringly antithetical to Tolkien's original. Both Faramir and his brother Boromir share a dream, which prompts them to "Seek for the Sword that was broken …" (Tolkien 1994:239-41). Upon hearing of this dream Aragorn stands amidst the Council and casts the Sword before Elrond: "Here is the Sword that was Broken" (Tolkien 1994:240). After Frodo reveals the Ring, the history of the sword, too, is revealed by Aragorn:

> For the Sword that was Broken is the Sword of Elendil that broke beneath him when he fell. It has been treasured by his heirs when all other heirlooms were lost; for it was spoken of old among us that it should be made again when the Ring, Isildur's Bane, was found. (Tolkien 1994:241)

Jackson allows Rivendell to be the keeper of this now-forgotten heirloom, changing its status in Aragorn's life and its importance in the fight against Sauron, thus also changing the mission of Boromir. By disconnecting Aragorn from the sword, Jackson loses touch with the sagas, like Sigurd, which inspired Tolkien. When Aragorn tells Boromir "… it was spoken of old among us that it should be made again when the Ring, Isildur's Bane, was found" he is telling

---

13 Most notably in the *Saga of the Volsungs* and the wishes of King Sigmund as he lay dying, "Guard well the broken pieces of the sword. From them can be made a good sword, which will be called Gram. Our son will bear it and with it accomplish great deeds, which will never be forgotten. And his name will endure while the world remains." (Byock 1990:54).

us that the sword will assist in the fight against the Dark Lord. The re-forging of the Sword that was Broken is inherently tied to the finding of the Ring and their ancient past. This is the reason Tolkien had it re-forged in Rivendell immediately after the Ring is revealed. In the Jackson interpretation, Aragorn is given the re-forged sword in *RotK* by Elrond, and its importance is only to identify Aragorn to the Dead King on the Paths of the Dead. This reflects the screenwriters' need to bring Aragorn from the heights of romantic mode to a more common mode of pathos, and their first step is to distance him from the symbol of valor and ancestry, his sword.

Another means of stripping away the hero in Aragorn is to remove his enchantment. In the film as theatrically released (at the writing of this article the authors had no access to any extended versions of *RotK*) Aragorn is not a healer. In "The Houses of Healing" Tolkien links this ability to heal – not merely apply salves or mend wounds but to heal by divine Providence – with his royal heritage: "The hands of the King are the hands of a healer. And so the rightful King could ever be known" (Tolkien 1994:935). Jackson's view of Aragorn makes him an adept herbalist, nothing more. Just after Frodo's wound on Weathertop, Aragorn enlists the aid of Sam to find *athelas* or kingsfoil, which the Ranger chews like so much tobacco and jabs into Frodo's wound. The ability to heal is reserved for the Elves alone.

Aragorn in the books does not merely use the herb to heal. The healing comes from within himself; he speaks to the patient, breathes on the *athelas*, crushes the leaves, sprinkles them on boiling water, and calls the spirit of the afflicted back from the Darkness: all rituals forgotten to Jackson (Tolkien 1992:192-194; 846-850). Aragorn is reduced and his bloodline is only connected to a failed Isildur, rather than possessing this enchanted connection, which is his legacy recognized by the wise: "He is Aragorn son of Arathorn,' said Elrond; 'and he is descended through many fathers from Isildur Elendil's son of Minas Ithil. He is the Chief of the Dúnedain in the North, and few are now left of that folk" (Tolkien 1994:240). Jackson *et al.* have created a disunity between the hero of the high romantic mode that was the unadulterated Aragorn of Tolkien's original epic and the flattened hero of the pathos-driven *low mimetic* mode, evident in the film trilogy. But Jackson doesn't limit the diminution of Aragorn to what we've already stated. Creating another of Frye's "factitious appeals" to the "tear-jerking" *low mimetic* mode (Frye 2000:39), he furthers Aragorn's humiliation. After an anti-climatic battle (which never happened in the books) with the Warg Riders in *TTT*, Aragorn's character is pushed into the ironic mode by literally falling over a cliff. This action not only diminishes the horrific loss of Gandalf at the Bridge of Khazad-Dûm, but stands crude testimony, pointing to the screenwriter's version of tragic irony. Frye says:

> Tragic irony ... does not necessarily have any tragic hamartia or pathetic obsession: he is only somebody who gets isolated from his society. This the central principle of tragic irony is that whatever happens to the hero should be causally out of line with his character. (Frye 2000:41)

Jackson *et al.* have built a momentum behind Aragorn's character, a momentum hinged on his prowess in battle. But, in an attempt to isolate him – and give a few moments of screen time for Liv Tyler's character Arwen – this episode completely disparages the cinematic hero we – the audience – have grown accustomed to. This entire episode, this isolation at once disallows Aragorn's presence, his being, the symbol of who and what he is as easily as Boromir, in the Council of Elrond scene, dismisses Aragorn as the return of Gondor's King. This repudiation of Aragorn embodies the film character's reluctance to accept his own status as King. In the final film, Jackson *et al.* abandons the theme of the reluctant heir of Isildur to have Aragorn disrespect the crown and the people of Gondor by barging into the city, disregarding the then Steward, Faramir, and taking the crown without any thought to honor, fealty, or ritual. This is contrary to an Aragorn revealed as embarrassed during Elrond's Council when Legolas reveals the lineage as the heir of the throne of Gondor. But Jackson hasn't simply changed Aragorn into a lower form of hero by having him essentially usurp the crown. Faramir is another character humiliated by the screenwriter's desire for pathos. Perhaps the extended version of *RotK* will alter our perception, but to have Aragorn disregard Faramir's position, the filmmaker's have done a grave disservice to the meaning of heroism in this tale. Compare the film version to the ritualized acceptance of the returned king:

> Faramir met Aragorn ... and he knelt and said: 'The last Steward of Gondor begs leave to surrender his office.' And he held out a white rod; but Aragorn took the rod and gave it back, saying: 'That office is not ended, and it will be a thee and thine heirs' as long as my line shall last. Do now thy office!'

> Then Faramir stood up and spoke ...: 'Men of Gondor hear now the Steward of this Realm! Behold! One has come to claim the kingship again at last. Here is Aragorn son of Arathorn, chieftain of the Dúnedain of Arnor, Captain of the Host of the West, bearer of the Star of the North, wielder of the Sword Reforged, victorious in battle, whose hands bring healing, the Elfstone, Elessar of the line of Valandil, Isildur's son, Elendil's son of Númenor. Shall he be king and enter into the City and dwell there?'
>
> And all the host and all the people cried *yea* with one voice. (Tolkien 1994:945-46)

Here the people of Gondor and Faramir must first accept Aragorn in order for him to be their rightful king. Jackson's version allows his victory in battle and the insistence of Elrond[14] to be the deciding factor for his ascension to king-hood. Tolkien also includes the ancient crown of Gondor's last king to be brought forth signifying that the coming of Aragorn is indeed the return of the king:

> '... using the authority of the Steward, I have today brought hither from Rath Dínen the crown of Eärnur the last king, whose days passed in the time of our long fathers of old.' Then the guards stepped forward, and Faramir opened the casket, and he held up an ancient crown. (Tolkien 1994:946)

When Faramir announces to the people Aragorn's names, titles, and expected station, bringing forth the crown, his reverence for and knowledge of his people's history is evident. He exhibits his wisdom when he speaks to Frodo in "Window on the West". Garth discusses Faramir's importance: "Faramir, of course, is an officer but also a scholar, with a reverence for the old histories and sacred values that help him through a bitter war" (Garth 2003:310). The scholarly officer ideal in Faramir is a model drawn from Tolkien and his colleagues during the bitterness of WWI. "As far as any character is 'like me' it is Faramir – except that I lack what all my characters possess (let psychoanalysts note!) Courage!" (*Letters* 232). Tolkien's humility precedes him, for it took great courage to face the atrocities of World War I described in Garth's *Tolkien and the Great War*. The comparison of Tolkien to Faramir deepens when Tolkien reveals

---

14 When bringing Aragorn the reforged blade, Elrond coaxes Aragorn to be all he can be – to become the Returned King. Yet again Jackson *et al.* have written themselves into the proverbial corner. In the extended version of *FotR*, Elrond challenges Gandalf's assertion that the realm of Men will succeed. Elrond then refutes Aragorn and denies the Ranger's ability to accept his own legacy. Are we to believe the harsh castigation has been countered for the sake of Elrond's daughter alone? The manner of the hypocrisy smacks not of a change of heart, but of an incompetence on the part of the screenwriters.

when "Faramir appeals of his private vision of the Great Wave, he speaks for me. That vision and dream has been ever with me ..." (*Letters* 232) Tolkien's dream spoke of a Great Wave "towering up and coming in ineluctably over the trees and green fields", which "always ends by surrender" (*Letters* 213; 347). The dream translated into Faramir's discussion with Frodo of the downfall of Númenor and his fears for his people (Tolkien: 1994:662-65). Both men, who served during the bitterness of war, shared the overwhelming vision of their people being swallowed up by Darkness (Tolkien 1994: 651). Tolkien invested in Faramir qualities any soldier would possess when away from home: sharing good conversation, education, knowledge, and the missed comforts with kindred spirits. He shares food and drink with Frodo and Sam. He is a vision of the chivalric knight, a light for them in dark places, he is "a Prince of Ithilien, the greatest noble after Dol Amroth" (*Letters* 324). The culture Tolkien presents is more antiquated than that of the high medieval romances of King Arthur, but one that is "less corrupt" and, in many ways, nobler (*Letters* 324). In essence, Faramir would not so desire the Ring as his brother Boromir had because of the wisdom Faramir himself possessed (Shippey 1983:106). His knowledge of how man can fall from Grace, as the Númenoreans had, did not allow him to succumb to the 'spell' of the Ring. He understood the 'peril of Men,' unlike his brother who desired this 'weapon' for Gondor: it was this desire that was Boromir's Fall (Tolkien 1994:665). Faramir knew that "there are some perils from which a man must flee" (Tolkien 1994:666). The differences in these two Gondorian brothers were what made them unique and apart from one another, at least philosophically and hierarchically. Faramir's knowledge of himself and his people elevate him above the tragic flaw of Boromir's desire and Fall.

The deviation of Faramir's character from book to film harkens to the screenwriters' desire for pathos in Aragorn – resulting in the 'Brego the Wonder Horse'[15] scene in *TTT*: an isolation of character into irony. The screenwriters decided to insert the Cirith Ungol and Shelob sequences into the beginning of the third film. Their reasoning: the huge battle sequence of Helm's Deep undercut Shelob's impact making her anti-climatic in the second film. Feeling left with a huge gap in the story-line, how then would they fill the gap? Boyens

---

15 The scene of Aragorn falling over the cliff, as so affectionately named over the Internet.

gives her explanation for Faramir's total delineation: "That is why Faramir had to become an obstacle, which is why he takes them to Osgiliath." When they decided to shift the scenes, why must Faramir become an obstacle? Wouldn't the Osgiliath scenes be anti-climatic as well? Boyens' intent is to create a Ring at the center of their tale, which is "one of the most evil things ever created." It is a Ring that supposedly corrupts all who know of it or come in contact with it within this universal structure. They do not observe their own laws though when Legolas, Gimli, Merry, and Pippin, all protagonists who journey for hundreds of miles in the constant company of the Ring, are not corrupted, or even desire it in the least. Earlier, during the Council of Elrond scene, Gimli even makes the attempt to destroy it. Tolkien tells his son Christopher in a 1944 letter that Faramir "… is holding up the 'catastrophe' by a lot of stuff about the history of Gondor and Rohan (and some very sound reflections no doubt on martial glory and true glory)" (*Letters* 79). Here is a character of upstanding stature, educated and knowledgeable of the fault of Men and exemplifies the spirit of free will (*Letters* 280):

> 'Alas for Boromir! It was a sore trial!' he said. How you have increased my sorrow, you two strange wanders from a far country, bearing the peril of Men! But you are less judges of Men than I of Halflings. We are truth-speakers, we men of Gondor. We boast seldom, and then perform, or die in the attempt. *Not if I found it on the highway would I take it* I said. Even if I were such a man as to desire this thing, and even though I knew not clearly what this thing was when I spoke, still I should take those words as a vow, and be held by them.
>
> But I am not such a man. Or I am wise enough to know that there are some perils from which a man must flee. Sit at peace! And be comforted, Samwise. If you seem to have stumbled, think that it was fated to be so. Your heart is shrewd as well as faithful, and saw clearer than your eyes. For strange though it may seem, it was safe to declare this to me. It may even help the master that you love. It shall turn to his good, if it is in my power. So be comforted. But do not even name this thing aloud. Once is enough. (Tolkien 1994:665-66)

This particular moment parallels Galadriel's test in Lothlórien. The quality of Faramir is exploited in the film to suit the needs of the screenwriters who felt that he needed to go on a journey, a journey which would isolate him from his society and bring pathos into the tale. This change allows him to be as desirous of the Ring as his brother Boromir, as compared in the two scenes of Boromir holding the Ring on Caradhras, and Faramir holding it with his sword in Henneth Annun, thereby unsettling the dynamic of their characters.

The carefully balanced dichotomy, written by Tolkien, illustrates the attributes of wisdom and desire. Boyens and David Wenham, the actor who portrayed Faramir, lead us to believe that Faramir needed to go on a journey to actualize the power of the Ring, and acknowledge what it did to Boromir. Tolkien, however, structures his character in order to define and provide us with this crucial information throughout the tale. Tolkien also endows Faramir with qualities reminiscent of Gandalf. Faramir's function in Tolkien's tale is to parallel the hospitality of another virulent force within the book, a force with whom the Ring has no effect at all: Tom Bombadil.

Upon announcing the exclusion of Tom Bombadil in the films, Jackson and specifically Boyens mention Bombadil's resistance to the Ring which wouldn't work in the pace of the film. Bombadil offers similar comforts to the hobbits as Faramir does in Henneth Annun – food, drink, rest, knowledge, good conversation, and safety from the encroaching Darkness. Boyens claims that the screenwriters were trying to "up the tension" by removing Bombadil's safe-haven between the pursuing Black Riders and the introduction of the mysterious Strider. In the same breath she says it would be "death on film" if you have a puzzling chap offer Frodo and Sam a cup of tea saying 'I'll do anything to help' – she refers simultaneously to Bombadil and to Faramir. In this line of thinking, by not having either character tempted by the Ring, "the Ring [is stripped] of all power". Why, then, include Faramir at all? Why change him rather than Tom? Wenham explains that "Phillipa, Fran and Peter gave their reasons as to why they thought the character should go along a different journey and a very believable journey as well." The journey he speaks of refers to the physical act of shanghaiing the hobbits, but it again refers to Frye's "tear-jerking" desire for sensationalism. Which is more sensational, having Faramir calmly resist the Ring as Gandalf does, or have him drag the hobbits miles off course to Osgiliath at sword's point, with the promise of taking them to Gondor? Boyens defends her interpretation as "something people can relate to".

The changes undermine not only how Tolkien structured the tale, but it also renders Faramir as less than Boromir and disrespects the connection Faramir has to Tolkien himself. Why would the audience not be intelligent enough to believe that Faramir has the ability to resist the Ring through wisdom alone rather than a melodramatic need to overcome his desire for it (Frye 2000:40)? These changes for the films' purposes and the comments made concerning them subtly hint that Tolkien's writing is less than believable. In defense of his choices and quality Faramir states: "I had no lure or desire to do other than I have done" (Tolkien 1994:667). It is in support of this quality and his choices that Sam replies: "But I can say this: you have an air too, sir, that reminds me of, of – well, Gandalf, of wizards" (Tolkien 1994:667). This is the catastrophe he upholds that Tolkien spoke of, the catastrophe of Númenor and his people, and a reflection of his role as a hero of the *high mimetic* mode.

The beauty of Tolkien's heroes is that he draws on and populates Middle-earth with numerous hero types (Petty 2003:260). Many critics from Tom Shippey to Anne Petty to John Garth, all range Tolkien's heroes from high myth to the ironic mode. In Tolkien's fiction, there are many levels of heroism, as well as many levels of evil. Tolkien displays characters from all of Frye's categorizations, yet pushes beyond hinting at a sixth mode above and outside Frye's categorizations: evangelium (Shippey 2000:223) which is the combination of all Frye's mode woven into a tapestry of fluid characterizations. By not adhering to Tolkien's heroic structures, Jackson demoralizes and diminishes each of Tolkien's characters, reducing their impact, making them flat, unstructured, thereby robbing them of their deeper meaning.

About the authors

Anthony Scott Burdge (Founder, Chairman and Webmaster of Heren Istarion) was born in 1972 in Los Angeles, California and is a decorated United States Navy, Desert Storm Veteran. He has walked the paths of Middle-earth since an early age and currently majors in Literature at Hunter College NYC. His studies range includes Norse Mythology, Medieval Literature, and Judeo-Christian ideology and text. His interest in Tolkien grew from the age of eight, when he received his first copy of *The Hobbit*. Over the last decade Mr. Burdge has delved into the mythological world while studying the works of J.R.R. Tolkien. He is an aspiring writer and a contributor to the forthcoming *Encyclopedia of Children's Literature* by Oxford University Press

Jessica Burke (Co-Chair Heren Istarion, Editor-in-Chief Parma Nölé) was born in 1974 in Brooklyn, New York. She has her Bachelor's Degree in English Literature from Brooklyn College, and is attending C.U.N.Y. for her Master's in English. Ms. Burke has studied anthropology, folklore, Medieval Literature, Mysticism, 19th Century literature and Judeo-Christian theology. She also has written an undergraduate thesis on the nature of light and darkness in the universe, which delved into the history and literary evolution of the vampire, along with exploration of the modern fantasy epics *The Lord of the Rings* and *Star Wars*. Ms. Burke is an aspiring author of medieval fantasy, much influenced by the works of J.R.R Tolkien. Her first experience with his writing came after an excursion to the N.Y. Public Library at the age of five, where she borrowed a recording of Professor Tolkien reading the chapter 'Riddles in the Dark' from *The Hobbit*.

References

BECKER, Alida (ed.), *A Tolkien Treasury* (second edition), Philadelphia: Running Press Book Publishers, 1989.

BYOCK, Jesse L. (trans.), *The Saga of the Volsungs*, Berkeley, Los Angeles and London: University of California Press, 1990.

CAMPBELL, Joseph (ed.), *The Portable Jung*, (reprint, first edition 1971), New York: Penguin Books, 1976.

CARPENTER, Humphrey (ed. with the assistance of Chr. Tolkien), *The Letters of J.R.R. Tolkien*, (first U.S. trade paperback edition) Boston: Houghton Mifflin Company, 2000.

FRYE, Northrop, *Anatomy of Criticism*, (fifteenth printing, with a new foreword), Princeton: Princeton University Press., 2000

GARTH, John, *Tolkien and the Great War*, (first U.S. edition), Boston: Houghton Mifflin Company, 2003.

JACKSON, Peter (dir.), *The Lord of the Rings: The Fellowship of the Ring*, (New Line Cinema, 2001), starring Elijah Wood, Viggo Mortensen, Sean Astin, Liv Tyler, Sir Ian McKellen and Christopher Lee, 2001.

The Lord of the Rings: The Two Towers, (New Line Cinema, 2002) Starring Elijah Wood, Viggo Mortensen, Sean Astin, Liv Tyler, Sir Ian McKellen, David Wenham, Bernard Hill, and Christopher Lee, 2002.

The Lord of the Rings: The Return of the King, (New Line Cinema, 2003) Starring Elijah Wood, Viggo Mortensen, Sean Astin, Liv Tyler, Sir Ian McKellen, David Wenham, Bernard Hill, David Wenham, and John Noble, 2003.

LOBDELL, Jared (ed.), *A Tolkien Compass*, (first Ballantine edition), New York: Ballantine Books, 1980.

PETTY, Anne, *Tolkien in the Land of Heroes: Discovering the Human Spirit*, (first U.S. edition), New York: Cold Spring Press, 2003.

REILLY, R.J., 'Tolkien and the Fairy Story', In: Neil D. Isaacs and Rose A. Zimbardo (eds.), *Tolkien and the Critics: Essays on J.R.R. Tolkien's The Lord of the Rings*, (first U.S. edition), Indiana: University of Notre Dame Press, 1968. Accessed via: http://80-galenet.galegroup.com.proxy.library.csi.cuny.edu. on February 2004.

ROGERS, Deborah, 'Everyclod and Everyhero', In: Jared Lobdell (ed.), *A Tolkien Compass*, (first Ballantine edition), New York: Ballantine Books, 1980, pp. 73-81.

SHIPPEY, Tom A., *The Road to Middle-earth*, (first U.S. edition), Boston: Houghton Mifflin Company, 1983.

J.R.R. Tolkien: Author of the Century, (first U.S. edition), Boston: Houghton Mifflin Company, 2000.

TOLKIEN, J.R.R., *The Hobbit*, (centenary edition), Boston: Houghton Mifflin, 1997.

The Lord of the Rings, (movie-tie edition), Boston: Houghton Mifflin Company, 1994.

YEATS, William Butler, *The Cutting of an Agate*, (first UK edition, 1919), London: Macmillan.

Øystein Høgset

The Adaptation of *The Lord of the Rings* – A Critical Comment

Abstract

This article presents the principal theories of adaptation and then moves on to discuss whether or not Peter Jackson has succeeded in adapting *The Lord of the Rings* according to these criteria. Based on the theories of Dudley Andrew, the article explores key aspects of the three films and attempts to illuminate any lack of fidelity to the spirit J.R.R. Tolkien's novel evident in the adaptations.

I

Basing a movie on an acclaimed novel is by no means a groundbreaking enterprise. In spite of this, when Peter Jackson's attempt to adapt J.R.R. Tolkien's *The Lord of the Rings* became reality, the entire 'art' of adaptation became the object of public scrutiny. In December 2003, Peter Jackson's mastodon project culminated in the release of The Return of the King,[1] completing the transformation of Tolkien's words into moving images and sound. Yet the question remained – was this a successful adaptation? Has *The Lord of the Rings* survived the transfer to the cinematic medium? And could an adaptation ever measure up to the unparalleled qualities of the novel?

Such questions may seem unavoidable when dealing with adaptations and adapted literature. However, they often fail to do justice to the specific challenges of the 'art of adaptation'. As of today very little research has been published on the subject, and the general discussion of the problems related to this particular field of study often suffers from ignorance and misunderstandings. While many seem to believe that a successful adaptation has to be entirely truthful to the words of the novel and to include as many scenes as possible

---

[1] The Lord of the Rings, The Fellowship of the Ring, The Two Towers and The Return of the King refer to Peter Jackson's adaptations, while *The Lord of the Rings*, *The Fellowship of the Ring*, *The Two Towers* and *The Return of the King* (cursive) refer to the original texts by J.R.R. Tolkien.

from it, this remains an extreme over-simplification of how to approach an adaptation.

In order to examine any adaptation closer it is necessary to categorise and deal with the film according to how it approaches the original text. Dudley Andrew (1992) presents three major modes of adaptation that illustrate how a director may approach a novel when attempting to adapt it. The first category, entitled *Borrowing*, indicates that the text is merely regarded as a source of inspiration, where the adaptation recreates or captures nuances of the novel. The second mode, on the other hand, represents a far more restricted approach, where a fragment of the original text is incorporated in the adaptation without undergoing any significant alterations, thus the "… uniqueness of the original text is preserved to such an extent that it is intentionally left unassimilated in the adaptation" (Andrew 1992:422). The final mode of adaptation, *Fidelity and Transformation*, is an equally complex and challenging form of text transition, and indicates that the entire text is adapted – encompassing the written words, the meaning behind these words and other significant aspects of the text. But while the words of a text may correspond with the written script of a film, the other rather elusive qualities of a text are far more challenging. As Andrew puts it:

> More difficult is fidelity to the spirit, to the original's tone, values, imagery, and rhythm, since finding stylistic equivalents in film for these intangible aspects is the opposite of a mechanical process. The cinéast presumably must intuit and reproduce the feeling of the original. It has been argued variously that this is frankly impossible, or that it involves the systematic replacement of verbal signifiers by cinematic signifiers, or that is the product of artistic intuition (Andrew 1992:423-24).

One problem that Andrew fails to acknowledge, but which Jakob Lothe addresses in his book *Narrative in Fiction and Film*, is the fact that there need not necessarily be a clear transition from one mode of adaptation to another. Furthermore a single film may contain more than one mode, which somewhat undermines the tripartite distinction presented by Andrew (Lothe 2000:87). Thus we have a variety of valid approaches within the art of adaptation. Nevertheless, Andrew's categories still suffice to make a general classification of how the original text is treated by the director. In the case of Peter Jackson's adaptation of *The Lord of the Rings*, the films appear at first to be entirely cast in the mode of *Fidelity and Transformation*. Nonetheless, I assume that the other two modes are present as well, thus acknowledging the limitations of Andrew's categories. Yet since the mode of *Fidelity and Transformation* appears to be the dominant mode, the adaptation needs to retain its fidelity to the spirit of the original text, which will be the focus of this article.

Bearing in mind the theoretical foundations presented above, there remains yet one fundamental principle that needs to be taken into account when discussing an adaptation: it is absolutely necessary to make a distinction between the original text and the film. The two should be considered separate pieces of art and products of specific artistic processes, even though they necessarily share certain similarities. Although an adaptation is based on a text, it undergoes a significant number of changes in the transition to a visual medium, not to mention the fact that it becomes the subject of interpretation. Hence the adaptation can be expected to differ to such an extent that it should be considered as independent (though derived) from the text upon which it is based. The importance of this fact is further illustrated when one considers documentaries such as National Geographic's recently released *Beyond the Movie: The Lord of the Rings: The Return of the King* (2003), which intends to explore the similarities between the history of the real-world and the fictional story of Middle-earth. This is in many ways an interesting undertaking, but the documentary fails to make a distinction between Tolkien's *The Lord of the Rings* and Peter Jackson's interpretation and adaptation. The documentary blends the two, often letting the adapted motion picture represent the original text, not taking into consideration any changes brought about in the process. The actors' interpretation of the characters in the novel and the visual depiction of the narrative suddenly constitute the basis for understanding the story Tolkien created in the first half of the 20th century. In this sense the documentary contributes to the blurring of the borders between the original text and the adaptation, because it fails to acknowledge the innate differences of the two media and does not consider whether or not the adaptation has been successful. This documentary embodies in many ways the most common problem when dealing with an adaptation and an original text – the failure to make a clear distinction between the two! In order to avoid such a 'confusion' of the two, one needs to focus on the director's presence in this process and the significance, in this case, of Jackson's contribution. Peter Jackson himself made this point very clear when answering questions related to the release of The Fellowship of the Ring – "You shouldn't think of these movies as being *The Lord of the Rings*. *The Lord of the Rings* is, and will always be, a wonderful book – one of the greatest ever written. Any films will only ever be an *interpretation* of the book. In this case my interpretation."[2]

As I have already mentioned the transition from one medium to another is bound to cause changes, especially when dealing with a work as complex as *The Lord of the Rings*. Therefore it was only to be expected that certain omissions and alterations would be evident in the adaptation, and as the artist behind the work, Peter Jackson is entitled to do this. Even when one recognises the mode of *Fidelity and Transformation* as the dominant approach to the original text, one must still accept the changes undertaken in the process and acknowledge the fact that the two media differ to such a great extent that it would be impossible to transfer the complete contents of the novel unaltered. Therefore I intend to focus on a selection of key aspects present in the adaptation, thereby both acknowledging Peter Jackson as the artist behind the work, and separating the adaptation from the novel upon which it was based. By comparing these aspects with the corresponding literary analysis I will illustrate whether or not the adaptation misrepresents the spirit of the original text, according to the theoretical principles presented by Dudley Andrew. The primary focus will then not be on the changes, but on how the film accomplishes the depiction of central aspects in the novel, and based upon the theory of adaptation, whether or not one can truly call Peter Jackson's movie a success.

II

Although J.R.R. Tolkien's epic story of the battle between Good and Evil was published more than fifty years ago, the conflict itself remains timeless. But even so the task of transferring the complexity of the conflict and the myriad of nuances with which Tolkien imbued his work, is by no means an easy task. Peter Jackson has opted to keep the macro structure of the narrative unaltered, thereby making visible the duality of the conflict and presenting all the major

---

[2] www.aint-it-cool-news/lordoftherings.html Q&A part 1, p. 4.

events of the novel. The final part of the adaptation culminates in the destruction of the One Ring[3] and the downfall of Sauron, concluding the battle. But it is at the very ending of the adaptation that one comes to understand that a vital element is missing. Throughout all three parts of the adaptation the film has struggled to capture the nuances of the conflict, and constantly reverted to the original duality, consisting of two distinct factions – either good or evil. In the end the good side is victorious and leads the peoples of Middle-earth into a new golden era, devoid of shadow and evil. It is this aspect that makes the adaptation deviate from the original text. In the novel Evil persists, even though its master is cast down and destroyed. Saruman serves as the ultimate example of how evil will remain in one guise or another, and rather than the complete downfall presented in the adaptation, Tolkien shows us a far more realistic world of fantasy, where the existence of lesser forms of Evil is both recognised and incorporated in the narrative. Tolkien's novel has constantly developed this particular aspect, illustrating how free will, choice and the seductiveness of power are but some of the factors that may guide ones actions. Apart from the One Ring, that remains the absolute incarnation of Evil, all other participants in the story are defined as either good or evil as a result of their choices and actions. The adaptation, however, fails to make the same point. In the end Evil is banished from Middle-earth, and as far as the audience is concerned, all the characters live happily ever after, either in the Undying Lands, Gondor or in the Shire. Compared to the novel, the adaptation omits a significant part of the conflict between Good and Evil.

This is perhaps the most serious deviation in the adaptation's depiction of the battle between Good and Evil, and as I have already pointed out, the film has difficulties in doing justice to the nuances of this particular aspect. Peter Jackson's loyalty to the narrative of the original text constantly fails to take into account the alterations he has made – thus creating logical breaches in the narrative of the films. This is perhaps made most evident in the depiction of Boromir in The Fellowship of the Ring. While Tolkien presents the character of Boromir as one of the truly great heroes of mankind, and shows how the seductive powers of the Ring gradually corrupt and contaminate him until he finally gives in and tries to take the Ring, the adaptation does no such thing.

---

3 The Ring (capitalised) refers to the ruling ring crafted by Sauron.

The audience is made aware of Boromir's flawed character from the moment Jackson introduces him. Instead of being presented as a hero, all the scenes depicting Boromir do nothing but reinforce the first impression of him being a villain. A scene that clearly illustrates this point is presented as the Fellowship ascends Caradhras. Frodo falls in the snow, and in doing so the Ring slips off his neck, only to be retrieved by Boromir. Eventually he returns it to Frodo, who hurriedly, and with an anguished look, again places the chain about his neck. Yet it is not so much in Boromir's actions, but in that of his companions, that the alteration of his character is revealed. Apparently, as Boromir picks up the Ring, Aragorn immediately places a hand upon the hilt of his sword, and even Gandalf turns to the scene with some apprehension. These obvious signs of distrust clearly illustrate that the character of Boromir is not to be trusted, and that it is almost expected that he will attempt to take the Ring, if given the chance. The adaptation reinforces this view when Galadriel later on warns Frodo of the threat that Boromir poses to the Ring. In the end, the inevitable takes place, whether premeditated or not, and he tries, and fails, to take the Ring from Frodo. Up to this point the alterations could easily have been explained as part of Jackson's changes in order to adapt the complex narrative of the novel and due to the necessity to somewhat simplify the supporting characters. But when Jackson chooses to include the scene where Boromir is given a hero's burial he creates a discrepancy that remains unexplained by the narrative of the adaptation. His self-sacrifice as he tries to save Merry and Pippin hardly seems to justify such an honour. For why should Boromir be treated as a hero after having confirmed everyone's suspicion and lack of confidence in his character? This discrepancy makes the film misrepresent an important part of the original text, because it fails to take into account the changes made in the process of adapting the novel.

Throughout *The Lord of the Rings* we witness the complete corruption of only two characters in detail, namely those of Boromir and Frodo. While the narrative of the adaptation struggles with the changes made to the character of Boromir, the fall of Frodo, as found in the novel, remains largely unaltered. Yet I would like to make one point. Tolkien emphasises free will in his story of the Ring, although the seductive powers of Evil at times overshadow ones ability to make a choice. As Boromir gives in to temptation, so does Frodo in the end, and only chance saves Middle-earth from being cast under the shadow. In her essay "Power and the meaning in *The Lord of the Rings*", Patricia Meyer Spacks makes an interesting point when she illustrates how Frodo uses the language of free will the moment he decides to keep the Ring, rather than to destroy it. However, this is done in an environment where free will ceases to exist (Spacks 1969:94). Frodo, apparently, believes this to be his own choice, not realising that it is under the evil influence of the Ring. The adaptation, however, fails even to hint at this paradox of free will. Whereas Frodo in the novel calmly proclaims "I have come … but I do not choose now to do what I came to do. I will not do this deed. The Ring is mine!"[4] The adaptation shows a determined Frodo announce, "The Ring is mine!"[5] and then place the Ring upon his finger – the aspect of free will completely removed. The alterations in the adaptation seem unnecessary, and obscure a point that is vital to the understanding of evil in the story of the Ring. The sense of free will has been a constant element throughout Tolkien's *The Lord of the Rings*, giving evidence to the fact that predetermination is but a minor factor in life, and that the individual is to some extent capable of shaping his own fate. Through this alteration Jackson undermines this theme and deviates from the spirit of the original text, making the adaptation leave out a vital aspect of the novel.

Of the main characters in the story of the Ring there are two that stand out from the rest, namely Aragorn and Frodo. Both carry the fate of the entire world upon their shoulders, and if either of them should fail, Middle-earth will be devastated by the armies of Sauron. The concept of the reluctant hero is a central part in *The Lord of the Rings*, emphasising the moral obligation to fight evil, even when victory seems impossible to achieve. This innate sense of responsibility is connected with the abovementioned characters, who relate to their tasks in very different manners. The adaptation introduces Aragorn as a brave and valiant warrior, but it soon becomes evident that there is more to this ranger from the North. As the Ring reaches Rivendell the true lineage of Aragorn is revealed, but so is his reluctance to accept his birthright. This becomes clear in a conversation between Elrond and Gandalf:

---

4 J.R.R. Tolkien, *The Return of the King* (London:Harper Collins Publishers, 1999), p. 265. The following abbreviations will be used when referring to Tolkien's novels: *FotR* – *The Fellowship of the Ring*, *TTT* – *The Two Towers*, *RotK* – *The Return of the King*.
5 Excerpt from the dialogue in The Return of the King.

> *Elrond*: There is no strength left in the world of Men. They are scattered, divided and leaderless.
> *Gandalf*: There is one who could unite them. One who could reclaim the throne of Gondor.
> *Elrond*: He turned from that path a long time ago. He has chosen exile.[6]

And in the very next scene, Aragorn reveals why he has not claimed that which is rightfully his:

> *Arwen*: Why do you fear the past? You are Isildur's heir, not Isildur himself. You are not bound to his fate.
> *Aragorn*: The same blood flows in my veins. The same weakness.
> *Arwen*: Your time will come. You will face the same evil. And you will defeat it.[7]

Haunted by the failure of his ancestors he has chosen to turn his back on that which could have been his by right, but as the film progresses the character of Aragorn changes. When Gandalf plummets to his death and the Fellowship loses its leader, Aragorn takes on the task of leadership. Towards the end of The Fellowship of the Ring he has both withstood the temptation of the Ring and truly taken on the burden of leadership, but there is still little evidence of the King that will lead men to victory. This aspect is developed considerably throughout the second part of the trilogy, and Aragorn emerges as the heroic general that inspires and leads his men. But even so, the reluctance appears to linger, and although Aragorn is intent on fighting the evil of Sauron, he still avoids his heritage. Nothing changes until he stands on the threshold of battle, and Elrond approaches him, bearing with him Andúril, a sword re-forged from the shards of Narsil – the very symbol of Aragorn's lineage, and explains why he no longer can escape the fate connected with his birthright:

> I come on behalf of one whom I love. Arwen is dying. She will not long survive the evil that now spreads from Mordor ... As Sauron's powers grow, her strength vanes. Arwen's life is now tied to the fate of the Ring. The Shadow is upon us Aragorn ... You ride to war, not to victory ... Put aside the ranger, become who you were born to be.[8]

The army needed to secure victory in battle will only answer to the King of Gondor, and in order to save both Middle-earth and Arwen, Aragorn overcomes

---

6 Excerpt from the dialogue in The Fellowship of the Ring.
7 Excerpt from the dialogue in The Fellowship of the Ring.
8 Edited excerpt from the dialogue in The Return of the King.

his fears, draws Andúril and embraces his destiny. From this point on Aragorn shoulders his moral obligation as the Leader of Men. But compared to Tolkien's presentation of the same character, the adaptation deviates considerably, because in the novel Aragorn never tries to flee from his duty as heir of Isildur. The shards of Narsil belong to him, they remain a constant reminder of who he truly is. For years he has chosen to live in obscurity and bide his time, but when the true peril of the Ring is unveiled, he no longer ignores his heritage. The weapon is re-forged, and he leaves Rivendell a man more conscious of both his true nature and his moral obligation. Aragorn does not turn into a glorious King over night, but Tolkien rather lets the reader gradually witness his growth in character. As the story progresses it becomes evident that Aragorn is coming to terms with his heritage, and his true nature is revealed to all those who behold him. By the time he reaches Minas Tirith he is the Leader of Men. The importance of this development is to a certain extent lost in the adaptation, as is his motivation. When Peter Jackson changes the narrative and ties Arwen's fate to the outcome of the battle, he undermines the aspect of heritage, destiny and obligation. Aragorn suddenly appears to accept his birthright because it is the only way he can save Arwen, not because he is destined to rule men. His motives have become personal and are an attempt to save the woman that he holds dear. He is no longer governed by his sense of duty. Again the original text is severely misrepresented.

While Aragorn flees from his destiny, only to accept it when threatened with the prospect of losing the person he loves, the depiction of Frodo is drastically different. Throughout the entire adaptation Frodo appears governed by fear. He plays the role of the Ring-bearer, yet does so with extreme reluctance. The fear of failing in his quest appears to be his sole motivation, and most of the time he resembles a scared child, faced with an impossible task. As the quest progresses Frodo grows more attached to the Ring, yet even this aspect is very often eclipsed by the fear he expresses. Instead the adaptation presents Sam as the true driving force of the quest, constantly supporting and urging his friend onwards. The only part of the narrative where Frodo is consequently depicted as something other than scared, is in his growing attachment to Gollum. But falling victim to Gollum's sinister plot to regain the Ring, Frodo sends Sam away, walks right in to the trap and reverts to being scared again. Although there are scenes within the three parts of the adaptation where Frodo is depicted as either a true friend, as brave, determined or even angry, these scenes are so few in number that they cannot be considered representative of his character. The novel, however, treats the character of Frodo very differently. In Tolkien's text it becomes natural to consider the foundation of Frodo and Sam's relationship as that of master and servant. And even though Frodo would never have succeeded in his quest without his friend and servant by his side, Sam still, in one sense, remains inferior to his master throughout the story. Furthermore Frodo is the true reluctant hero. Frodo shoulders the burden of the Ring and sets out on the quest for its destruction (*FotR* 74) as soon as the true nature of the Ring is revealed, and the fact that it has not come into his possession by chance, but due to providence or fate. He constantly faces great challenges, but he never gives up nor does he admit defeat. Instead his will and moral obligation to fight the evil of Mordor carry him on. Fear is, of course, an emotion that Frodo has to deal with, yet it never seems to dominate his character, but rather appears a natural reaction to the circumstances created by the context of the narrative. In his adaptation, Peter Jackson has altered both the character of Frodo and Sam. First of all he has removed the class barrier that is present in the novel, and in doing so he shifted the balance between the two. While he has reduced Frodo, he has strengthened Sam, making him far more capable of dealing with the challenges they face on their journey. These alterations could have been justified if Frodo had retained some of the qualities from the original text. But instead the adaptation depicts him as a scared child – a misrepresentation of hobbits in general and of Frodo in particular, making it seem impossible for him to muster the moral determination and strength of will needed to accomplish the task he sets out to do. There is of course the possibility that the actor portraying Frodo, Elijah Wood, is incapable of acting out the nuances of the character, or that Peter Jackson has chosen to reduce this particular aspect of the narrative – the result remains the same.

By excluding these aspects in the characters of Frodo and Aragorn, a vital part of the original text is lost and the adaptation does not remain faithful to the spirit of the original text.

III

According to Andrew's definition, the spirit of the text extends beyond the mere thematic aspects of the narrative, and it is here that Peter Jackson's adaptation deviates most prominently from the original text. When acknowledging the adaptation as a separate piece of art one must accept that changes are bound to occur, but even so I would like to point out a few particular differences that are no longer due solely to the different stylistic characteristics of the two media.

The basic concept of the adaptation is to divide *The Lord of the Rings* into three parts, as is very often done with the novel. But unlike the adaptation, the novel has never been planned as a trilogy, but rather an 'epic novel' of more than a thousand pages. And even though the text is divided into six books, that are, in turn, further subdivided into numerous chapters, there is a unity to the narrative that a film-trilogy must retain. The adaptation, however, presents a trilogy where the three parts are clearly centred around different aspects of the story. The Fellowship of the Ring focuses on establishing the epic structure of the narrative, and the visualisation of Middle-earth. The Two Towers narrows the focus and explores the emotional aspect of some of the characters, yet at the same time it introduces the grand and brutal battle scenes of the story. The Return of the King, the final part in the trilogy, to a great extent highlights the epic battle scenes, but it also remains the most sentimental of the three parts, devoting much time to the depiction of the characters' sense of agony, loss, despair and dwindling hope. Furthermore, the first part of the adaptation remains the least traditional film, in the sense that it focuses on the story and the world it is set in, rather than on the individual characters. It therefore shows strong parallels to the literary genre of the epic. The second and third parts of the trilogy are more traditional. In addition to focusing more on the characters within the story, they also contain a number of clichés originating from modern cinema and action films. Both Sam and Éowyn face superior foes, and their bold heroics are accompanied by phrases very much like those found in modern Hollywood productions. In Tolkien's novel, Sam takes on Gollum as the dreadful Shelob attacks him and Frodo (*TTT* 417-18). But in the adaptation Sam's adversary is none other than Shelob herself, and as he faces this ancient evil he loudly exclaims: "Let him go, you filth!"⁹ This momentary bravery may be explained by Sam's devotion to his friend, yet it resembles the type of catch phrase that many modern actors use today. Perhaps even clearer is a scene that is present in Tolkien's novel and remains largely unaltered in the movie. In the novel Éowyn faces the Witchking Angmar on the fields outside Minas Tirith. Standing between the Lord of the Nazgûls and the crippled King Théoden, she bravely proclaims:

> But no living man am I! You look upon a woman. Éowyn am I, Éomund's daughter. You stand between me and my lord and kin. Begone, if you be not deathless! For living or dark undead, I will smite you, if you touch him. (*RotK* 129)

And then faces and defeats Angmar. The adaptation depicts the same scene, but with a significant alteration. Rather than keeping the original dialogue and sequence of events, Éowyn shouts, "I am no man!"¹⁰ and slays the fatally wounded Witchking. So rather than speaking her warning and then miraculously defeating her foe, Éowyn is depicted as the modern action heroine, finishing off her enemy with a quick thrust of her sword and a catch phrase. It may be possible to argue that these aspects represent the modern film genre and are therefore equivalent to the verbal signifiers of the novel, yet the first part of the adaptation is to a large extent devoid of such elements. My claim is therefore that these elements change the spirit of the original text to the worse and add a dimension that does not belong to the story of the Ring.

Although each of the three parts of the adaptation has its own distinctive feel, all three share certain similarities that create a sharp contrast to the original text. Peter Jackson has managed to visualise his selection from *The Lord of the Rings* in three instalments totalling a little over nine hours, and even though a three-hour film is considered above average running time, Jackson has still had to compress the narrative in order to fit it all in. As a result, each part of the adaptation consists of a closely linked series of successive climaxes so that the audience hardly finds the time to catch their breath. And unlike Tolkien, who excels at gradually introducing and developing tension before letting it reach its peak, Jackson lets the action explode on screen from the very first second. The

---

9 Excerpt from the dialogue in The Return of the King.
10 Excerpt from the dialogue in The Return of the King.

subtlety with which Tolkien introduces new elements into the story is replaced by a host of special effects and sounds. The prime example is the Nazgûls, whom Tolkien deliberately introduces as hooded riders, but then gradually discloses the horrifying truth that has been shrouded by their cloaks. Jackson, however, employs the Nazgûls in all their horrific splendour, introducing them to the audience in a bombardment of visual effects and sound, thereby drastically reducing their effect and deviating from the style of the original text. It may, of course, be argued that Jackson was pressed for time and could not progress at Tolkien's leisurely pace. But when an adaptation deviates to such an extent from the original text, it distorts an important element of the narrative.

Another related topic is how Peter Jackson has chosen to deal with magic. He stated, prior to the release of The Fellowship of the Ring, that he wanted above all to escape the clichés of movie magic and pyrotechnics, and instead focus on the more psychological side of magic that Tolkien had presented prominently in *The Lord of the Rings*.[11] Yet very little of Tolkien's subtlety survives in the adaptation. Instead Jackson has apparently used many of the familiar clichés of the genre.

Of the many examples in the adaptation, I would like to single out three specific scenes to prove this point. In the prologue of The Fellowship of the Ring, Sauron is shown in battle, wearing the One Ring as a kind of magical weapon. His foes are crushed beneath his mighty mace, and the camera constantly focuses on the Ring – making the viewer aware of the fact that Sauron's overpowering strength emanates from it. A significant alteration, since the power of Tolkien's Ring was based mainly on the corruptive lure of evil and the power to bend the will of others.

Gandalf, who represents the forces of good, also falls victim to a rather crude visualisation of magic. When Gandalf is confronted with the treachery of Saruman in The Fellowship of the Ring, the two wizards immediately commence flinging each other into the walls, until Saruman secures Gandalf's staff and pivots him to the top of the tower – a stark contrast to the more resigned non-violent surrender in the original text (*FotR* 338-42). Jackson's presentation

---

[11] www.lordoftherings.net – taken from a session of questions and answers with Peter Jackson regarding the adaptation of *The Lord of the Rings*.

of the scene strongly resembles both the Force in the science fiction trilogy *Star Wars* and the visualisation of magic in the movie *Willow*, which contradicts Jackson's claim of originality.

Just as representative is Gandalf's exorcism of King Théoden in The Two Towers. As Gandalf the White reveals himself and attempts to free Théoden, Saruman manifests himself in the body of his victim. In a contest of power, supported by a blinding flash of light, Théoden and Saruman are both flung backwards. Gandalf emerges victorious, and Théoden slowly transforms from a haggard old man to the proud king he used to be, while an obviously hurt Saruman carefully regains his footing in the Tower of Isengard. Tolkien, however, describes no visible magic in the corresponding scene in the novel. But even so the reader immediately understands that the powers of Gandalf are at work. The reader witnesses Théoden's gradual recovery, all brought about by Gandalf, and yet done in a very subtle and discreet way. Tolkien's magic is, in this instance, closer to psychological treatment than wonderworking.

Even though the adaptation is presented in a visual medium it does not mean that all the effects must remain purely visual. There are a number of ways by means of which the psychological aspect of magic could easily have been enhanced, especially when the cast consists of such recognised actors as Ian McKellen and Christopher Lee. I would thus have expected Peter Jackson to avoid such clichés and to retain the depiction of magic as found in the original text. The visualisation of magic deviates to such an extent from Tolkien's description that the adaptation presents an entirely different understanding of magic and constitutes a serious breach of the expected faithfulness to the original text.

IV

Peter Jackson completed his film trilogy in December 2003 as The Return of the King was released. Yet in the wake of each movie Jackson has released an extended version that include a number of new and extended scenes, thus adding about half an hour to the length of each of the films. The extended version of The Return of the King is expected to come out sometime in autumn 2004.

According to the latest news it will add fifty minutes of footage to the original movie.

The extended versions give Peter Jackson room for a number of scenes that he had to exclude from the cinematic versions of the films and he can now add elements he considers important to the narrative. Unfortunately, the extended versions do not necessarily contribute to the strengthening of the adaptation's faithfulness to the spirit of the original text. Although they do include a number of elements that where sorely missed in the first editions of the films, the adaptation still struggles with the aspects I have discussed in this paper. The extended version of The Fellowship of the Ring and The Two Towers do much to make these films a more wholesome experience, and the added scenes bridge important gaps in the narrative. Yet they still deviate to such an extent that the extended versions do not improve the adaptation significantly and it remains doubtful whether the final part of the extended trilogy will be able to correct the shortcomings of the preceding films.

Peter Jackson's movie trilogy has visualised the world that Tolkien created more than fifty years ago, a world that has captivated the imagination of the millions of people that have read the book ever since it was first published. The sheer immensity of this task alone must ask for our respect, for Jackson presents Middle-earth in great detail, almost rivalling that of Tolkien's literary work. The commercial success of the completed trilogy is unsurpassed, and at the Oscars 2004 The Return of the King made a clean sweep, winning eleven prizes out of a possible eleven. Today the films stand as a pinnacle in film history, and have more or less dethroned the *Star Wars* trilogy that has reigned unchallenged for twenty years. But is Peter Jackson's trilogy a successful adaptation according to the theoretical criteria? In this case, the answer simply has to be 'No'. Even though Peter Jackson has chosen to adapt just the core elements of Tolkien's work, his depiction misrepresents the spirit of the original text to such an extent that, although the films are in many ways extremely successful, the trilogy cannot be considered a successful adaptation.

About the author

Øystein Høgset completed his Master's Degree in English at the University of Oslo in 2002, presenting the dissertation *The Unavoidable Comparison – The Fellowship of the Ring Presented in Fiction and Film*. His thesis provides an in-depth study of the first part of Peter Jackson's adaptation, exploring in detail how it visualises central thematic aspects of the original text upon which it was based. Øystein Høgset is currently teaching English and Comparative Religion, while doing research for a possible doctorate on the theory of adaptation, based on Peter Jackson's visualisation of *The Lord of the Rings*.

Primary sources

TOLKIEN, J.R.R., *The Fellowship of the Ring* [1954], London: Harper Collins Publishers, 1999.

The Two Towers [1954], London: Harper Collins Publishers, 1999.

The Return of the King [1955], London: Harper Collins Publishers, 1999.

The Fellowship of the Ring (2001).

The Fellowship of the Ring – Extended version (2002).

The Two Towers (2002).

The Two Towers – Extended version (2003).

The Return of the King (2003).

(Director/Producer/Writer, Peter Jackson, Writer/Producer, Fran Walsh, Writer, Stephen Sinclair, Writer, Philippa Boyens, Director of Photography, Andrew Lesnie, Camera Operator, Peter McCaffrey, Weta Digital – Animation Designed & Supervised by Randall William Cook, Weta Workshop – Head of Department, Richard Taylor. With Sean Astin (Sam), Sean Bean (Boromir), Cate Blanchett (Galadriel), Orlando Bloom (Legolas), Billy Boyd (Pippin), John Rhys-Davies (Gimli), Ian Holm (Bilbo), Christopher Lee (Saruman), Ian McKellen (Gandalf), Dominic Monaghan (Merry), Viggo Mortensen (Aragorn), Liv Taylor (Arwen), Elijah Wood (Frodo), Production: New Line Cinema).

Secondary sources

ANDREW, Dudley, 'Adaptation', In: Gerald Mast, Marshal Cohen, and Leo Braudy (eds.), *Film Theory and Criticism*, Oxford: Oxford University Press, 1992, 420-28.

HØGSET, Øystein, *The Unavoidable Comparison – The Fellowship of the Ring Presented in Fiction and Film*, Oslo: University of Oslo, 2002.

LOTHE, Jakob, *Narrative in Fiction and Film*, Oxford: Oxford University Press, 2000.

SPACKS, Patricia Meyer, 'Power and meaning in *The Lord of the Rings*', In: Neil D. Isaacs and Rose A. Zimbardo (eds.), *Tolkien and the Critics*, London: University of Notre Dame Press, 1969, 81- 99.

NATIONAL GEOGRAPHIC *Beyond the Movie: The Lord of the Rings: The Return of the King* (2003).

www.aint-it-cool-news/lordoftherings.html

www.lordoftherings.net

James Dunning

The Professor and the Director and Good vs. Evil in Middle-earth

Abstract

The article discusses aspects of philosophical or spiritual *Weltanschauung* behind Tolkien's Middle-earth: The Thermodynamics of Middle-earth, The Encroaching of the Shadow, Benevolent Serendipity (Divine Providence), and certain other manifestations of Good vs. Evil in *The Lord of the Rings*. How these factors play out, in the original vs. Peter Jackson's film trilogy, is explored.

An epic cinematic trilogy for the new millennium is upon us. I am awestruck by brilliant characterizations: the Hobbits, Gandalf, Saruman, Aragorn, Arwen, Galadriel. Burned into my memory are scenes of exquisite grandeur that closely follow, and realize what J.R.R. Tolkien certainly must have intended. The Shire is portrayed lovingly, green and rolling, with architecture cozy and quaint. Strider in the Prancing Pony at Bree, shrouded in his shadowy hood, veiled in smoke, appears menacingly like a Black Rider, and *exactly* as this reader had imagined. The enchantment of Rivendell, suggesting the Elves' weaving their love for all things in Middle-earth into their craft, made me gasp with recognition. Isildur and Anarion the Argonath, Rauros Falls, Minas Tirith and Mount Doom, all took my breath away.

And Mr. Jackson's cinematic triumph, for all its condensations and departures from Tolkien's plot, still contains compelling spiritual lessons on the dignity and responsibility of the little man, the joys and benefits of enjoying a quiet life and simple pleasures, the beauty of love between friends, the necessity of perseverance in resisting evil, the role of pity and understanding in human ecology, and the hidden benign force of Divine serendipity.

Therefore I feel that the basic grasp of characters and spirit is *usually* correct throughout Peter Jackson's film(s) *The Lord of the Rings*. I am fond of the films, and will certainly watch them again and again, gripping the arms of my chair and grabbing the popcorn. Having said this frankly, I must now disclose my membership among the *Elder* race of Tolkien aficionados. Consistent with status as Elder (or *Eldar*, if you will pardon me) is my conviction that in translating Tolkien into Jackson, something *philosophical* is inevitably lost. And here I will concentrate chiefly on manifestations of Good and Evil in Middle-earth, *books* vs. *films* (1-9), and close by including some 'general' contrasts and observations (10).

Middle-earth: The Director's Cut

Long-brooders over Tolkien's works (Eldar) as a rule know little of Hollywood and filmmaking. However even to this armchair cinema gawker, it is apparent that Peter Jackson possesses a genius at *getting into and behind* Middle-earth and realizing its characters, landscapes and artifacts in exquisite detail. Even to approach *The Lord of the Rings* is a courageous act, for capturing both body and spirit of Tolkien's world cinematically is a formidable *gamble*.

On the one hand, there are the increasingly cynical movie-goers, who are jaded toward great cinematic events, and merely yawn at gargantuan (and costly) displays of pyrotechnics or special effects. Mr. Jackson also had to reckon with a very good chance that the *hoi polloi* of 2001 might well lose patience with the intricate and complex world this Professor of mediaeval languages **sub-created**, to house his Elven languages. And *sub-created* from *what*? [...] from Men of a long-gone Heroic Age, from far-off (and therefore *legendary*) creatures celebrated in preliterate and just-barely-literate cultures of northern Europe, and from improbable anthropomorphic imaginary creatures, including *hemianthropoids*, and even *anthropoflora*!!

On the other hand, those *Eldar* (as above) are a difficult lot. While not *everyone* (alas!) loves *The Lord of the Rings*, the elect initiates in the craft love their Middle-earth with the fierce, undying love of the Elves. Starry-eyed dervishes learn Elvish as living languages. Modern Shire genealogists memorize ancestry of the Hobbits (who would approve with a toast of proper 1420!). There are even some souls who can recite Tolkien's entire novel *verbatim*, with the zeal of a *hakim* reciting his Holy Book from *memory*. There might even be some plotting to tar-and-feather your humble narrator for presuming to label

Tolkien's *magnum opus **a novel!*** Such zealots are unlikely to bear the slight with impunity, if a pet character is omitted, or if 'blasphemous' plot revisions fracture Tolkien's story for posterity.

So, between such terrible alternatives, for accepting the challenge of ***sub-directing*** Middle-earth, *and* for succeeding so marvelously in many respects, my heart swells with admiration for Mr. Jackson. But *The Lord of the Rings* is *more* than its characters, landscapes, artifacts, and plot. There are *spiritual* imperatives operating behind the scenes in Middle-earth. And Hollywood is typically *action*.

So how in Middle-earth does Tolkien translate into cinema? I begin by exploring the *Weltanschauung*, the world-view *behind the scenes* in Tolkien's Middle-earth.

The Weltanschauung of Tolkien's Middle-earth

Tolkien was born a Roman Catholic in Anglican Britain. Tolkien's faith was sincere, and he maintained it with intense conviction; his Christianity surfaces at odd moments throughout the tapestry of *The Lord of the Rings*, however it does so *without preaching*. Tolkien's faith erupts with great force in *The Silmarillion*, much of which is narrated in quasi-Biblical tone. Several scholars have discussed the *spiritual* background behind the books. In my own view there are three basic *leitmotifs* (1-3) that run systematically like clockwork behind events in Middle-earth, and I will discuss other recurrent *motifs* (4-9), *book* vs. *film*.

1. The thermodynamics of Middle-earth

As in our world, thermodynamics runs everything. The cosmos was created pure and beautiful, beyond imagining; but this cosmos is losing energy, gaining entropy, winding down like a clock. Nothing is the same as it used to be. How do we know this? We receive fleeting glimpses of the Elder Days, bright and magical, from Bombadil and Elrond of Rivendell, and a veritable *epiphany* in Lórien.

Tom Bombadil, the Eldest of all living things in Middle-earth, who was there when the Elves arrived, has powers over flora and fauna. Moreover, the Ring has no power over him. Tom conveys the spirit of the Elder Days through his singular communion with living things, and through his rhythmic and melodic use of language:

> Tom sang most of the time, but it was chiefly nonsense, or else perhaps a strange language unknown to the hobbits, an ancient language whose words were mainly those of wonder and delight. (I. 202)

Elrond inhabits Rivendell. *'Evil things did not come into that valley'* (H. 61). Elrond is the keeper of Vilya, mightiest of the Three Elven Rings (III. 381). Elrond commands the forces of nature in his valley, to sweep away the assaulting Black Riders, and to heal Frodo's Morgul wound. A spirit of Elder-Days peace and healing rules the house of Elrond (I. 297).

Lórien, maintained by Galadriel's ring Nenya (I. 472), is the most poignant witness to the undimmed beauty and power of the Elder Days. Frodo the Elf-friend becomes our window.

> [...] it seemed to him that he had stepped over a bridge of time into a corner of the Elder Days, and was now walking in a world that was no more. In Rivendell there was memory of ancient things; in Lórien the ancient things still lived on in the waking world. Evil had been seen and heard there, sorrow had been known; the Elves feared and distrusted the world outside: wolves were howling on the wood's borders: but on the land of Lórien no shadow lay. (I. 453)

One final taste of the Elder Days is Galadriel's parting gift to Sam. To heal the Shire, Sam distributes the contents of his magic box from Lórien around the Shire.

> Altogether 1420 in the Shire was a marvellous year. Not only was there wonderful sunshine and delicious rain, in due times and perfect measure, but there seemed something more: an air of richness and growth, and a gleam of a beauty beyond that of mortal summers that flicker and pass upon this Middle-earth. (III. 375)

On film:

Galadriel delivers the opening monologue *'The world is changing [...],'* as our monolithic reference to 'thermodynamics.' The basic principle is not stated in *words*. However one visualizes, from the beauty of the landscape, the intricacy of artifacts of Rivendell and of Lórien, and from the otherworldly musical score, how blessed and haunting is the world of the Elves, *and* their Elder Days. And one senses their loss.

The Elder Days are not re-seeded in the Shire.

2. The Encroaching of the Shadow

We have seen the operation in Middle-earth of *Time*:

> This thing all things devours:
> Birds, beasts, trees, flowers;
> Gnaws iron, bites steel;
> Grinds hard stones to meal;
> Slays king, ruins town,
> And beats high mountain down.
> (H. 84; Riddles in the Dark)

Gollum's cruel riddle proves the 'thermodynamics of Middle-earth.' Things are bad enough; but the tale of woe is just begun. Since Ilúvatar's Creation, since the Music of the Ainur (S. 3), the influence of Evil, *The Shadow*, accelerates decline in Middle-earth. The preface to *The Lord of the Rings*, verse translated from the Black Speech, sets the ominous keynote:

> Three Rings for the Elven-kings under the sky,
> Seven for the Dwarf-lords in their halls of stone,
> Nine for mortal Men doomed to die,
> One for the Dark Lord on his dark throne
> In the Land of Mordor where the Shadows lie.
> One Ring to rule them all, One Ring to find them,
> One Ring to bring them all and in the darkness bind them
> In the Land of Mordor where the Shadows lie.

Sauron covets power over all living things. Sauron learned Ring-making from the Eldar, however perverted it to evil uses, deceiving the Eldar. But Elrond tells of the *original* Three Elven Rings:

> 'The Three were not made by Sauron, nor did he ever touch them. [...] But they were not made as weapons of war or conquest: that is not their power. Those who made them did not desire strength or dominion or hoarded wealth, but understanding, making, and healing, to preserve all things unstained. [...] But all that has been wrought by those who wield the Three will turn to their undoing, and their minds and hearts will become revealed to Sauron, if he regains the One. It would be better if the Three had never been. That is his purpose.' (I. 352)

Glóin asks what will happen to the Three if Sauron's One Ring is destroyed. Elrond again:

> We know not for certain. Some hope that the Three Rings, which Sauron has never touched, would then become free, and their rulers might heal the hurts of

the world that he has wrought. But maybe when the One has gone, the Three will fail, and many fair things will fade and be forgotten.' (I. 352)

Galadriel advises Frodo of the impending conundrum: whether the Ring stands or falls, the Elder Days will fade, along with the Eldar (I. 472).

When the Ring is destroyed, indeed the Elder Days are numbered; and Elves, Dwarves, Wizards, and perhaps the Ents will fade. Treebeard says to Celeborn and Galadriel:

> 'It is sad that we should meet only thus at the ending. For the world is changing: I feel it in the water, I feel it in the earth, and I smell it in the air. I do not think we shall meet again.' (III. 320)

The Shadow, or Evil, embodied in Sauron's compulsion to dominate all living things, accelerates the decline of much that is good and pure in Middle-earth.

On film:

From Galadriel's voice in Lórien comes our warning that destroying the One Ring will cause many fair things to fade and be forgotten: 'Do you not see that your coming is to us as the footsteps of doom?' Elrond tells us that Arwen will fade and lose the life of the Eldar if she remains behind. The Three Elven Rings are mentioned in the introduction, but their preservative role is not emphasized.

3. Benevolent serendipity: The silver lining of providence

The evil of the Dark Lord has jeopardized Middle-earth throughout history. And yet an unmistakable thread of silver lining is woven throughout Middle-earth's tapestry. A Power behind the scenes shapes its destiny.

It begins quietly in *The Hobbit*, when Bilbo and the Dwarves leave the forest-path, and all but Bilbo are taken prisoner by the Wood-elves. Bilbo frees them and brings them down the river to Esgaroth. It was lucky they left the old Forest Road *against advice* (H. 183-84).

At the conclusion of *The Hobbit* old friends Gandalf and Balin visit Bilbo in the Shire. Gandalf tells Bilbo:

> 'You don't really suppose, do you, that all your adventures and escapes were managed by mere luck, *just for your sole benefit*? You are a very fine person, Mr. Baggins, and I am very fond of you: but you are only quite a little fellow in a wide world after all!' [Author's italics] (H. 286)

This remark is the final intimation of Fate/Providence on the threshold of *The Lord of the Rings*. Gandalf, conducting investigations on his own, confirms that Bilbo's magic ring is the One Ring, which has *a mind of its own*. Says Gandalf:

> 'There was more than one power at work, Frodo. The Ring was trying to get back to its master. [...] it abandoned Gollum, only to be picked up by the most unlikely person imaginable: Bilbo from the Shire!
>
> Behind that there was something else at work, beyond any design of the Ring-maker. I can put it no plainer than by saying that Bilbo was *meant* to find the Ring, and *not* by its maker. In which case you were also *meant* to have it, and that may be an encouraging thought.' (I. 87-88)

Providence arranged for the Ring to fall into the hands of a kindly agent of good. In turn, Frodo asks Gandalf why *he* was chosen.

> 'Such questions cannot be answered,' said Gandalf. 'You may be sure that it was not for any merit that others do not possess; not for power or wisdom, at any rate. But you have been chosen, and you must therefore use such strength and heart and wits as you have.' (I. 95)

Elrond echoes likewise. Providence chooses its own prime movers in any cause. Questioning its operation is in vain.

During their flight from the Shire, the hobbits leave the road just in time, for a Black Rider approaches, dismounts and creeps toward the hobbits. Frodo is nearly betrayed but saved by the appearance of a company of passing Elves. *By strange chance* the hobbits meet Gildor Inglorion with the Elves. The Black Riders shun them and the Elves are alarmed that the hobbits are pursued, and provide them memorable food, safety, and rest. Gildor warns Frodo unequivocally against the Black Riders, and offers unexpected aid:

> 'In the morning we shall have gone; but we will send our messages through the lands. The wandering companies shall know of your journey, and those that have power for good shall be on the watch. I name you Elf-friend; and may the stars shine upon the end of your road!' (I. 124)

This incident establishes the pattern: Frodo and Company will encounter unexpected aid. Elrond predicts likewise (I. 360).

In the Old Forest Merry and Pippin are swallowed alive into the cracks beneath Old Man Willow (I. 166). Tom Bombadil frees Merry and Pippin. Later he rescues the hobbits from the Barrow-wight, and breaks the Wight's spell; he gives Merry a *providential* sword. He welcomes the hobbits to his house for three days' safety and rest. Frodo asks Tom if he heard Frodo calling. Says Tom:

> '[...] Nay, I did not hear: I was busy singing. *Just chance brought me here, if chance you call it. It was no plan of mine, though I was waiting for you.*' [Author's italics] (I. 175)

In Rivendell Gandalf watches at Frodo's bedside. Frodo, dismayed at Gandalf's absence, says he did not know what to do without him.

> 'I was delayed,' said Gandalf, 'and that nearly proved our ruin. *And yet I am not sure: it may have been better so.*' [Author's italics] (I. 290)

Gandalf is attuned to 'reversals' which hold disguised blessings: during his absence, something unforeseen and providential may have happened. Indeed, Merry receives his sword of the Barrow-downs.

The Ring must go to the Fire. Silence reigns, and deep dread: *who* will do this deed? Frodo breaks the fateful silence.

> At last with an effort he spoke, and wondered to hear his own words, *as if some other will was using his small voice*.
>
> 'I will take the Ring,' he said, 'though I do not know the way.' [Author's italics] (I. 354)

Elrond knows Frodo's Ring-bearing is a fortuitous consequence of Bilbo's long stewardship of the Ring.

> '[...] I think that this task is *appointed* for you, Frodo; and that if you do not find a way, no one will. This is the hour of the Shire-folk, when they arise from their quiet fields to shake the towers and counsels of the great. *Who of all the wise could have foreseen it?*' [Author's italics] (I. 354)

In Lórien on the night before their departure the wisdom of Galadriel comforts the Fellowship.

> 'Do not trouble your hearts overmuch with thought of the road tonight. *Maybe the paths that you each shall tread are already lain before your feet, though you do not see them.* Good night!' [Author's italics] (I. 476)

At the breaking of the Fellowship, Sam voices the likelihood that Frodo will bolt for Mordor, *alone* if need be. Pippin is alarmed, and pleads with Aragorn to stop Frodo.

> 'I wonder,' said Aragorn. 'He is the Bearer, and the fate of the Burden is on him. I do not think that it is our part to drive him one way or the other. Nor do I think that we should succeed, if we tried. *There are other powers at work far stronger.*' [Author's italics] (I. 522)

Merry and Pippin enter Fangorn Forest and meet Treebeard the Ent. They make Treebeard aware of the desperate game for the fate of Middle-earth. Théoden would say, *Oft evil will shall evil mar*. For paradoxically the Orcs have but succeeded in escorting Merry and Pippin to Fangorn in the nick of time and thus cause the involvement of the Ents. Consequently Gandalf foresees disaster for Saruman the tree-killer (II. 131). When the Huorns (Ents gone tree-ish and *wild*) scour the battlefield of Orcs, onlookers view the trees with alarm, suspecting Gandalf's wizardry is at work.

> 'The trees?' he said. 'Nay, I see the wood as plainly as you do. But that is no deed of mine. It is a thing beyond the counsel of the wise. Better than my design, and better even than my hope the event has proved.' (II. 189)

In the Battle of the Pelennor Fields the Lord of the Nazgûl upon his winged steed threatens Théoden, fallen beneath Snowmane. Lady Éowyn bravely resists. Merry masters his terror and pierces the Nazgûl from behind. The Nazgûl utters a wailing cry and vanishes from the earth. Later Merry tries to retrieve his belongings, but the blade of his sword, wrought slowly long ago in the North-kingdom when the Dúnedain were young, dissolves in front of his eyes.

> *No other blade*, not though mightier hands had wielded it, would have dealt that foe a wound so bitter, cleaving the undead flesh, breaking the spell that knit his unseen sinews to his will. [Author's italics] (III. 146)

Oft evil will shall evil mar. Had the Barrow-wight not seized the hobbits, Merry would never have gained his sword of destiny.

Below (9) is described Tolkien's **greatest** providential event, the intervention of Gollum during Frodo's unforeseen lapse, resulting in the Ring's destruction.

In the contest of Good and Evil in Middle-earth, the action of Divine Providence is implied through all. Evil may have its day, but Light triumphs over Shadow. Tolkien's *eucatastrophe* (his coined word: *the sudden, joyous turn, a good catastrophe, a sudden and miraculous grace*), is a foretaste of Christian eschatology: God playing with loaded dice; the world redeemed (see S. 6).

On film:
In *FotR* acts of unexpected aid are missing; significantly, the rescue by Gildor and the Elves (I. 116). Although in the extended version of *The Fellowship* a ghostly cavalcade of Elves passes by, we lose Elven exposure. Farmer Maggot aids the hobbits leaving the Shire (I. 133). Maggot, Old Forest, Bombadil and the Barrow-wight are entirely missing. The hobbits jump straight from Brandywine to Bree. Therefore, some history and unexpected aid are lost, and Merry's sword of Númenor (I. 201) is not explained.

In Tolkien's Flight to the Ford Frodo is rescued by Glorfindel, a powerful Elf-lord. Frodo mounts his white steed Asfaloth, and gallops to the Ford of Bruinen *alone* (I. 284). On film Glorfindel is replaced by Arwen, who *bears* Frodo to Bruinen on Asfaloth.

Tolkien's Treebeard, oldest of living things, is well aware of Saruman the tree-killer. The hobbits make Treebeard aware of the great game for Middle-earth, with Saruman now a Power, and 'aligned' with the Shadow. Treebeard, having roots in the Elder Days, knows only too well that the Shadow must be vanquished *unconditionally*. On film (*TTT*), Treebeard stubbornly remains *neutral*, and only Pippin's ruse hoodwinks Treebeard into setting the hobbits down close to Isengard, to reveal that Orcs have axed his beloved trees, to arouse his anger at Isengard. This departure is *hobbit-centric*.

On film (*TTT*) Saruman's dam above Isengard was patrolled by Orcs, and destroyed by Ents. In the book Ents and Huorns dig great pits and trenches to channel the waters of Isen and other streams to flood Isengard (II. 222).

Still the notion of Providence working behind the scenes emerges loud and clear. But one must still accept responsibility and get on with the task at hand. Frodo says: 'I wish the Ring had never come to me.' Gandalf's words echo several times:

> 'So do all who live to see such times; but that is not for them to decide. All we have to do is decide what to do with the time that is given to us. There are other forces at work in this world, Frodo, besides the will of evil. Bilbo was *meant* to find the Ring. In which case you were also *meant* to have it. And that is an encouraging thought.'

Most important of all is the role of pity and understanding, and the hidden force of Divine serendipity.

4. Tolkien on the nature of Good and Evil

Tolkien has chosen the metaphor of Light versus Shadow to illustrate elemental morality. As Light and Shadow define each other in dramatic chiaroscuro, Good and Evil are likewise defined by comparison: one against the other.

In Lothlórien Frodo ascends a height. After the radiance and peace of Lórien from the Elder Days, he is struck by contrast with the ordinary world. Sud¬denly he perceives the opposing Shadow of Dol Guldur, where the Enemy long hid as the Necromancer. Haldir comments:

> 'We fear that now it is inhabited again, and with power sevenfold. A black cloud lies often over it of late. In this high place you may see the two powers that are opposed one to another; and ever they strive now in thought, but whereas the light perceives the very heart of the darkness, its own secret has not been discovered. Not yet.' (I. 456)

The trees fight with each other as they rot and wither. The Shadow of Sauron is poisonous for all living things. This comes to stark realization in Mordor's desolation.

Melkor of the Valar, mightiest in knowledge and power, became the first Dark Lord of Middle-earth, and was given the name Morgoth, the 'Dark Enemy' (see S. 71). Sauron became one of his emissaries to Middle-earth. Morgoth's evil is *perennial* (III. 190). In squandering his powers in self-interest, Morgoth diminishes in power and vision, like Sauron and Saruman (see S. 25). Evil is *self-limiting. Oft evil will shall evil mar.* The self-limiting nature of Sauron's malice becomes more apparent. Gandalf says:

'Despair or folly? [...] Let folly be our cloak, a veil before the eyes of the Enemy! For he is very wise, and weighs all things to a nicety in the scales of his malice. But the only measure that he knows is desire, desire for power, and so he judges all hearts. Into his heart the thought will not enter that any will refuse it, that having the Ring we may seek to destroy it.' (I. 352)

On film:

The Nine kings of Men fall to Sauron through their lust for *power* (*FotR*). The Orcs kill and cannibalize their dead comrade: *'Meat's back on the menu, boys!'* (*TTT*). They likewise reduce Men to *'man-flesh.'* The Nazgûl mow down the night-watch in the Shire and in Bree (*FotR*). We see Orcs and Nazgûl as ruthless, and as showing no respect for living things. Saruman's army is for one purpose: *'[...] to destroy the world of Men'* (Aragorn, *TTT*). They will kill men, *women* and *children*. The metaphor of the Shadow is intact. Gandalf tells the Balrog: *'Go back to the Shadow!'* Galadriel says of Gandalf: *'He has fallen into Shadow.'* We learn from Gandalf's words that Sauron's malice is self-limiting (*RotK*). It is the Free Peoples who exhibit love, hope, and loyalty.

5. Refusers of the Ring

Sauron's One Ring is an instrument of malice. The Ring is evil by nature, and *cannot* produce good, no matter who wields it and it corrupts its wearer. When Frodo in his anxiety offers the Ring to Gandalf:

> 'No!!' cried Gandalf, springing to his feet. 'With that power I should have power too great and terrible. And over me the Ring would gain a power still greater and more deadly.' His eyes flashed and his face was lit as by a fire within. 'Do not tempt me! For I do not wish to become like the Dark Lord himself. Yet the way of the Ring to my heart is by pity, pity for weakness and the desire for strength to do good. Do not tempt me! I dare not take it, not even to keep it safe, unused. The wish to wield it would be too great for my strength. I shall have such need of it. Great perils lie before me.' (I. 95)

Gandalf becomes the first member of an elect society: those possessing wisdom and foresight from the Elder Days, *to refuse the Ring*. Also Elrond refuses to take the Ring into his keeping (I. 350).

Evil is perilously seductive, even to the Wise. Frodo, now more anxious than before, offers the Ring to Galadriel in Lothlórien.

'And now so it comes. You will give me the Ring freely! In place of the Dark Lord you will set up a Queen. And I shall not be dark, but beautiful and terrible as the Morning and the Night! Fair as the Sea and the Sun and the Snow on the Mountain! Dreadful as the Storm and the Lightning! Stronger than the foundations of the earth. All shall love me and despair!' (I. 473)

Tolkien arouses our deadliest fears, that we understand the peril of the Ring's temptation. But Galadriel masters herself, and does not leave the path of wisdom.

Sam looks in the Mirror of Galadriel, and receives horrible premonitions of destruction in the Shire. Sam recognizes Galadriel's goodness and protests:

'I wish you'd take his Ring. You'd put things to rights. You'd stop them digging up the gaffer and turning him adrift. You'd make some folk pay for their dirty work.'

'I would,' she said. 'That is how it would begin. But it would not stop with that, alas!' (I. 474)

Faramir of Gondor, brother of Boromir, who was corrupted by lust for the Ring, confronts the Ring, reads Boromir's heart, and *refuses the Ring*.

'[…] *Not if I found it by the highway would I take it* I said. […]. I am wise enough to know that there are some perils from which a man must flee. Sit at peace! And be comforted, Samwise. […] For strange though it may seem, it was safe to declare this to me. It may even help the master that you love. It shall turn to his good, if it is in my power.' [Author's italics] (II. 367)

'Sleep, both of you – in peace, if you can. Fear not! I do not wish to see it, or touch it, or know more of it than I know (which is enough), lest peril perchance waylay me and I fall lower in the test than Frodo son of Drogo.' (II. 368)

Sam recognizes Faramir's wisdom of the Elder Days.

'You have an air too, Sir, that reminds me of, of – well, Gandalf, of Wizards.' (II. 369)

Faramir is true to his word. At considerable personal risk, he releases Frodo, Sam, and Gollum. Moreover, he aids them on their way with provisions, and by providing staves of *lebethron* wood, which bear a virtue of finding and returning.

Last of the members is Sam, who tearfully takes the Ring, believing Frodo is dead from Shelob's venom. On the edge of Mordor, Sam puts on the Ring.

> Already the Ring tempted him, gnawing at his will and reason. Wild fantasies arose in his mind; and he saw Samwise the Strong, Hero of the Age, striding with a flaming sword across the darkened land, and armies flocking to his call as he marched to the overthrow of Barad-Dûr. And then all the clouds rolled away, and the white sun shone, and at his command the Vale of Gorgoroth became a garden of flowers and trees and brought forth fruit. He had only to put on the Ring and claim it for his own, and all this could be. (III. 216)

In the end, the evil allure of the Ring was quenched, conquered by Sam's love for his master, and also by plain hobbit-sense, as he intuits that the Ring's visions are a cheat to betray him. At about the same time, the Steward Denethor, lamenting Boromir's death, tells Gandalf that his elder son would have brought him 'a mighty gift'. Gandalf replies:

> 'You are strong and can still in some matters govern yourself, Denethor; yet if you had received this thing, it would have overthrown you. Were it buried beneath the roots of Mindolluin, still it would burn your mind away, as the darkness grows, and the yet worse things follow that shall soon come upon us.' (III. 105-06)

In stark contrast to the refusers, Gollum's self-serving fantasies tempt him in the Dead Marshes.

> 'See, my Precious: if we has it, then we can escape, even from Him, eh? Perhaps we grows very strong, stronger than Wraiths. Lord Sméagol? Gollum the Great? *The* Gollum! Eat fish every day, three times a day, fresh from the Sea. Most Precious Gollum! Must have it. We wants it, we wants it! (II. 304)

Gollum in the end fails his test. He seizes the Precious, and perishes.

On film:
In the book first *Sam* peers into the Mirror, and sees events that enrage him. Galadriel's response (I. 474) is instructive about the power of the Ring (see above). This is missing on film, where only Frodo looks in the Mirror.

Gandalf vehemently refuses the Ring. Galadriel's temptation is intact and *dramatic*; we see her metamorphosis into a queen of *dread*, but she quietly refuses the Ring. On film we do not see Sam put on the Ring. Unexpectedly, Aragorn *declines* the Ring atop Amon Hen.

On film (*TTT*), Faramir drags Frodo, Sam and Gollum against their will into Osgiliath: '*A chance for Faramir, Captain of Gondor, to show his quality.*' He would, *like Boromir,* bring his father *'a mighty gift'*. He releases them only after Frodo, on the edge of madness, confronts a winged Nazgûl. Faramir's deputy-sheriff heavy-handedness on film, dragging unwilling Frodo and Company along into Osgiliath, fractures the plot, and *obscures* Tolkien's intent.

In *Tolkien's* 'The Last Debate', Legolas and Gimli enter Minas Tirith, and observe its architecture.

> 'And doubtless the good stone-work is the older and was wrought in the first building,' said Gimli. 'It is ever so with the things that Men begin: there is a frost in spring, or a blight in summer, and they fail of their promise.'
>
> 'Yet seldom do they fail of their seed,' said Legolas. 'And that will lie in the dust and rot to spring up again in times and places unlooked for. The deeds of Men will outlast us, Gimli.'
>
> 'And yet come to naught in the end but might-have-beens, I guess,' said the dwarf.
>
> 'To that the Elves know not the answer,' said Legolas. (III. 182)

Tolkien knows the answer: he drops numerous hints that Faramir, *unlike* Boromir, evokes Númenor and the Elder Race.

> Boromir, five years the elder, beloved by his father, was like him in face and pride, but in little else. Rather he was a man after the sort of King Eärnur of old, taking no wife and delighting chiefly in arms; fearless and strong, but caring little for lore, save the tales of old battles. Faramir the younger was like him in looks but otherwise in mind. He read the hearts of men as shrewdly as his father, but what he read moved him sooner to pity than to scorn. He was gentle in bearing, and a lover of lore and of music, and therefore by many in those days his courage was judged less than his brother's. But it was not so, except that he did not seek glory in danger without a purpose. He welcomed Gandalf at such times as he came to the city, and he learned what he could from his wisdom; and in this as in many other matters he displeased his father. (Appendix A; III. 419)

Tolkien's Faramir is a foil to his corruptible brother Boromir. Faramir refuses the Ring, *as would Gandalf,* understands and accepts Frodo's mission, and speeds him on his way. Here is the indication of Elven nobility surviving in the remnants of Númenor's race. Tolkien is forecasting the future of Men: *one is lost, but one remains.*

Someone remains to pass the torch. The rest is up to us Lesser Men of Latter Days.

6. The randomness of evil things

There are many workers of evil in Middle-earth. Exponents of evil are but *self-servers*, and thus not all evil things in the world are allied with Sauron.

After Caradhras defeats the Fellowship, Aragorn and Gimli philosophize, based on their experiences in Middle-earth.

> 'There are many evil and unfriendly things in the world that have little love for those that go on two legs, and yet are not in league with Sauron, but have purposes of their own. Some of them have been in the world longer than he.' (I. 378)

> 'Caradhras was called the Cruel, and had an ill name,' said Gimli, 'long years ago, when rumour of Sauron had not been heard in these lands.' (I. 403)

At Moria's Gate the Watcher in the Water assails the Fellowship. We do not know whether the creature is aligned with Sauron, however it seizes Frodo first; hence it may sense the Ring.

> 'I do not know,' answered Gandalf; 'But the arms were all guided by one purpose. Something has crept, or has been driven out of dark waters under the mountains. There are older and fouler things than Orcs in the deep places of the world.' (I. 403)

Gandalf the White has returned from the abyss beneath Durin's bridge, and tells the Three Hunters of his struggle with the Balrog beneath the earth.

> 'Far, far below the deepest delving of the Dwarves, the world is gnawed by nameless things. Even Sauron knows them not. They are older than he. Now I have walked there, but I will bring no report to darken the light of day.' (II. 134)

On film:

Evil appears more *centralized*. In Eregion *crebain* from Dunland spy upon the Fellowship (I. 373). The book never identifies the source of espionage ('*being watched*'); *Sauron* is the likely assumption. Later the Fellowship ascends the pass of Caradhras. Tolkien explains that many *unaligned* unfriendly things are the world (I. 378). On film (*FotR*), however, the source is *Saruman*. We see Saruman receiving the birds' tidings, or with raised staff atop Isengard, invoking the storm with a sinister incantation.

7. White wizards: Old and new

When Gandalf the Grey seeks Saruman's counsel on the Ring, he notices that the robe of Saruman "The White" is now composed of many colors which shimmer and shift as the lighting changes (I. 339). Gandalf fears that Saruman has left the path of wisdom.

Gandalf the *White* returns to Isengard. He confronts Saruman regarding his evil deeds, giving him one last chance to leave Isengard, abandon his self-seeking devices, and aid in Middle-earth's defence. But Saruman, being treacherous himself, does not trust Gandalf and refuses his offer to go free (II. 240), spewing pride and hatred. Gandalf reveals himself as Gandalf *the White*, breaks Saruman's staff, the focal point of a wizard's powers, and casts Saruman from the Council. Pippin asks Gandalf what he will do to Saruman.

> 'I? Nothing!' said Gandalf. 'I will do nothing to him. I do not wish for mastery. What will become of him? I cannot say. I grieve that so much that was good now festers in the tower.' (II. 243)

Here are contrasted the ways of evil and good. Saruman is mastered by rage, pride and hatred, and fails to recognize his last chance of escape from the Shadow. Saruman has lusted after the Ring, which corrupts the hearts of all who covet it. Gandalf has no desire for domination. And he remains, throughout the book, the character most capable of pity and understanding (see II. 353, S. 24-25).

The returning hobbits must evict evil from the Shire. Gandalf senses trouble. But the hobbits must be self-reliant, for Gandalf, after appealing to their self-reliance and pointing out their ability to take care of themselves now, bows out (III. 340).

Indeed the hobbits have gained stature from their adventures. The Shire is raised, the thugs are routed. The mysterious totalitarian boss "Sharkey" pillaging the Shire is *Saruman*. After the hobbit uprising, Saruman, turned adrift by the hobbits, stabs Frodo, but his blade is deflected by Frodo's mithril coat. Sam draws his sword, but Frodo holds him back and lets Saruman depart unharmed (III. 369). Saruman, still dogged by Wormtongue, kicks

Wormtongue viciously in the face and orders him to follow. Finally Wormtongue snaps, and slits Saruman's throat from behind. Wormtongue is shot dead by hobbits; as for Saruman, his body disintegrates as it betrays *years* of living death. Saruman's spirit looks West, whence it came. But his spirit, dissipated through evil pursuits, has lost its birthright there, and its eternal home. But Gandalf leaves Middle-earth from the Grey Havens for the Blessed Lands in the West, to dwell with the Valar.

On film:
Saruman says from the caverns of Isengard in *TTT*:

> 'The old world will burn in the fires of industry. The forests will fall. A new order will arise. We will drive the machine of war with the sword and the spear and the iron fist of the Orc.'

This is entirely in keeping with Tolkien's nightmare: Saruman betrays the Elder Days, falling to blind militarism and foul industrialism.

As the Three Hunters meet Gandalf the White in Fangorn (*TTT*), Gandalf's voice at first sounds frighteningly like that of Saruman. This may be a device for suspense, but also may be intended to demonstrate the kinship of the two White Wizards, or the ascendancy of the new one: Gandalf is now what Saruman *should have been* (see II. 125).

The confrontation between Gandalf and Saruman, culminating in the breaking of Saruman's staff, is missing, along with a lesson on Good, on Evil and its consequences in Middle-earth.

Missing from *RotK* is the 'Scouring of the Shire'. The death of Saruman, Sharkey's End, is also missing, so we lose an important lesson on the wages of evil. Moreover, we do not see the hobbits roused to independence, nor the torch passed to the heroes of the Fourth Age.

8. The perils of seeing afar

Saruman was once noble and far-sighted. How did Saruman turn to evil? The Tower of Orthanc holds a *palantír*, one of the Seeing Stones of Númenor, forged in the Elder Days. At first Saruman wisely refrained from using the Stone, but thirst for knowledge, pride, and ambition to become a power in Middle-earth mastered Saruman. But the Stones are interlinked, and the *palantír* of Minas Ithil (now Minas *Morgul*, Tower of Sorcery) is now in the hands of Sauron, who like Smaug, possesses *rather an overwhelming personality* and traps the roving eye of Saruman (II. 259).

Denethor the Steward of Gondor likewise uses a *palantír*. Sauron's despairing visions seduce Denethor to cremate himself and Faramir *alive*. Gandalf, about to challenge the Witch-king, is summoned and saves Faramir. Denethor burns alive, with the *palantír* in his hands and though Gandalf has prevented the worst, he is troubled by the Enemy's long reach and laments the fall of Denethor (III. 161).

Clearly the palantír is just as perilous as the Mirror of Galadriel, wherein images are often *not as they seem* (I. 470).

Comparing the Mirror and the *palantíri*, one easily imagines the danger of a *palantír*, if Sauron the master of lies and treachery feeds propaganda on the other end.

Pippin, overcome by curiosity, purloins the *palantír* from under sleeping Gandalf's elbow. He fares poorly with the Stone, and is revealed to the Eye of Sauron! Gandalf tells Pippin that he has been "saved mainly by good fortune, as it is called" (II. 254).

Gandalf himself hesitates to use the *palantír*.

> 'Strange powers have our enemies, and strange weaknesses!' said Théoden. 'But it has oft been said: *oft evil will shall evil mar.*'
>
> 'That many times is seen,' said Gandalf. 'But at this time we have been strangely fortunate. Maybe, I have been saved by this hobbit from a grave blunder. I had considered whether or not to probe this stone myself to find its uses. Had I done so, I should have been revealed to him myself. I am not ready for such a trial, if indeed I shall ever be.' (II. 255)

Only Aragorn succeeds with the *palantír*, just barely. He looks in the Stone not for self-serving purposes, but to distract Sauron, to aid the Ring-bearer (III. 190).

As Frodo and Sam approach Mount Doom, we learn the consequences of Aragorn's seizing the Stone, as Sauron's Eye is diverted from his own land (III. 245).

On film:
Saruman's consulting the *palantír*, inferred after the fact by Gandalf in the book, is demonstrated on screen, with Saruman playing Sauron's obedient servant (*FotR*, *TTT*). We see Pippin's disastrous flirting with the *palantír*. But at the Pyre of Denethor, where is the *palantír*? Tolkien's Denethor is a noble character, albeit *corruptible* like Boromir. Tolkien establishes a common link between the fall of Saruman and Denethor: both dared use the *palantír* and were ensnared. The *palantír* is not evil like the Ring. It is like a video-telephone, however one is on line with Sauron the Base Master of Treachery, who deals in lies and intimidation (see III. 205).

9. Pity and Prophecy

The only way to possess the Ring unscathed is through pity and understanding. Bilbo, after finding the Ring, is desperate to escape from Gollum and the Goblins. Gollum crouches menacingly, blocking Bilbo's exit. Bilbo debates whether to kill Gollum with Sting. However:

> A sudden understanding, a pity mixed with horror, welled up in Bilbo's heart: a glimpse of endless unmarked days without light or hope of betterment, hard stone, cold fish, sneaking and whispering. All these thoughts passed in a flash of a second. He trembled. And then quite suddenly in another flash, as if lifted by a new strength and resolve, he leaped. (H. 93)

And Bilbo escapes with the Ring. When Gandalf reveals it is the One Ring, and that Gollum has leaked the name 'Baggins' to Sauron under torment, Frodo exclaims, and Gandalf replies:

> 'What a pity that Bilbo did not stab that vile creature, when he had a chance!'

> 'Pity? It was pity that stayed his hand. Pity and Mercy: not to strike without need. And he has been well rewarded, Frodo. Be sure that he took so little hurt from the evil, and escaped in the end, because he began his ownership of the Ring so. With pity.' (I. 92)

Gandalf knows the Ring is evil, and that Bilbo survived only by resisting its evil whisperings. He advises Frodo against exacting vengeance, and his advice becomes a turning-point for Middle-earth.

> 'Deserves it! I daresay he does. Many that live deserve death. And some that die deserve life. Can you give it to them? Then do not be too eager to deal out death in judgement. For even the very wise cannot see all ends. I have not much hope that Gollum can be cured before he dies. But there is a chance of it. *And he is bound up with the fate of the Ring. My heart tells me that he has some part to play yet, for good or ill, before the end. And when that comes, the pity of Bilbo may rule the fate of many – yours not least.*' [Author's italics] (I. 92-93)

Gollum attacks Frodo and Sam in the Emyn Muil, and the hobbits are alarmed. They debate whether to kill Gollum or bind him to die in the waste; Frodo hears Gandalf's voice out of the past, pleading pity (II. 281).

Frodo does come to pity Gollum. Despite Sam's misgivings, Frodo enlists Gollum as guide, forcing Gollum to swear on the only thing he respects: the *Precious*. This becomes Gollum's turning-point. Later Gollum begs Frodo for the Ring. Frodo, in a stern and masterful voice Sam has never heard before, warns Gollum that the Ring will wreak his undoing (II. 313-14).

Still Frodo does not forget Gandalf's message of pity. At Henneth Annûn, Frodo saves Gollum from certain death at Faramir's hands, not least since he feels that "[…] this creature is in some way bound up with my errand" (II. 374).

Prophet Frodo appears once more on the slopes of Mount Doom, when he challenges Gollum: "If you touch me ever again, you shall be cast yourself into the Fire of Doom!" (III. 272).

It is Sam's turn to kill Gollum. He certainly deserves killing, plotting Frodo's death for selfish ends, *exactly* as Sam projected. But Sam, having *grown* bearing the Ring, also pities Gollum, and perhaps has learned pity and understanding (III. 273). He spares Gollum's life with chagrin. Meanwhile Frodo has entered the Chambers of Fire and claims the Ring: "'I have come,' he said, 'but I do not choose now to do what I came to do. I will not do this deed. The Ring is mine!'" (III. 274).

The Ring, now most powerful at its origin, has *seized* Frodo. Worst of all, Sauron's realm is shaken; the Enemy is suddenly *aware* of Frodo, and of his enemies' designs. But the unexpected happens.

> Suddenly Sam saw Gollum's long hands draw upward to his mouth, his white fangs gleamed, and then snapped as they bit. Frodo gave a cry, and there he was, fallen upon his knees at the chasm's edge. But Gollum, dancing like a mad thing, held aloft the Ring, a finger still thrust within its circle. It shone now as if verily it was wrought of living fire.
>
> 'Precious, Precious, Precious!' Gollum cried. 'My Precious! O my Precious! And with that even as his eyes were lifted up to gloat on his prize, he stepped too far, toppled, wavered for a moment on the brink, and then with a shriek he fell. Out of the depths came his last wail *Precious*, and he was gone. (III. 275-76)

On film:
In the Emyn Muil (*TTT*), Frodo warns Gollum of impending retribution if he betrays his oath on the Precious. The message of pity emerges intact, that most eloquently brought to life on film. Gandalf says to Frodo:

> 'Pity? It was pity that stayed Bilbo's hand. Many that live deserve death. And some that die deserve life. Can you give it to them, Frodo? Then do not be too eager to deal out death in judgement. For even the very wise cannot see all ends. *My heart tells me that Gollum has some part to play yet, for good or ill, before the end. Before this is over, the pity of Bilbo may rule the fate of many.*' [Author's italics] (see I. 92-93)

The Ring is unmade, Barad Dûr is cast down in ruin, and Sauron perishes beyond hope of return.

Frodo failed at the end, for in Mount Doom the power of the Ring proved too strong for his will. But Gollum stepped in as if *summoned*, and destroyed the Ring in his stead. Gollum, spared by the pity and foresight of Gandalf, *and* by the pity of many others, becomes the unwitting instrument of Providence to destroy Sauron's realm in Middle-earth.

10. Flotsam and Jetsam

Other film amendments / omissions:
The plot deviations on film are too many to mention here. After Bilbo's Long-Expected Party, Bilbo departs not with Dwarves (I. 62), but *alone*. When

Frodo's peril is revealed, Gandalf says, 'You ought to go quietly, and you ought to go soon.' But not *'instantly'* (I. 99). On film Gandalf says, 'You must leave quickly!' Frodo, Sam and *Peregrin* leave Hobbiton together, without Gandalf, who *should have come* (I. 105); on film it is only Frodo and Sam, dispatched by Gandalf.

In the book: before Moria's Gate Boromir casts a stone into the water and thus awakens the Watcher, who seizes Frodo first. Frodo, fearing the water, admonishes him (I. 401). This episode is consistent with Boromir's role, for he will cause Frodo further trouble; perhaps it is a *foreshadowing*. On film Merry casts the first stone, and when Pippin starts to throw, Aragorn tells him: "Do not disturb the water!'

When Gandalf releases Théoden on film (*TTT*), Gandalf drives out Saruman's spirit, as a Biblical casting-out of demons. Suddenly Théoden loses *forty years* to become a 'young' Bernard Hill. Compare Tolkien's scene (II. 151): Théoden remains aged, because later in *The Return of the King* he laments that his age is an ill no leech can wholly cure.

RotK is the most climactic and emotionally wrenching of the three films. Strangely, at opening we witness a flashback to the finding of the Ring in the River Anduin. A large fish pulls Déagol into the river; he loses the fish, but grabs the Ring. Sméagol covets Déagol's Ring, and brutally murders Déagol on the spot. We witness Sméagol's horrifying metamorphosis into the Gollum that we know and loathe so well: Andy Serkis' finest hour.

The final five chapters of *The Two Towers* are in the film *RotK*. Gollum leads the hobbits up the Stair of Cirith Ungol. But on film Gollum drives a wedge of deceit between Frodo and Sam; Gollum drops their *lembas* bread onto the stair below while the hobbits are asleep, blaming Sam. Sam's eyes stream with tears as Frodo sends him home. Sam returns with I bread which Gollum has let fall; but Frodo must face terror in Shelob's lair *alone*, not together with Sam, as in the book.

On film Elrond comes to Aragorn at Dunharrow, bringing Narsil/Andúril, the Sword-that-was-Broken, reforged by Elves. Tolkien's Aragorn leaves Rivendell with the sword (I. 362), and does not see Elrond until his coronation.

On film Gandalf asks Pippin to scale Mount Mindolluin and light the war-beacon. This is *hobbit-centric*, and a discredit to Denethor's military readiness. Tolkien's Denethor is prepared: the war-beacons are alight as Gandalf and Pippin ride Shadowfax to Gondor (III. 20).

Frodo is wounded and worn down fighting Evil. On film we miss Frodo's pining and illness. But he completes the Red Book, passing it to Sam. He travels to the Grey Havens with Bilbo, Elrond, Galadriel and Gandalf, where the hobbits' farewell is among the most poignant ever witnessed on screen. The passengers board ship, and the three hobbits return to the Shire. But we miss the last voyage through Frodo's eyes.

> And the ship went out into the High Sea and passed on into the West, until at last on a night of rain Frodo smelled a sweet fragrance on the air and heard the sound of singing that came over the water. And then it seemed to him that as in his dream in the house of Bombadil, the grey rain-curtain turned all to silver glass and was rolled back, and he beheld white shores and beyond them a far green country under a swift sunrise. (III. 384)

But in the film *RotK* Gandalf speaks these words to tell Pippin why he need not fear death.

Insertions and expansions:
It is heart-warming hearing so much Elvish, Sindarin and Quenya, on film, with English language sub-titles: the director respects the origin of Tolkien's sub-creation in *language*. This inclusion must have been daunting for screenwriters. For like Illyrian or Tocharian, known only in fragments from isolated inscriptions, the Elven tongues are likewise *defective*, or at least our knowledge of them.

Although, regrettably, many songs from *The Lord of the Rings* are not heard on film, still Elven Tongues are heard at sporadic moments, notably when Arwen, Aragorn, Elrond, Legolas and Galadriel converse.

Aragorn and Elrond in the garden of Rivendell behold a statue of Gilraen, Aragorn's mother. He quotes his mother's words before she died:

> 'Ónen i-Estel Edain, ú-chebin estel anim.'
> (I gave hope to the Dúnedain, I have kept no hope for myself).
> (Appendix A. III. 427)

Actors sometimes stumble over syllables or words: in *FotR* Gandalf says *Cáradhras*, and a few moments later Saruman says *Carádhras*. Haldir in the extended version says Caras *Galadhon* instead of Caras *Galadon*. Perhaps a conversation with a screenwriter's consultant will reveal how they got Gimli's scurrilous Dwarvish curse, when he withers the Elves in Lórien. The map in Henneth Annûn has *Dagorland* instead of *Dagorlad*.

The Eldar communicate also *mind-to-mind*, without words (*FotR*, *TTT*). The chief telepath is Galadriel, who speaks to Aragorn, Frodo and Boromir. Elrond and Arwen also communicate mind-to-mind. Arwen and Aragorn communicate in dream sequences, as Arwen intervenes when Aragorn is in danger (*TTT*). The film demonstrates this power in episodes *beyond* those in the book.

Gollum was an awesome first in cinematic history. One quite forgets that Gollum is *digital*, and not a *living* character. Andy Serkis, his actor prototype, actually constitutes Gollum's movements. Mr. Serkis' body and face are rubber-like, for he captures Gollum's sinewy twistings and turnings, and his repulsive grimaces, surely like Tolkien intended. The film *TTT* shows a masterful debate between Slinker and Stinker.

One's heart is greatly warmed, where Elrond sends Haldir and Elven archers to the aid of Rohan at Helm's Deep.

One also finds brilliant insertion of material found outside *The Lord of the Rings proper*, actually from elsewhere in Tolkien, from *The Hobbit*, the Appendices, or *The Silmarillion*. One recurrent *motif* is Arwen's renouncing Eldar immortality in order to remain beyond death with Aragorn, the love of her life. *The Tale of Aragorn and Arwen* facilitates the *motif*. As we see Aragorn in state:

> Then a great beauty was revealed in him, so that all who after came there looked on him in wonder; for they saw that the grace of his youth, and the valour of his manhood, and the wisdom and majesty of his age were blended together. And long there he lay, an image of the splendour of the Kings of Men in glory undimmed before the breaking of the world. (Appendix A. III. 428)

Elrond speaks some of these words, as before our eyes the body of Aragorn on his bier becomes a stone effigy.

There are delightful insertions from *The Hobbit*. The introduction to *FotR* shows Bilbo finding the Ring. When Bilbo receives Gandalf at Bag End: while Gandalf is getting his bearings in the diminutive hobbit-dwelling, Bilbo putters about in the kitchen, muttering about cold chicken, pickles, tart, etc., the same fare at the Unexpected Party! (H. 24). In the evening, before the Long-Expected Party, Bilbo and Gandalf are smoking; and Gandalf spears Bilbo's large smoke-ring with an elaborate clipper-ship of smoke (see H. 25-26).

When Gandalf confides to Bilbo that Frodo *suspects something*, Bilbo replies:

> 'Of course he does! He's a *Baggins*; not some blockheaded Bracegirdle from Hardbottle!'

This is a sly dig at the Sackville-Bagginses! (See III. 372, Appendix 474).

As Saruman confronts his new Uruk-hai, he reveals how the race of Orcs came to be: 'They were Elves once, taken by the Dark Powers, tortured and mutilated, a ruined and terrible form of life;' compare *The Silmarillion*:

> [...] all those of the Quendi who came into the hands of Melkor, ere Utumno was broken, were put there in prison, and by slow arts of cruelty were corrupted and enslaved; and thus did Melkor breed the hideous race of the Orcs in envy and in mockery of the Elves, of whom they were afterwards the bitterest of foes. [...] And deep in their heart of hearts the Orcs loathed the Master whom they served in fear, the maker only of their misery. (S. 50)

Marching to Helm's Deep Gimli reveals to Éowyn how the world believes there are no Dwarf-women, but there are.

> It was said by Gimli that there are few dwarf-women, probably no more than a third of the whole people. They seldom walk abroad except at great need. They are in voice and appearance, and in garb if they must go on a journey, so like to the dwarf-men that the eyes and ears of other peoples cannot tell them apart. This has given rise to the foolish opinion among Men that there are no dwarf-women, and that the Dwarves 'grow out of stone.' (Appendix A; III. 449)

Aragorn interjects with a wry grin: 'It's *the beards*.' Éowyn tries to maintain a straight face. With bearded *women*, no wonder poor Gimli finds Lady Galadriel so beautiful!

Alas, poor Gimli is the butt of several jokes on film, usually because of his physical stature. The wickedest occurs when Legolas and Gimli await the attack atop the rampart at Helm's Deep. Legolas asks Gimli, should he describe what is happening, or should he find him a *box* (to stand upon)!

Actually Gimli, portrayed by John Rhys-Davies, is right on the mark, and retains Gimli's Dwarvish integrity on film. Gimli is forthright and vehement, with a long and deadly memory for injuries, a hearty laugh, wry gallows-humour, and he is zealous for combat in a righteous cause, *particularly* when there are Orc-necks to hew.

Dialogue shuffle: Whose line is this, anyway?
Tolkien's characters are replaced by others on film. In some cases quotations from one character are assigned as lines to another, or sometimes a character keeps his lines, but utters them in another context.

Treebeard's line 'The world is changing [...]' goes to the narratress in the introduction to *FotR* (Galadriel?).

Legolas sees approaching *crebain* from Dunland, Gimli says 'a wisp of cloud,' and Boromir says, 'It's moving fast; against the wind.' This dialogue derives from another scene:

> Frodo looked up at the sky. Suddenly he saw or felt a *shadow* pass over the high stars, as if for a moment they faded and then flashed out again. *He shivered.*
>
> 'Did you see anything pass over?' he whispered to Gandalf, who was just ahead.
>
> 'No, but I felt it, whatever it was,' he answered. 'It may be nothing only a wisp of thin cloud.'
>
> 'It was moving fast then,' muttered Aragorn, *'and not with the wind.'* [Author's italics] (I. 374)

Imagery of the shadow, and the fact that Frodo sees it and shivers, is consistent with similar imagery elsewhere that suggests a *winged Nazgûl*.

Tolkien's Gandalf says to Éomer of Éowyn:

> 'But who knows what she spoke to the darkness, alone, in the bitter watches of the night, when all her life seemed shrinking, and the walls of her bower closing in about her, a hutch to trammel some wild thing in?' (III. 175)

On film Wormtongue hisses these lines to Éowyn alone at Theodred's bier (*TTT*). Gandalf blasts Wormtongue in the book:

> 'How long is it since Saruman bought you? When all the men were dead, were you to pick your share of the treasure, and take the woman you desire? Too long have you watched her under your eyelids and haunted her steps.' (II. 159)

On film Éomer uses similar words to Wormtongue.

Gollum's rhyme in the Dead Marshes (*TTT*) is adapted from the Barrow-wight's dreary incantation.

> 'Cold be heart and hand and bone
> And cold be travellers far from home;
> They do not see what lies ahead
> When sun has failed and moon is dead.' (see I. 195)

Film messages:
Owing to emphasis on action and cinematic brevity, chiefly the Elder Days and the mechanisms of Providence emerge less prominently, and perhaps other Tolkien messages emerge in lesser *intricacy*. Therefore to some viewers violence *appears* over-emphasized. And only Tolkien himself so deliberately *passes the torch*.

However, Mr. Jackson's triumph, for all its condensations and apparent departures from Tolkien's plot, still contains compelling spiritual lessons. Soliloquies by Gandalf, Sam and Galadriel help to fill in certain blanks.

One lesson is on the dignity and responsibility of the 'little man.' The diminutive hobbits arise from their quiet *Smials* to trouble the counsels of the Great and Wise.

Another is the joys and benefits of a quiet life and simple pleasures, close to nature with 'less noise and more green.' If we lose some lofty Elder-Days love for nature, we certainly gain satisfying visions of bucolic Shire life, with its quiet fields, its Bagginses, Boffins, Grubbs, Chubbs, Hornblowers, Bolgers and Proud-*feet*.

There is also the beauty of love and friendship; between Frodo and Sam especially, and the hobbits; members of the Fellowship bond despite differences:

Man and Halfling, Elf and Dwarf. Sam follows Frodo into Mordor. Merry and Pippin will not be left behind. The Three Hunters scour Rohan on foot with no sleep for three days, to save Merry and Pippin from torment and death. Legolas and Gimli form a fast friendship on screen, as in the book. Arwen forsakes the immortality of the Eldar to remain with Aragorn.

One learns the necessity of perseverance in resisting evil. Evil is a reality, from coveting power, without respect for Free Peoples, or for Middle-earth itself. Evil must be confronted if one will survive. And mighty Sauron is defeated by the quiet perseverance of *two little hobbits.*

Conclusion

The filmmakers use models and special effects to breathtaking advantage on film. The Shire, Rivendell, Moria, the flight to the Bridge of Khazad-Dûm, the Black Gate, Minas Tirith, Paths of the Dead, Barad-Dûr, and Mount Doom are awe-inspiring. The swooping of the winged Nazgûl is terrifying and imaginative. The Oliphaunts attacking the Riders of Rohan are a gripping addition, and hearts beat fast at the heroism of Legolas and Aragorn. The level of detail captured on film is phenomenal, often highly authentic.

But Middle-earth is not a land of special effects: it is the home of the *heart*. And Mr. Jackson knows this well. He seems at home in Middle-earth, as do actors, extras, technicians, etc. The epic is carried along by a rush of human emotion, as is the audience. Its monumental musical score augments the majesty and grandeur of the epic. It took this writer a full two days to recover emotionally from the aftermath of *RotK*. Many, even some of the *Eldar* (long-time devotees of Tolkien), will certainly revisit these films again and again.

But some of the *Eldar* remain alienated or incensed at Mr. Jackson for compromising Tolkien's plot occasionally, for omitting episodes, or for whatever reason. There is chagrin that many will now see the films and *think they know Tolkien*. But condensing a work longer than *War and Peace* into – *nine hours of film* requires adaptations, even if some make little sense to *Eldar*, who would have adapted differently. But I respect the film(s) as a triptych masterpiece, am grateful to have seen them, and to own them.

So render unto Jackson that which is Jackson's, and unto Tolkien that which is Tolkien's. The movies have broken, like a rip-tide of history. As an act of Fate/Providence, their positive messages of pity and understanding, life close to the earth, the necessity to resist evil, and trust in the serendipity of Divine Providence, are *perhaps* penetrating to the masses: even to many who might never otherwise penetrate Tolkien in print, a *forbidding* work for many. Many Orc-minded films have issued from Hollywood. But thanks to Mr. Jackson's cinematic icon, Hollywood *may* reveal Tolkien's positive lessons to moviegoers, imparting messages they sorely need, at a turning-point in history when they most need them. Sam imparts one such message:

> [...] *that there is some good in this world.*

It remains to be seen what future impact the films will have. May the success of the movies be like a manifestation of Ilúvatar, who *absorbs* variations to the Divine music, to weave a mightier harmony. And Tolkien's messages are too powerful to be contained only in the literary realm, or in the phantasms of Hollywood special effects: *there are powers at work far stronger*. Watch and see what transpires. Whatever may betide, whatever variations it must witness, I am confident that J.R.R. Tolkien's *original* work will not fade during my lifetime, nor for many lifetimes to come, while the thrones of the Valar endure.

About the author

James Dunning earns bread using his pharmaceutical background, and works outside Atlanta, GA, USA. But he has also accumulated a body of undergraduate and graduate work in Germanic and Slavic languages, and in linguistics. Dr. Dunning became a devotee of J.R.R. Tolkien's work in 1966, has completed the 20th reading of *The Lord of the Rings*, and has published in *Beyond Bree* (Newsletter of American Mensa's Tolkien Special Interest Group) and in *Lembas* (Journal of Nederland's Tolkien Society). He is also mentioned in the Acknowledgements of *The Annotated Hobbit*.

Note:

Quotations from *The Hobbit* (H) and *The Lord of the Rings* (I, II, III) cite page numbers from the Ballantine paperback edition, forty-sixth printing, December 1973.

Quotations from *The Silmarillion* (S) cite page numbers from the Ballantine paperback edition, third printing, December 1982.

The author gratefully acknowledges proofreading and encouragement from Ms. Lisa Dunning and Mr. Mark T. Hooker.

Conventions (abbreviations)

LotR	*The Lord of the Rings* (Film Trilogy)
FotR	*The Fellowship of the Ring* (Film)
TTT	*The Two Towers* (Film)
RotK	*The Return of the King* (Film)
Mr. Jackson	*Peter Jackson and Company* (i.e., his collaborators in filmmaking)

Alexandra Velten

The Soundtrack Lyrics of Peter Jackson's *The Lord of the Rings* – A Legitimate 'Translation' of Tolkien?

Abstract

This article deals with the texts accompanying the orchestral score to the Peter Jackson films. The texts are presented in an overview and examined according to their contents and form, discussing the question whether or not they can be seen as true to Tolkien's textual legacy. Remarkable parallels can be drawn between the function of non-English texts in the book and in the films.

> If I had considered my own pleasure more than the stomachs of a possible audience, there would have been a great deal more Elvish in the book.
> (Tolkien 1995:216)

Introduction

As an introductory remark, I would like to stress that this article is not intended as a musicological treatment of the score of the recent films based on *The Lord of the Rings*, but rather a literary and linguistic assessment of the texts used as lyrics. Out of necessity, this study is more of an overview than an in-depth treatment, as all available songs shall be presented. Page numbers referring to *The Lord of the Rings* are taken from the one-volume edition published by Harper Collins in 1994, and referred to as *LotR*:page number.

A unique opportunity is offered to the philologist, as the lyrics are not only English texts, but also use several of Tolkien's conceived languages. We find Quenya, Sindarin, Rohirric, Adûnaic, Black Speech, and Khuzdul; English does not figure largely in the corpus of lyrics at all. The songs that are provided with English lyrics, which are 'May it be' from *The Fellowship of the Ring*, 'Gollum's Song' from *The Two Towers*, and 'Into the West' from *The Return of the King*, are not part of this study, as they are not part of the soundtrack proper, but additional 'pop songs' that accompany the end titles of the respective films. The only English text is part of the track 'The Steward of Gondor', on *The Return of the King* soundtrack album. Some of the lyrics examined were not published on the available CDs at all.

Although some of the lyrics were published in the CD booklets of the several different (i.e., limited 'collectors' or normal) editions of the soundtrack albums, there is the added difficulty of several textual versions available. Thankfully, a part of the very active linguistic Internet community of Tolkien fans has created a collection of all available lyrics, complete with linguistic comments. Some of the lyrics have been published in the accompanying sheet music for the films, and due to them not being available in Germany, I have used the texts as published by Ryszard Derdzinski at *Gwaith-i-Phethdain* (Derdzinski 2004), and I am indebted to him and those who have worked on this web site for compiling the full set of texts of all three films. Translations of the lyrics can be found either in the sheet music or the CD booklets, some only on the website available to owners of the limited edition CDs, and some can be found on the bonus DVD that was shipped with the limited edition soundtrack CD of *The Return of the King*. For ease of reference, the translations I use in this article were taken from *Gwaith-i-Phethdain* as the most comprehensive source available. The texts from different sources sometimes differ from each other, and we find that some of them do not appear on the available CDs at all. This is, of course, due to late changes and decisions about what to include on the CD and/or the films themselves. I do not attempt to rival the above-mentioned website's collection of linguistic information but, instead, refer the reader to it for any in-depth grammatical discussion about specific Sindarin or Quenya questions. Other useful references the reader may wish to consult are given in the bibliographical references.

With these preliminary observations and explanations out of the way, we will now have a closer look at the texts themselves – are they the rightful heirs of Tolkien's textual legacy? The translator working on Peter Jackson's films, David Salo, is one of the pre-eminent experts on Elvish and founded the Elfling List. He was also responsible for translating the soundtrack lyrics into Sindarin, Quenya, Rohirric and several other languages. We are dealing with several different categories here: The score uses original lyrics or quotes from *The Lord of the Rings* by Tolkien, as well as lyrics by Tolkien that have been translated and/or adapted, and, of course, original lyrics created especially for the film.

Interestingly, most of the titles of the tracks on the CDs have been taken directly from chapter headings of *The Lord of the Rings* or from closely related sources.

On *The Fellowship of the Ring*, the following tracks have titles from the *The Lord of the Rings* novel: 'Concerning Hobbits', 'The Ring Goes South', 'A Journey in the Dark', 'The Shadow of the Past', 'The Black Rider', 'At the Sign of the Prancing Pony', 'A Knife in the Dark', 'Flight to the Ford', 'Many Meetings', 'The Council of Elrond', 'The Bridge of Khazad-dûm', 'Lothlórien', 'The Great River', and 'The Breaking of the Fellowship'. The last eleven contain lyrics, the others are instrumental symphonic works. Of the remaining tracks, 'The Treason of Isengard' took its title from the volume of *The History of Middle-earth* of the same title. 'The Prophecy' is titled according to Malbeth the Seer's prophecy from *The Return of the King* (*LotR*:764). 'Amon Hen' took its title from the hill of the same name and is used in scenes in the film that are part of the chapter 'The Breaking of the Fellowship'.

On the album accompanying *The Two Towers*, we find the following tracks titled according to book chapters: 'The Taming of Sméagol', 'The Passage of the Marshes', 'The Black Gate is Closed', 'The Riders of Rohan', 'The Uruk-hai', 'The Forbidden Pool', 'The King of the Golden Hall', 'Treebeard', 'The White Rider', and 'Helm's Deep'. Here, the latter four contain lyrics. 'Isengard Unleashed', 'Foundations of Stone', 'Breath of Life', 'Evenstar', and 'Samwise the Brave' are not taken from chapter headings, but the latter is a variation on a quote from *The Lord of the Rings*: "But you've left out one of the chief characters: Samwise the stouthearted," (*LotR*:697) which also appears in the film as dialogue, again in the adapted version. 'The Hornburg' obviously refers to the building, whereas 'Forth Eorlingas' is a quote again, taken from *The Lord of the Rings*, from Théoden's Call to Arms:

> Arise now, arise, Riders of Théoden!
> Dire deeds awake, dark is it eastward.
> Let horse be bridled, horn be sounded!
> Forth Eorlingas! (*LotR*:506)

The Return of the King CD gives the following titles reusing chapter headings from the novel: 'Minas Tirith, 'The Black Gate Opens', 'The Ride of the Rohirrim', 'Shelob's Lair', and 'The Grey Havens'. 'Cirith Ungol' has been adapted from 'The Stairs of Cirith Ungol', and 'The Fields of the Pelennor' is a variation on 'The Battle of the Pelennor Fields'. 'The Return of the King', obviously, refers to the title of the third part of *The Lord of the Rings*. 'A Storm is Coming' is using a quote from the book (*LotR*:581) that Gandalf uttered when beholding the approaching Nazgûl. 'The White Tree', 'The Steward of Gondor', 'Minas Morgul', and 'Andúril' are mere referrals to the respective people, places, or objects. 'Hope and Memory', 'Ash and Smoke', and 'Twilight and Shadow' obviously play with the parallelism in their titles, using important topoi from the novel as well as the film. 'Hope Fails' seems to be a general sentiment, not a quote, whereas 'The End of All Things' is taken from a quote by Frodo (*LotR*:926).

Most of the texts we are dealing with were composed in English and then translated into Sindarin and Quenya, closely followed in quantity by Rohirric. Most of the texts in Adûnaic, Khuzdul, and Black Speech are not based on Tolkien's texts but to a large amount on David Salo's reconstructions. For a further discussion of this topic see also Salo (2003).

Observations on the Respective Texts

The Fellowship of the Ring

We will now take a closer look at the texts themselves, in the order in which they appear in the three films, starting with *The Fellowship of the Ring*. The first track that shall concern us is 'The Prophecy'. As has been remarked earlier, it refers to Malbeth the Seer's Words in *Return of the King*.

The Prophecy (version published in the CD booklet)

Quenya	*English*
Yénillor morne	Out of the Black Years
tulinte i quettar	come the words
Tercáno Nuruva	[the] Herald of Death.

| Hlasta! Quetis | Listen! It speaks |
| Ilfirimain | to those who were not born to die ... |

The Prophecy: Sheet Music Version

Quenya	*English*
Hlasta!	Listen!
Quetis Ilfirimain:	It speaks to those
	who were not born to die:
Corma turien te	[One] Ring to rule them [all]
Corma tuvien	[One] Ring to find [them]
Corma tultien te	[One] Ring to bring them [all]
Huines se nutien.	[And] in the Darkness bind it
Tercáno Nuruva.	[The] Herald of Death
Tuvien Corma tultien te	to find [One] Ring, to bring them [all]
Huinesse nutien	[And] in the Darkness bind it
Corma turien te Corma.	[One] Ring to rule them [all],
	[One] Ring

The version of this track published in the CD booklet is not the actual recorded version one can hear on the CD. The sheet music version seems to be the same as the text sung on the CD and was thus the version of this track that I had a closer look at. The lyrics are in Quenya, and, as all other lyrics not in Present-day English, were translated by David Salo, who, as has been mentioned in the introduction, worked as a language consultant and translator on the films. Out of necessity, the translated lyrics do not only contain attested words that can be found in the Tolkien canon, but also Salo's own creations. For further information on which parts of the lyrics (and also of the non-English dialogue from the films) are purely Tolkien and which are words created or derived by Salo, refer to Derdzinski (2004). I would also like to refer the reader to this web page for further discussion of the grammar of the texts discussed here. Space restrictions forbid a discussion of these in this paper.

The text these Quenya lyrics refer to are 'Malbeth the Seer's Words', a prophecy uttered in the days of the last king of Fornost (*LotR*:764):

> "Thus spoke Malbeth the Seer, in the days of Arvedui, last king at Fornost," said Aragorn:
>
> Over the land there lies a long shadow,
> westward reaching wings of darkness.
> The Tower trembles; to the tombs of kings

> doom approaches. The Dead awaken;
> for the hour is come for the oathbreakers;
> at the Stone of Erech they shall stand again
> and hear there a horn in the hills ringing.
> Whose shall the horn be? Who shall call them
> from the grey twilight, the forgotten people?
> The heir of him to whom the oath they swore.
> From the North shall he come, need shall drive him:
> he shall pass the Door to the Paths of the Dead.

"Quetis Ilfirimain" refers to the oathbreakers from Malbeth's words. The text is not an adaptation of the poem, but uses it as a thematic backdrop, which is underlined by calling the track 'The Prophecy'. It indeed deals with a prophecy that is only referred to again during the course of the third film, when Aragorn receives Andúril from Elrond and is reminded by him of this prophecy and that he, Aragorn, is supposed to call the oathbreakers forth to battle.

The track is used to introduce the Second Age prologue scenes in the first film and thus sets the theme for the remainder of the film trilogy. The Ring Poem is also included in the second version of the lyrics, to create a musical backdrop to the scenes that show why the One Ring was not destroyed then, and to show the other Rings of Power.

The most interesting aspect, though, about most of the soundtrack lyrics is that they cannot be understood initially. One might be a scholar of Old English or even Sindarin or Quenya, but even then it is often impossible to understand the choral pieces without the further aid of a lyrics sheet. This is in keeping with Tolkien himself, who, intentionally, left some of his poems and other fragments in *The Lord of the Rings* untranslated, most famously 'A Elbereth'. Another example of such a fragment would be Aragorn in Lórien:

> For the grim years were removed from the face of Aragorn, and he seemed clothed in white, a young lord tall and fair; and he spoke words in the Elvish tongue to one whom Frodo could not see. *Arwen vanimelda, namárië!* he said, and then he drew a breath, and returning out of his thought he looked at Frodo and smiled. (*LotR*:343)

In the case of the three films, it is nigh impossible to understand all the lyrics to the musical score while watching the film. They create a backdrop and set the scene for the story, but can only be understood in their entirety by studying the texts afterwards. Whatever one's opinion of the score as such might be, the creation of its lyrics is an achievement of its own.

"Both offer the assurance that there is more to Middle-earth than can immediately be communicated," says Shippey (1992:102) about untranslated names such as Gil-galad and Nobottle. "Tolkien used them [the names, maps, and myths] in an extremely peculiar, idiosyncratic and daring way, which takes no account at all of predictable reader-reaction" (Shippey 1992:102). He then gives the song to Elbereth as an example of this idiosyncratic way of dealing with non-English texts: "However no reader of *The Lord of the Rings* can actually know that, since it is sung in the elvish language Sindarin and not offered in translation till p. 64 of *The Road Goes Ever On*, the song-cycle published in 1968. As they stand in *The Fellowship of the Ring*, they are nonsense syllables" (Shippey 1992:102f.). He traces Tolkien's 'private theory' about the beauty of certain sounds back to 1926, when Tolkien first mentioned something he called *Lautphonetik*, but which Shippey (1992:103) prefers to call "'an aesthetics of sounds': a science that would explain why certain sounds or combinations of sounds produced different effects from others." We thus have to conclude that the makers of the films made a conscious decision to use the same technique as Tolkien himself did.

Snow White! Snow White!

Sindarin

A Bereth thar Ennui Aeair!
Calad ammen i reniar
Mi 'aladhremmin ennorath.
A Elbereth Gilthoniel
i chin a thûl lín míriel ...

English

O Queen beyond the Western Seas!
O light to us that wander
Amid the tree-woven middle-lands.
O Elbereth Star-kindler
the eyes and breath your [are] shining like jewels ...

In the extended edition of the first film on DVD, a scene with Frodo and Sam watching Elves going to the Grey Havens is included, and the lyrics for this enchanting little scene are a direct translation of Tolkien's English poem 'Snow White! Snow White!' (*LotR*:78), which appeared in the same scene in the book (with the difference that Pippin was also present). The lyrics consist of a translation of the first stanza and two lines of the second stanza.

The Treason of Isengard

Black Speech

Shre nazg golugranu kilmi-nudu
Ombi kuzddurbagu gundum-ishi
Nugu gurunkilu bard gurutu
Ash Burz-Durbagu burzum-ishi
Daghburz-ishi makha gulshu
darulu.
Ash nazg durbatulûk,
ash nazg gimbatul,
ash nazg thrakatulûk agh
burzum-ishi krimpatul
Daghburz-ishi makha gulshu
darulu.

English

Three rings for-Elven-kings under-sky
Seven for-dwarf-lords in-halls
Nine for-mortals doomed to-die
One for-Dark-Lord in-darkness
in-Mordor where shadows lie.

One Ring to-rule-them-all,
One Ring to-find-them,
One Ring to-bring-them-all and
in-the-Darkness bind-them
in-Mordor where shadows lie.

Gû kîbum kelkum-ishi, burzum-ishi. Akha – gûm-ishi ashi gurum.
Nubin sherkuk, rakhizinash, matizinashûk, matizin Umbrûk.

There-is-no life in-the-cold, in-the-dark. Here – in-the-void only death.
I-smell your-blood. I-shall-devour-it, eat-it-all – eat-all the-world.'

This text is a combination of Tolkien's Ring Poem (LotR:v) and two lines by Philippa Boyens, both translated into Black Speech by David Salo. The ring inscription, of course, is used in Tolkien's translation. The remainder of the text is a combination of the few words we know of Black Speech and some creations or derivations by Salo.

The track itself is used as a musical backdrop to Saruman's betrayal. As such, it underlines the might of Sauron in turning Saruman to betrayal by using both his own language and the poem about the fateful Rings of Power. The two lines by Philippa Boyens might seem a trifle melodramatic in this context: "There-is-no life in-the-cold, in-the-dark. Here – in-the-void only death. I-smell your-blood. I-shall-devour-it, eat-it-all – eat-all the-world." Nevertheless, they underline both Sauron's and Saruman's desire to overthrow the Free Peoples and rule Middle-earth by evil.

The Black Rider / At the Sign of the Prancing Pony / A Knife in the Dark / Flight to the Ford

Adûnaic

Nêbâbîtham Magânanê
Nêtabdam dâurad

English

We deny our maker.
We cling to the darkness.

Nêpâm nêd abârat-aglar	We grasp for ourselves power and glory.
îdô Nidir nênâkham	Now we come, the Nine,
Bârî 'n Katharâd	Lords of Eternal Life.

This text in Adûnaic appears, in fragments, in all three of the above-mentioned tracks. It always serves as a 'theme' for the Black Riders, both in its tune and in the use of Adûnaic for the lyrics (the lyrics for the Black Riders are the only instance of Adûnaic in the soundtrack.) The text itself is, again, by Philippa Boyens, translated by David Salo. The lyrics stress the Ringwraiths' lust for power and their denial of everything that is associated with light: "We grasp for ourselves power and glory [...] Lords of Eternal Life." The text shows the Ringwraiths as perversions and corruptions of Men that have turned against their maker, i.e. Eru Ilúvatar himself: "We deny our maker." Using fragments from the text in conjunction with the appropriate 'theme music' assures continuity in the film's narrative – the viewer will connect both the tune and the (for him or her) 'incomprehensible' text of this particular language with the Black Riders.

The only proper fragments of Adûnaic and a grammar that remained incomplete can be found in Tolkien (1992:413-440). It is part of a larger group of writings centring on the *Akallabêth*, the Downfall of Númenor, which is written from a then modern point of view of a group of contemporary scholars modelled on the group of writers called the Inklings. Here, Tolkien said that he wanted to create Adûnaic as a language with a "faintly Semitic flavour" (Tolkien 1992:240), i.e. basing it on such phenomena as triconsonantal roots for semantically related words.[1] *Akallabêth* itself is one of the few instances of an Adûnaic word that has been published in the context of *The Lord of the Rings*; it is the title of the *Silmarillion* chapter on the Downfall, meaning 'She that is Fallen', i.e. Númenor itself. By using Adûnaic for the Ringwraiths, the Downfall due to human folly is repeated as a topos. As Númenor had to fall through the hubris of Man, the Nazgûl themselves fell under Sauron's spell through their lust for power.

---

[1] It has been remarked that Adûnaic differs from languages such as Arabic in that it does not only rely on triconsonantal roots. Interestingly enough, the languages that the Ancient Egyptians used, i.e. Old, Middle, and Late Egyptian, also had biconsonantal and triconsonantal roots as well as words based on four consonants.

Song to Tinúviel

Sindarin

Tinúviel elvanui
Elleth alfirin edhelhael
O hon ring finnil fuinui
A renc gelebrin thiliol ...

English

Tinúviel [the] elven-fair,
Immortal maiden elven-wise,
About him cast [her] night-dark hair,
And arms [like] silver glimmering ...

This is sung by Aragorn in the film, also only in the extended DVD version, and is based on a few lines of Tolkien's English version of the so-called 'Lay of Leithian' (*LotR*:188), the story of Beren and Lúthien:

> As Beren looked into her eyes
> Within the shadows of her hair,
> The trembling starlight of the skies
> He saw there mirrored shimmering.
> Tinúviel the elven-fair,
> Immortal maiden elven-wise,
> About him cast her shadowy hair
> And arms like silver glimmering.

Aragorn sings part of this poem about a mortal man falling in love with an elven woman, foreshadowing later scenes in the film where the viewer sees him in love with Arwen. Although the song in this context seems very logical, the casual viewer of the film will not even be aware of the connection.

Sindarin

Tinúviel elvanui
Elleth alfirin

English

Tinúviel [the] elven-fair,
Immortal maiden

These two lines are sung in the beginning of the track 'Flight to the Ford', which also features fragments of the Black Riders' Adûnaic lyrics. The original text is, again, from the 'Lay of Leithian', as mentioned above, the poem about Beren and Lúthien that Aragorn tells the Hobbits while they are resting at Weathertop (*LotR*:188), and it is used here, in a Sindarin translation, to introduce Arwen in the first film. Interestingly enough, the viewer will most certainly only notice the ethereal, 'elvish' music in the background, and only a more thorough immersion in the film's textual corpus will show that we are dealing with a very interesting intertextual link to Tolkien. Arwen was often seen in her relation to Lúthien and has often been compared with her, as both were, of course, in love with a mortal man. In the film, Frodo first sees her as an ethereal, glowing elvish being come straight out of legend, and the reference to Lúthien shows Arwen's legacy.

Many Meetings (A Elbereth Gilthoniel)

Sindarin	English
A Elbereth Gilthoniel, silivren penna miriel	O Elbereth Star-kindler, (white) glittering slants-down sparkling-like-jewels
o menel aglar elenath,	from firmament glory [of] the star-host,
na-chaered palan diriel o galadhremmin ennorath nef aear, sí aearon,	to-remote-distance after-having-gazed from tree-tangled middle-lands, on-this-side [of] ocean, here [on this side of] the Great Ocean,
Fanluilos, le linnathon Nef aear, sí aearon!	Fanuilos, to thee I will chant on-this-side [of] ocean, here [on this side of] the Great Ocean!

In the book, this song to Elbereth is sung at Rivendell during Frodo's introduction to the Hall of Fire (*LotR*:231). We find the track at more or less the same place in the film, as it is used during the introductory shots in Rivendell. This is one of the texts that were not translated for the lyrics, as Tolkien himself used its Sindarin version. It is one of the best-known examples of Tolkien's strategy of not translating non-English texts in *The Lord of the Rings*. He did, indeed, provide notes and a translation of the poem later on in Swann/Tolkien (1968:72), which also included Tolkien's own calligraphy of the poem in Tengwar; but in *The Lord of the Rings* itself, Tolkien did not provide any explanation exceeding Bilbo's cryptic "It is a song to Elbereth" (*LotR*:232). Fauskanger (2004) provides an excellent linguistic introduction to both the version of the song to Elbereth sung at Rivendell as well as the lines Sam is using when confronting Shelob.

Aníron (The Council of Elrond)

Sindarin	English
O môr henion i dhû: Ely siriar, êl síla. Ai! Aníron Undómiel.	From darkness I understand the night: dreams flow, a star shines. Ah! I desire Evenstar.

Tiro! Êl eria e môr.	Look! A star rises out of the darkness.
I 'lîr en êl luitha 'úren.	The song of the star enchants my heart.
Ai! Aníron ...	Ah! I desire ...

This is, in fact, one of the few 'proper' songs from the soundtrack, this one being sung by the Irish singer Enya. It is used as a traditional 'love theme' for Aragorn and Arwen in Rivendell, and its lyrics were apparently not translated by David Salo, but by Roma Ryan, the lyricist of Enya. In this text, we hear Aragorn speaking about his love and desire for Arwen, the Evenstar, of course referring to the 'nightfall' of the elves in Middle-earth that is soon to come, and Arwen as the last 'star' shining among her people. The song might be simple in structure and wording, but provides a poetic rendition of Arwen and Aragorn's situation in *The Lord of the Rings*. "From darkness I understand the night" then refers to a world without the elves.

The Bridge of Khazad-dûm

Khuzdul	*English*
Urus ni buzra!	Fire in the deep!
Arrâs talbabi fillumâ!	Flames lick our skin!
Ugrûd tashniki kurdumâ!	Fear rips our heart!
Lu! Lu! Lu!	No! No! No!
Urkhas tanakhi!	The demon comes!

This is one of the few instances that Dwarvish is used in the soundtrack, which has to remain as constructed as the lyrics in Adûnaic or Black Speech. The text itself deals with the dwarves' fear of the Balrog and is, in its construction, deliberately kept simple both to represent the 'earthy' dwarves, resembling the 'Song of Durin' that Gimli sang in Moria (*LotR*:308f.), which Shippey (1992:176) called "dwarvishly plain and active", and the stomping rhythm of the choral piece in which the text is sung. These drums are referring to the Book of Mazarbul and the mentioning of "drums, drums in the deep" by Ori (*LotR*:314). In the second film, another piece in Dwarvish can be heard at the beginning during Gandalf's battle with the Balrog.

Salo (2003) says about his creation of these lyrics:

> It's based on or inspired by the few Dwarvish words and names which Tolkien created and which have been published; but since Tolkien did not provide us anything regarding the grammar of Dwarvish (except a vague hint that it

might be like Hebrew), and only gave us a very small vocabulary, something like 90% of this language is a new invention – by me. It *sounds* like Khuzdul, but I am sure that in structure and vocabulary it is much more different from what Tolkien would have created than any of the Elvish. [...] So there is real linguistic structure there, and an homage to Tolkien's languages; but very little of it is genuine Tolkien.

Lament for Gandalf (Lothlórien)

Quenya

A Olórin i yáresse
Mentaner i Númeherui
Tírien i Rómenóri,
Maiaron i oiosaila
Manan elye etevanne

Nórie i malanelye?

English

Olórin whom long ago
sent the Lords of the West
to guard the Lands of the East,
ever-wise of the Maiar
what drove you to leave
[lit. 'why you left']
land which you loved?

Sindarin

Mithrandir, Mithrandir!
A Randir Vithren!
Ú-reniathach i amar galen

I reniad lín ne môr, nuithannen

In gwidh ristennin,
i fae narchannen
I Lach Anor ed ardhon gwannen
Calad veleg, ethuiannen.

English

Mithrandir, Mithrandir,
O Pilgrim Grey
No more you will wander the
world green
Your journey in darkness stopped

The bonds cut, the spirit broken

The Flame of Anor has left this World
Great light has gone out.

Version from the Sheet Music

Sindarin

In gwidh ristennin,
i fae narchannen
I Lach Anor ed ardhon gwannen

Mithrandir, Mithrandir!
A Randir Vithren!
Ú-reniathach i amar galen

I reniad lín ne môr, nuithannen

English

The bonds cut,
the spirit broken
The Flame of Anor has left this World

Mithrandir, Mithrandir,
O Pilgrim Grey!
No more you will wander the
world green
Your journey in darkness stopped.

Quenya	English
Ilfirin nairelma nauva i nauva	Undying [is] our regret, [it] will be what will be [or What should be shall be]
Ilfirin nairelma ar ullume nucuvalme	Undying [is] our regret and yet we will cast all away,
Nauva i nauva melme nóren sina nairelma	[It] will be what will be, love for this land [is] our regret.

A very apt lament for Gandalf, who fell in Moria, is presented with this song in both Sindarin and Quenya. Gandalf is, in the Quenya part of the lament, named as Olórin, his original name when he was sent to Middle-earth early in the Third Age. It is an extrapolation of what is said in *The Lord of the Rings*:

> *Mithrandir, Mithrandir* sang the Elves, *O Pilgrim Grey*! For so they loved to call him. But if Legolas was with the Company, he would not interpret the songs for them, saying that he had not the skill, and that for him the grief was still too near, a matter for tears and not yet for song. (*LotR*:350)

In the film, Legolas also uses words to this effect – a refusal to translate the Elvish words, thus leaving the viewer as well as the members of the Fellowship who do not speak Quenya or Sindarin in doubt about the contents of the lament.

The verse in Quenya displays another strategy the writer of the lyrics employed: She took fragments of Galadriel's words (*LotR*:356) about the destiny of the elves and formed them into a poem, thus assuring textual coherency with Tolkien's original creation and strengthening the bond between book and film:

> The love of the Elves for their land and their works is deeper than the deeps of the Sea, and their regret is undying and cannot ever wholly be assuaged. Yet they will cast all away rather than submit to Sauron: for they know him now. For the fate of Lothlórien you are not answerable but only for the doing of your own task. Yet I could wish, were it of any avail, that the One Ring had never been wrought, or had remained for ever lost. (*LotR*:356)

The Great River

Quenya	English
Ai! laurie lantar lassi súrinen, yéni únotime ve ramar aldaron!	Alas! golden leaves fall in the wind, long years numberless as [the] wings of trees!
yéni ve linte ...	Long years like swift ...

Quenya	English
Et Eärello Endorenna utúlien.	Out of the Great Sea to Middle-earth I am come.
Sinome maruvan ar Hildinyar tenn'Ambar-metta!	In this place I will abide, and my heirs, unto the ending of the world!

With this Quenya text, we have a part of the other important and well documented Elvish text by Tolkien on the soundtrack: Galadriel's lament, 'Namarië' (LotR:368). Linguistic details can, again, be found in Swann/Tolkien (1969:58ff.). Like 'A Elbereth', the film uses a poem in the same scene as the book, in this case when the fellowship leaves Lórien. The latter part, then, are Elendil's words when he came to Middle-earth – these can be heard in the film during the moment when the fellowship reaches the Argonath and Aragorn says, in the book, "Behold the Argonath, the Pillars of the Kings!" (*LotR*:383). Although few viewers will have realised this, the moment is repeated at Aragorn's coronation, in the book as well as *The Return of the King* film, providing a kind of subtle foreshadowing that Tolkien would surely have approved of.

The Two Towers

Foundations of Stone

Quenya	English
Cuiva Olórin	Awake Olórin
Nárendur	Servant of fire
Tira nottolya	Face your foe
Tulta tuolya	Summon forth your strength
An mauya mahtie	For you must fight
Ter oiomornie	Through endless dark
Ter ondicilyar.	Through chasms of stone.
Mettanna.	To the end.
Nurunna!	To the death!

Khuzdul	English
Irkat-lukhud ma katabrikihu	No shaft of light Can breach it
Ulfat-atam ma tanakhi uduhu	No breath of air Comes from it
bin-nât aznân tarsisi	Only an endless dark rises

Bazar udu agânî-furkhîn	Deep from the beginnings
	Of the world.
Gurd!	Have fear!
Ma nîd sakhu!	Do not look down!
Ma satf unkhai!	Nor step too close!
Atkât zatagrafizu	The silence will take you.
Zatablugi sulluzu	It will swallow you whole.

This is the companion piece to the first film's lament for Gandalf, showing his 'rebirth', and is also sung in Quenya. Most of the pieces in the soundtrack sung in Quenya use this language for the same purpose as Tolkien did: to show the antiquity of the far-reaching history of Middle-earth. The latter part of this track is in Dwarvish again, also a continuation of the first film's depiction and soundscape of Moria. Here, the fear and respect of the dwarves for Khazad-dûm is recounted, although they overstepped the boundary and awakened the Balrog.

The King of the Golden Hall

Rohirric/Old English

English

He laered hine ridan	He taught him to ride,
And wealdan mece	To wield a sword.
And standan fæst	To stand strong
And feond ne forhtian.	And show his enemy no fear.
Nu he sceal leornian	Now he must learn
þæt hearde soþ:	The hard truth:
He raerede his cnapa	That he had brought his boy
Of cilde to menn	From childhood
þæt he his deaþ geseo.	So that he might face his death.
Se feond wæs simble mid heom.	The enemy was always with them.
Se feond ne reccede ege.	The enemy did not care about fear.

This is the first of a series of Old English, i.e. Rohirric, pieces for the Rohirrim. Here, Théoden grieves for his fallen son Théodred. The form of the text is not in the typical Anglo-Saxon poetic form, though. It appears to be a prose text without any intentional alliterative rhyme. The contents are not strictly an Anglo-Saxon topic as well, as the father grieves for his dead son, but are, nevertheless, in an appropriately sad mood.

Éowyn's Dirge

Rohirric/Old English

Bealocwealm hafaþ *f*reone *f*recan *f*orth onsended
*g*iedd sculon *s*ingan *g*leomenn *s*orgiende
on *M*eduselde þæt he *m*a no wære
his *d*ryhtne *d*yrest and mæga *d*eorost.
Bealo ... .

English

An evil death has sent forth the noble warrior
A song shall sing sorrowing minstrels
in Meduseld that he is no more,
to his lord dearest and kinsmen most beloved.
An evil death ...

In a rather brave decision, the extended version of the second film shows the actress Miranda Otto as Éowyn in a scene not explicitly mentioned in the book, singing a lament for her dead cousin Théodred, in a voice broken by sadness. In this text as well some of the following Old English/Rohirric texts, I have italicised possible alliterations.[2] For most viewers, the grief is shown in the sad melody and the whole setting, even if they do not understand the words. The text itself is a clever adaptation of some lines from the great Anglo-Saxon poem *Beowulf* (von Schaubert 1946:68; line 2265): "Bealocwelm hafaþ fela feorhcynna forþ onsended" ("Baleful death has sent many of my living kin forth.")

Evenstar

Sindarin	*English*
Ú i vethed nâ i onnad.	Not the end [it] is the beginning.
Si boe ú-dhanna.	Now it-is-necessary [that] don't-fall
Ae ú-esteli, esteliach nad.	If you don't-trust some-thing.
Ú i vethed nâ i onnad.	Not the end [it] is the beginning.
Nâ boe ú i.	[It] is necessary don't that.
Estelio han, estelio han, estelio, estelio han, estelio veleth.	Trust this, trust this, trust Trust this, trust love.
[Es]teliach nad, estelio han.	You trust some-thing, trust this.

---

2 Obviously, one can argue whether, in the line "giedd sculon singan gleomenn sorgiende" the <g> is used for an alliteration, as, in the first instance, it is pronounced /j/, and in the second one /g/. Nevertheless, even the *Beowulf* poet used such allophones as alliterations.

In this text, Arwen is mourning for Aragorn. The track is used in the second film to show Aragorn's future as king and his death, as Elrond wants to discourage his daughter from choosing a life as a mortal woman by showing her the grief that awaits her when her prospective husband dies. Nevertheless, the text does not only show sadness and grief, but also death as a new beginning: "Ú i vethed nâ i onnad."

It is the end of Aragorn and Arwen, and of the Age of the Elves, of course, but also a new beginning as the Age of Man. The text is thus more encouraging than the scene the track is accompanying, as Arwen will die of her grief. In a sense, the text is thus not appropriate for this scene, as the music itself also centres on a very sad and melancholic melody, and the text is the only hint of something positive in a negative context.

Treebeard

Sindarin

Naur vi eryn,
lanc i dalaf.
Mathach vi geven?
Nostach vi 'wilith?
Mâb le i nagor,
Bâd gurth vi ngalad firiel.
Dorthach vi mar han?
Dagrathach go hain?

English

The woods are burning,
the ground lies bare.
Do you feel it in the earth?
Can you smell it in the air?
The war is upon you,
Death moves in the fading light.
Are you part of this world?
Will you join their fight?

The text uses part of what Peter Jackson had Galadriel say in the prologue to the first film: "I amar prestar aen, han mathon ne nen, han mathon ne chae a han noston ned 'wilith." – "The world is changed; I can feel it in the water, I can feel it in the earth, I can smell it in the air," which is actually a quote of Treebeard (in *LotR*:959): "It is sad that we should meet only thus at the ending. For the world is changing: I feel it in the water, I feel it in the earth, and I smell it in the air. I do not think we shall meet again." He utters these words when he meets Galadriel. Effectively, this text asks the question whether the ents want to join the War of the Ring as their world is being changed and destroyed by Saruman's, and, in the end, Sauron's machinations. It is not given in Entish but Sindarin, either because Entish would have been too difficult to use with almost no source material, or because Entish would have been too long-winded to provide a text to be sung in the course of a few minutes. Nevertheless, an Elvish language is still fitting for ents as a part of nature.

The White Rider

Rohirric / Old English

Lim-strang wæs geboren
Bearn leod-cyninga
Magorinc Mearces.
Bunden in byrde to laedenne
Bunden in lufe to þegnunge
Lang beadugear cyþaþ
Lic onginneþ bugan.
Swift deadlic gear Stieppaþ geond willan.
Ac eagan giet lociaþ
Beorhtre gesihþe;
Heorte giet beateþ.

English

Strong-limbed he was born
This son of Kings;
This warrior of Rohan.
Bound by birth to lead.
Bound by love to serve.
Long years of war begin to show.
The body has begun to bend.
Swift mortal years outpace the will.

But the eyes still watch clear-sighted.

The great heart is beating still.

Another text in Old English, this piece accompanies Gandalf's 'exorcism' of Théoden. As the White Wizard drives out Saruman's evil influence, we hear about the Rohirric idea of a king, which is very much modelled on the Anglo-Saxon kingly ideal. The king is a leader of his people and not just commanding from his throne, but, furthermore, a fighting king, despite his old age. He is still competent, and even if his body is not that of a young man anymore, his spirit will always fight. This is, of course, reminiscent of Beowulf in his old age who sets out to fight a last battle against the dragon – he defeats his enemy, but dies as well. We can see this text, thus, as foreshadowing Théoden's destiny to die in battle later on, if we accept the parallel to Beowulf. Shippey (1992:182) called Tolkien's portrayal of the Rohirrim as a kind of pagans "bowdlerised. [...] They are so virtuous that one can hardly call them pagans at all." Thus, it is fitting indeed to use Old English texts for the films that stress these virtues. Again, the text itself is not in proper Old English metre, but we do find more lines in alliterative verse than in most of the other examples of Rohirric in the films. These are used intermittently with more modern, loose forms of composition.[3]

---

3 Again, one might argue that the alliteration in the line "Ac eagan giet lociaþ Beorhtre gesihþe" is not something an Anglo-Saxon poet would have done; we usually do not find alliteration relying on prefixes such as <ge->, as it was unstressed.

Helm's Deep

Rohirric / Old English

Heo naefre wacode dægred
To bisig mid dægeweorcum
Ac oft heo wacode sunnanwanung

þonne nihtciele creap geond moras

And on þaere hwile
Heo dreag þa losinga
Earla þinga þe heo forleas.
Heo swa oft dreag hire sawle sincende
Heo ne cuþe hire heortan lust.

English

She never watched the morning rising,
Too busy with the day's first chores,
But oft she would watch the sun's fading,
As the cold of night crept across the moors.

And in that moment
She felt the loss
Of everything that had been missed.
So used to feeling the spirit sink,

She had not felt her own heart's wish.

Rohirric / Old English

Hwær *c*wóm helm?
Hwaer *c*wóm byrne?
Hwær cwóm *f*eax *f*lówende?
Hwær cwóm *h*and on *h*earpestrenge?
Hwær cwóm *s*cir fýr *s*cinende?
Hwær cwóm lencten and hærfest?
Hwær *c*wóm héah *c*orn weaxende?
Hwá gegaderath *w*uduréc of *w*ealdholte byrnende?
Oþþe *g*esiehth of *g*ársecge
þá *g*éar *g*ewendende?

English

Where is the helm and the hauberk,
and the bright hair flowing?
Where is the hand on the harp string,
and the red fire glowing?
Where is the spring and the harvest
and the tall corn growing?
Who shall gather the smoke of
the dead wood burning?
Or behold the flowing years
from the Sea returning?

These two texts both feature in the track 'Helm's Deep'; the second text also appears in parts in the tracks 'The Hornburg' and 'Forth Eorlingas.' The first text is addressing Éowyn and her life; the second text deals with the more general topic of lamenting the Rohirrims' destiny.

In the first text, based on a poem by Philippa Boyens, we do not find alliterative metre; it is, again, a prose text.[4] It tries to convey Éowyn's melancholic view of her life as being in "[a] cage" (*LotR*:767), not being able to follow her true calling as a shield maiden and go fighting alongside her male relatives.

---

[4] The <h> in "hwær" does not alliterate with any of the other <h>-graphemes, as it is pronounced /x/ and not /h/.

The second text is far more interesting: It is a translation of Tolkien's poem (*LotR*:497) bemoaning the destiny of the Rohirrim in true Anglo-Saxon fashion in a lament of bygone times. In the novel, the original in modern English is recited at a wholly different point in the narrative; it is sung by Aragorn when Gimli, Legolas, Gandalf and he visit the grave mounds at Edoras, whereas in the film it is used for Théoden riding into battle. In my opinion, the positioning of the poem in battle scenes stresses the importance of this, essentially, pessimistic world view of the Rohirrim going to a battle against overwhelming odds even better.

Breath of Life

Sindarin

Uich gwennen na
'wanath ah na dhín.
An uich gwennen na
ringyrn ambar hen.
Boe naid bain gwannathar,
Boe cuil ban firitha.

Boe naer gwannathach.

English

You are not bound to loss and silence.

For you are not bound to the
circles of this world.
All things must pass away,
All life is doomed to fade …

Sorrowing you must go.

This text was apparently written by Fran Walsh and not translated by David Salo, showing yet another person working on the films as being capable of using Elvish. The song accompanies one of the scenes not in the book and one of those that were highly controversial: Aragorn's tumble into the river and subsequent daydream of Arwen, which, apparently, saved his life. Whatever one may think about this scene, the text is very appropriate, as it recalls images of mortality and immortality.

Isengard Unleashed

Sindarin

Rithannen i geven
thangen i harn
na fennas i daur
ôl dûr ristannen
eryn …

… echuiannen
i ngelaidh dagrar
ristar thynd, cúa tawar
dambedir enyd i ganed

English

Earth shakes
Stone breaks
The forest [is] at [your] door
The dark sleep is broken
The woods …

… have awoken
The trees have gone to war
Roots rend, wood bends
The Ents have answered the call

si linna i 'waew trin 'ylf	Through branches now the wind sings
Isto i dur i chuiyl	Feel the power of living things
i ngelaidh dagrar	The trees have gone to war
Quenya	*English*
Ar sindarnóriello caita mornie,	And grey-country-from lies darkness,
Ar ilye tier duláve lumbule	And all roads down-licked [the] clouds
...	...

This text accompanies the ents' march on Isengard in the film and also recalls the huorns coming to Helm's Deep – "the trees have gone to war", thus continuing in style and topic the lyrics to 'Treebeard'. In both texts, the style is rather terse, with short lines, and, in this track, accompanied by a slow marching rhythm to describe the ents' movements.

The second part of this track consists of two lines from Galadriel's lament in its original Quenya (*LotR*:368) to accompany another, very controversial, scene: the death of Haldir. Even though Tolkien did not write anything about elves in Helm's Deep, this scene and the text chosen to illustrate it serve one purpose rather well: to show that the time of the elves in Middle-earth is over. We see Haldir looking at his dead comrades, all fittingly clad in the colours of autumn, red-gold, accompanied by Galadriel's words about the dark road ahead. Again, a discussion of the whole text of Galadriel's lament can be found in Swann/Tolkien (1968:58).

The Return of the King

Minas Tirith

Sindarin	*English*
Revail vyrn dan minuial	Black wings against a pale morning
ú galad, ú vin anor hen	There is no more light, not in this sun
Cano an dregad	Call the retreat
ú natha ored	There will be no warning
Gwanwen ost in giliath	The citadel of the stars is gone
Dannen Osgiliath	Osgiliath is fallen

This text features as part of the track 'Minas Tirith' and deals with the retreat from Osgiliath in a descriptory fashion; describing the shadow cast by the fell beasts in its first two lines. Calling Osgiliath both by its normal name and as Ost-in-Giliath is a clever device of both repetition and variation.

The Steward of Gondor

Sindarin

Boe le henio
E sí câr athad iyn
Ane ah a phen
I ú athelitha.

English

You must understand.
He does the duty of two sons now.
For himself; and for the one
who will not return.

This text from the track 'The Steward of Gondor', which also features a short song in English by Billy Boyd in his role of Pippin, is a loose translation of a quote from *The Lord of the Rings*, referring to Faramir, who is burdened with fulfilling not only his duty, but also that of his fallen brother (and his father's favourite) Boromir: "The Lord drives his son too hard, and now he must do the duty of two, for himself and for the one that will not return" (*LotR*:798), uttered by some unknown Gondorian.

Pippin's song is an adapted version of the last stanza of the original walking song that Bilbo Baggins made, "and taught it to Frodo as they walked in the lanes of the Water-valley and talked about adventure" (*LotR*:76).

> Home is behind, the world ahead,
> And there are many paths to tread
> Through shadows to the edge of night,
> Until the stars are all alight.
> Then world behind and home ahead,
> We'll wander back to home and bed.
> Mist and twilight, cloud and shade,
> Away shall fade! Away shall fade!
> Fire and lamp, and meat and bread,
> And then to bed! And then to bed! (*LotR*:76)

The first four lines are taken over as a direct quote, and the remaining lines are adapted as:

> Mist and shadow
> Cloud and shade
> Hope shall fail
> All shall fade

Pippin sings it to Denethor, in an interesting change from the book, where he refrains from singing after the Steward asks him to sing a song:

> Pippin's heart sank. He did not relish the idea of singing any song of the Shire to the Lord of Minas Tirith, certainly not the comic ones that he knew best; they were too, well, rustic for such an occasion. He was however spared the ordeal for the present. He was not commanded to sing. (*LotR*:789)

In the film, Pippin does indeed sing one of those 'rustic' songs to a very disturbed Steward of Gondor, while the viewer also watches Faramir riding to his presumed doom – a very daring juxtaposition that elucidates not only the troubled relationship of Faramir and his father, but also emphasises the fact that hobbits, in this 'Great War', feel utterly lost.

Andúril

Sindarin

Elo! Andúril;
Lach en Annûn
I chatho asgannen,
Ad echannen!

English

Behold! Andúril;
Flame of the West
The blade [that was] broken,
[has been] remade!

This track is used to convey an atmosphere of dignity and hope as Elrond presents Andúril to Aragorn (at a different point than in the book, though). The text is a very good example of a situation adapted from the book and taken out of its context, but nevertheless fitting in the narrative situation of the film, when Aragorn's true destiny and the course he is about to take is surrounded with an air of dignity and importance. It is in this scene that the prophecy about the oath-breakers is mentioned again, which had been foreshadowed in the prologue of the first film.

Ash and Smoke

Sindarin

Go vegil tolo hi
Egor íriel firi
'Ni men hen ú veth 'war.

English

Come armed,
or prepared to die.
There is no other end to this road.

Hope Fails

Sindarin

Hollen i ven
In gyrth han agorer
a han beriar in gyrth
Hollen i ven.

English

The way is shut.
It was made by those who are dead
and the Dead keep it.
The way is shut.

These two short texts accompany the appearance of the Army of the Dead. They are rather simple both in style and contents.

The Black Gate Opens / The Fields of the Pelennor

Sindarin

Caedo, losto. Ú-erin davo.
Ú-erin davo.
Amman harthach?
Anim únad.
Le tûg nach..
O hon ú-wannathon
Ú-moe le anno nad.
Ónen a hon beth nín.
Gurth han ristatha.
Ta han narcho Gurth.
Gar vethed e-chúnen,
go hon bedithon na meth.

English

Lie down, sleep. –
I cannot yield.
Why do you still hope? –
I have nothing else.
You are a fool. –
I will not leave him.
You owe him nothing. –
I gave him my word.
Death will break it. –
Then let death break it.
He has the last of my heart.
I will go with him to the end.

This text is used both in 'The Black Gate Opens' and 'The Fields of the Pelennor'. It is written in the form of an argument, seemingly of Sam and his conscience, or even the evil influence of Sauron. One side argues that Samwise is a fool to still hope for a good ending and victory, the other side, probably Sam himself, argues that he will go with Frodo to the end and there is obviously still hope in the power of friendship. This text is, in my opinion, a very good example of a text written not by Tolkien, but conveying Tolkien's sense of the importance of friendship in times of war.

The End of All Things

Sindarin

Mi naurath Orodruin
Boe hedi i Vin.
Han i vangad i moe ben bango.
Sin eriol natha tûr în úgarnen
Sin eriol um beleg úgannen
Ú cilith 'war
Ú men 'war
Boe vin mebi
Boe vin bango

English

Into the fires of Orodruin
The One must be cast.
This [is] the price that must be paid.
Only thus its power will be undone,
Only thus a great evil unmade.
There is no other choice,
There is no other way.
One of you must take it,
One of you must pay.

Sindarin	English
Dannen le	You have fallen.
A ú-erin le regi	And I cannot reach you.
Rang ail le iestannen	Ever step I willed you on,
Lû ail le tegin na hen.	Every moment I lead you to this.
Gwannach o innen ului	You never left my mind,
Ú lû erui, ului.	Not once, not ever.

Sindarin	English
Anírach únad	You want nothing more
Egor gurth hen	Than this death.
Han cenin vi chen lín	I see it in your eye.
Egor ú-erin le devi	But I cannot let you
Tellin men achae	We have come too far
Brennin men anann	We have held on too long.
Rago! Ú-erich leithio,	Reach! You cannot let go,
Ú-erich o nin gwanno.	You cannot leave me.

Sindarin	English
Nu dalav	Beneath the ground
Úrui tuiannen na ruith	Swollen hot with anger
Leithia Orodruin oe in phan.	Orodruin releases all its ruin.
Ristannen i geven,	Earth rips asunder
Danna eliad morn.	Black rain falls.
Si, na vethed	Here at the end;
Meth i naid bain	The end of all things.
I wilith úria	The air is aflame,
I ardhon ban lacha!	All the world is on fire!

Sindarin	English
Orthannen im vi ól	In a dream I was lifted up.
Coll e dû	Borne from the darkness
Or hiriath naur	Above the rivers of fire.
Na rovail mae sui 'waew	On wings soft as the wind.
Man prestant i ardhon?	What's happened to the world?
Cerithar aen illiad dim úthenin?	Is everything sad going to come untrue?

These five texts all accompany the track 'The End of All Things', a very epic, fully orchestrated piece to illustrate the final destruction of the One Ring and the struggles of Frodo, Sam, and Gollum on the one hand, and Aragorn and his army on the other hand. The title of this track is a quote by Frodo, his last words at the end of the chapter 'Mount Doom': "I am glad you are here with me. Here at the end of all things, Sam." (*LotR*:926)

The words are used in a choral rendition of almost Wagnerian dimensions to stress the importance of these climactic scenes. The texts themselves deal with several situations. The first is emphasising the fact that destroying the Ring also means a sacrifice, and that someone has to pay this price. It puts the whole Quest in a few words – to destroy Sauron and his evil powers, the Ring has to be destroyed along with all the power of its own, and probably also destroying the one who carries it.

The second and third texts are dealing with a scene not in the book, as Frodo almost falls into the Cracks of Doom and Sam tries to save him, but Frodo obviously has suicidal tendencies and would rather let go and die. Although not in the book, this scene and its accompanying textual references in the soundtrack convey a strong sense of the doom that the influence of the One Ring has wrought. Again, the importance of friendship in dire situations is stressed.

The fourth text is a descriptive account of Orodruin's fires after the destruction of the Ring, whereas the last text describes the rescue by the Eagles and the hope Frodo and Sam feel during this moment, as if all evil had been undone.

The Return of the King

Quenya	*English*
Et Eärello Endorenna utúlien	Out of the Great Sea to Middle-earth I am come.
Sinome maruvan ar Hildinyar tenn' Ambar-metta	In this place I will abide, and my heirs, unto the ending of the world

Sindarin	*English*
Tinúviel elvanui	Tinúviel [the] elven-fair,
Elleth alfirin edhelhael	Immortal maiden elven-wise,
O hon ring finnil fuinui	About him cast [her] night-dark hair,
A renc gelebrin thiliol ...	And arms [like] silver glimmering ...

These two texts, to be heard during the scene of Aragorn's coronation, are a continuation of scenes from the first film where these lyrics have been featured before. The first part are, as has been mentioned above, Elendil's words, in the book also uttered by Aragorn at his coronation (*LotR*:946), whereas the second text refers to Arwen again, as was heard when she first appeared in the first film. By this, in repeating words and also musical themes, a sense of unity is achieved, connecting the three films, so that they, ultimately, might be seen as one film and not a trilogy – just as the book itself.

The Grey Havens

Sindarin

English

Dartha o nas a thar emyn
Men 'wain egor annon thurin
Ah ae anann erphennin hain
Na vedui cenithon aur wain
I badathon raid yriel
Amrûn n'Anor, Annûn n'Ithil.

Still round a corner there may wait
A new road or a secret gate;
And though I oft have passed them by,
A day will come at last when I
Shall take the hidden paths that run
West of the Moon, East of the Sun.

This is a Sindarin translation of a poem by Tolkien (*LotR*:1005), accompanying the scenes at the Grey Havens in the film, to mark both an end and a beginning when the Ringbearers leave Middle-earth and a new age begins. Sam called it a variation on "the old walking song" (*LotR*:1005) that Bilbo Baggins made and that Frodo is singing at that point:

Still round the corner there may wait
A new road or a secret gate,
And though we pass them by today,
Tomorrow we may come this way
And take the hidden paths that run
Towards the Moon or to the Sun. (*LotR*:76)

Summary

To sum up the textual and stylistic overview of the soundtrack lyrics to the Peter Jackson films, the following important points have to be stressed.

Whether or not one appreciates the changes and interpretations the films have made, one must acknowledge the amount of thought and detail that has gone into the creation of these texts. Not only do they present accurate translations into several of Tolkien's conceived languages and Old English, but they also manage to convey certain important ideas. As has been mentioned before, Tolkien's strategy of employing texts in non-English languages without translations has also been used in the film soundtrack.

> This was Tolkien's major linguistic heresy. He thought that people could feel history in words, could recognize language 'styles', could extract sense (of sorts) from sound alone, could moreover make aesthetic judgements based on phonology. [...] He clearly believed that untranslated elvish would do a job that English could not. (Shippey 1992:104)

In my opinion, using music together with untranslated texts actually 'does the job' that Shippey refers to, thus being a logical extension of Tolkien's ideas about his *Lautphonetik* and about translations.

Even the scenes not taken from the book have received appropriate renditions in Tolkien's languages, and have, in my opinion, been treated in the spirit of Tolkien, even if the scenes themselves might remain bones of contention.

Important motifs that Tolkien used, such as the destruction (and subsequent revenge) of nature, the importance of destiny, and, most of all, the importance of friendship in dire situations and of everlasting hope, have all been incorporated in the soundtrack lyrics. This is a feat that not many literary adaptations can claim for themselves, and is the more important as the average viewer of the films does not even appreciate all these details.

Thus, after examining the lyrics of the soundtrack to Peter Jackson's *The Lord of the Rings* trilogy, we may draw the following conclusion: Whether one likes Jackson's interpretation of Middle-earth or not, the textual legacy of Tolkien has been incorporated into the lyrics in an exemplary way.

About the author

Alexandra Velten studied English Linguistics, English Literature, and Egyptology at Johannes Gutenberg-University, Mainz. Her M.A. thesis centred on the semantic typology of Old English nominal compounds. She is currently writing her PhD thesis on the history of the LSP of Egyptology. Other research interests include word-formation, historical linguistics, the clash of religions in late Antiquity, and the history of Egyptology. She works as a lecturer in English linguistics at the University of Mainz.

Bibliographical references

DERDZINSKI, Ryszard, *Gwaith-i-Phethdain*, http://www.elvish.org/gwaith/movie.html (27-02-2004).

ELFLING MAILING LIST, http://groups.yahoo.com/group/elfling/ (27-02-2004).

FAUSKANGER, Helge K., 'A Elbereth Gilthoniel', http://www.uib.no/People/hnohf/elbereth.htm (27-02-2004a).

FAUSKANGER, Helge K., *Ardalambion*, http://www.uib.no/People/hnohf/ (27-02-2004b).

FAUSKANGER, Helge K., 'Namarië', http://www.uib.no/People/hnohf/namarie.htm (27-02-2004c).

HOSTETTER, Carl F., *The Elvish Linguistic Fellowship*, http://www.elvish.org (27-02-2004).

SALO, David, 'David Salo's Elvish Q&As', 2003, www.musefanpage.com/NewFiles/salo_ answers.html (27-02-2004).

SCHAUBERT, Else von (ed.), *Beowulf*, Paderborn: Schöningh, 1946.

SHIPPEY, Tom, *The Road to Middle-earth*, (First edition 1982), London: HarperCollins, 1992.

SWANN, Donald and J.R.R. Tolkien, *The Road Goes Ever On. A Song Cycle*, London: George Allen and Unwin, 1968.

The Lord of the Rings: The Fellowship of the Ring, 2001, Original Motion Picture Soundtrack, music composed, orchestrated and conducted by Howard Shore. CD with lyrics booklet.

The Lord of the Rings: The Two Towers, 2002, Original Motion Picture Soundtrack, music composed, orchestrated and conducted by Howard Shore. CD with lyrics booklet.

The Lord of the Rings: The Return of the King, 2003, Original Motion Picture Soundtrack, music composed, orchestrated and conducted by Howard Shore. CD with lyrics booklet.

TOLKIEN, J.R.R. and Christopher Tolkien, *Sauron Defeated: The End of the Third Age*, (The History of Middle-earth Volume 9), London: HarperCollins, 1992.

The Letters of J.R.R. Tolkien, (ed. by Humphrey Carpenter and Christopher Tolkien, first edition 1981), London: HarperCollins, 1995.

The Lord of the Rings, (First edition 1954/55), London: Harper-Collins, 1995

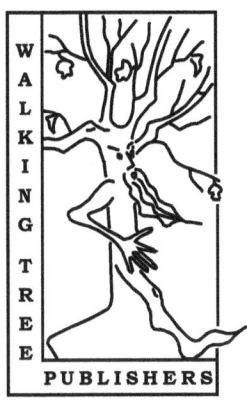

Walking Tree Publishers

Walking Tree Publishers was founded in 1997 as a forum for publication of material (books, videos, CDs, etc.) related to Tolkien and Middle-earth studies. Manuscripts and project proposals can be submitted to the board of editors (please include an SAE):

Walking Tree Publishers
CH-3052 Zollikofen
Switzerland
e-mail: info@walking-tree.org
http://www.walking-tree.org

Cormarë Series

The *Cormarë Series* has been the first series of studies dedicated exclusively to the exploration of Tolkien's work. Its focus is on papers and studies from a wide range of scholarly approaches. The series comprises monographs, thematic collections of essays, conference volumes, and reprints of important yet no longer (easily) accessible papers by leading scholars in the field. Manuscripts and project proposals are evaluated by members of an independent board of advisors who support the series editors in their endeavour to provide the readers with qualitatively superior yet accessible studies on Tolkien and his work.

News from the Shire and Beyond. Studies on Tolkien
Peter Buchs and Thomas Honegger (eds.), Zurich and Berne 2004, Reprint, First edition 1997 (Cormarë Series 1), ISBN 978-3-9521424-5-5

Root and Branch. Approaches Towards Understanding Tolkien
Thomas Honegger (ed.), Zurich and Berne 2005, Reprint, First edition 1999 (Cormarë Series 2), ISBN 978-3-905703-01-6

Richard Sturch, *Four Christian Fantasists. A Study of the Fantastic Writings of George MacDonald, Charles Williams, C.S. Lewis and J.R.R. Tolkien*
Zurich and Berne 2007, Reprint, First edition 2001 (Cormarë Series 3), ISBN 978-3-905703-04-7

Tolkien in Translation
Thomas Honegger (ed.), Zurich and Jena 2011, Reprint, First edition 2003 (Cormarë Series 4), ISBN 978-3-905703-15-3

Mark T. Hooker, *Tolkien Through Russian Eyes*
Zurich and Berne 2003 (Cormarë Series 5), ISBN 978-3-9521424-7-9

Translating Tolkien: Text and Film
Thomas Honegger (ed.), Zurich and Jena 2011, Reprint, First edition 2004 (Cormarë Series 6), ISBN 978-3-905703-16-0

Christopher Garbowski, *Recovery and Transcendence for the Contemporary Mythmaker. The Spiritual Dimension in the Works of J.R.R. Tolkien*
Zurich and Berne 2004, Reprint, First Edition by Marie Curie Sklodowska, University Press, Lublin 2000, (Cormarë Series 7), ISBN 978-3-9521424-8-6

Reconsidering Tolkien
Thomas Honegger (ed.), Zurich and Berne 2005 (Cormarë Series 8),
ISBN 978-3-905703-00-9

Tolkien and Modernity 1
Frank Weinreich and Thomas Honegger (eds.), Zurich and Berne 2006 (Cormarë Series 9), ISBN 978-3-905703-02-3

Tolkien and Modernity 2
Thomas Honegger and Frank Weinreich (eds.), Zurich and Berne 2006 (Cormarë Series 10), ISBN 978-3-905703-03-0

Tom Shippey, *Roots and Branches. Selected Papers on Tolkien by Tom Shippey*
Zurich and Berne 2007 (Cormarë Series 11), ISBN 978-3-905703-05-4

Ross Smith, *Inside Language. Linguistic and Aesthetic Theory in Tolkien*
Zurich and Berne 2007 (Cormarë Series 12), ISBN 978-3-905703-06-1

How We Became Middle-earth. A Collection of Essays on The Lord of the Rings
Adam Lam and Nataliya Oryshchuk (eds.), Zurich and Berne 2007 (Cormarë Series 13), ISBN 978-3-905703-07-8

Myth and Magic. Art According to the Inklings
Eduardo Segura and Thomas Honegger (eds.), Zurich and Berne 2007 (Cormarë Series 14), ISBN 978-3-905703-08-5

The Silmarillion - Thirty Years On
Allan Turner (ed.), Zurich and Berne 2007 (Cormarë Series 15),
ISBN 978-3-905703-10-8

Martin Simonson, *The Lord of the Rings and the Western Narrative Tradition*
Zurich and Jena 2008 (Cormarë Series 16), ISBN 978-3-905703-09-2

Tolkien's Shorter Works. Proceedings of the 4th Seminar of the Deutsche Tolkien Gesellschaft & Walking Tree Publishers Decennial Conference
Margaret Hiley and Frank Weinreich (eds.), Zurich and Jena 2008 (Cormarë Series 17), ISBN 978-3-905703-11-5

Tolkien's The Lord of the Rings: Sources of Inspiration
Stratford Caldecott and Thomas Honegger (eds.), Zurich and Jena 2008 (Cormarë Series 18), ISBN 978-3-905703-12-2

J.S. Ryan, *Tolkien's View: Windows into his World*
Zurich and Jena 2009 (Cormarë Series 19), ISBN 978-3-905703-13-9

Music in Middle-earth
Heidi Steimel and Friedhelm Schneidewind (eds.), Zurich and Jena 2010 (Cormarë Series 20), ISBN 978-3-905703-14-6

Liam Campbell, *The Ecological Augury in the Works of JRR Tolkien*
Zurich and Jena 2011 (Cormarë Series 21), ISBN 978-3-905703-18-4

Margaret Hiley, *The Loss and the Silence. Aspects of Modernism in the Works of C.S. Lewis, J.R.R. Tolkien and Charles Williams*
Zurich and Jena 2011 (Cormarë Series 22), ISBN 978-3-905703-19-1

J.S. Ryan, *In the Nameless Wood* (working title)
Zurich and Jena, forthcoming

Rainer Nagel, *Hobbit Place-names. A Linguistic Excursion through the Shire*
Zurich and Jena, forthcoming

The Broken Scythe. Death and Immortality in the Works of J.R.R. Tolkien
Roberto Arduini and Claudio Antonio Testi (eds.), Zurich and Jena, forthcoming

Christopher MacLachlan, *Tolkien and Wagner: The Ring and Der Ring*
Zurich and Jena, forthcoming

Renée Vink, *Wagner and Tolkien*
Zurich and Jena, forthcoming

Constructions of Authorship in and around the Works of J.R.R. Tolkien
Judith Klinger (ed.), Zurich and Jena, forthcoming

Tolkien's Poetry
Julian Morton Eilmann and Allan Turner (eds.), Zurich and Jena, forthcoming

Beowulf and the Dragon

The original Old English text of the 'Dragon Episode' of *Beowulf* is set in an authentic font and printed and bound in hardback creating a high quality art book. The text is illustrated by Anke Eissmann and accompanied by John Porter's translation. The introduction is by Tom Shippey. Limited first edition of 500 copies. 84 pages. Selected pages can be previewed on: www.walking-tree.org/beowulf
Beowulf and the Dragon
Zurich and Jena 2009, ISBN 978-3-905703-17-7

Tales of Yore Series

The *Tales of Yore Series* grew out of the desire to share Kay Woollard's whimsical stories and drawings with a wider audience. The series aims at providing a platform for qualitatively superior fiction with a clear link to Tolkien's world.

Kay Woollard, *The Terror of Tatty Walk. A Frightener*
CD and Booklet, Zurich and Berne 2000, ISBN 978-3-9521424-2-4

Kay Woollard, *Wilmot's Very Strange Stone or What came of building "snobbits"*
CD and booklet, Zurich and Berne 2001, ISBN 978-3-9521424-4-8

www.ingramcontent.com/pod-product-compliance
Lightning Source LLC
Chambersburg PA
CBHW070733160426
43192CB00009B/1417